Eritrea's Gold Rush

Eritrea's Gold Rush

Eritrea's Gold Rush

Western Mining Companies, Regional Wars, and Human Rights Abuses in Africa

Charlotte Touati

LONDON · NEW YORK · OXFORD · NEW DELHI · SYDNEY

Zed Books
Bloomsbury Publishing Plc
50 Bedford Square, London, WC1B 3DP, UK
1359 Broadway, 12th Floor, New York, NY 10018, USA
29 Earlsfort Terrace, Dublin 2, Ireland

First published in Great Britain 2025

Cover design by Toby Way
Cover image © sdmix/Adobe Stock

A catalogue record for this book is available from the British Library.

Library of Congress Cataloging-in-Publication Data
Names: Touati, Charlotte, 1982 – author.
Title: Eritrea's gold rush: western mining companies, regional wars, and human rights abuses in Africa / Charlotte Touati.
Description: London; New York: Zed Books, 2025. | Includes bibliographical references and index. | Summary: "Leading Horn of Africa expert Charlotte Touati exposes the role played by Canadian gold mining company Nevsun and other global actors in propping up the regime of Isayas Aferwerki, one of Africa's most dangerous dictators. In so doing, Touati shows how global capital networks help perpetuate economic and political instability in the Horn of Africa, which in turn is fostering violence and instability throughout other parts of the world" – Provided by publisher.
Identifiers: LCCN 2025020891 (print) | LCCN 2025020892 (ebook) | ISBN 9781350513556 (hardback) | ISBN 9781350513563 (paperback) | ISBN 9781350513570 (epub) | ISBN 9781350513587 (pdf)
Subjects: LCSH: Nevsun Resources (Firm) | Human rights--Eritrea. | Forced labor--Eritrea. | Gold mines and mining--Social aspects--Eritrea. | Eritrea- Politics and government--1993- | Eritrea--Foreign relations--20th century. | Eritrea--Foreign relations--21st century.
Classification: LCC JC599.E65 T68 2025 (print) | LCC JC599.E65 (ebook) | DDC 323.09635--dc23/eng/20250430
LC record available at https://lccn.loc.gov/2025020891
LC ebook record available at https://lccn.loc.gov/2025020892

ISBN: HB: 978-1-3505-1355-6
PB: 978-1-3505-1356-3
ePDF: 978-1-3505-1358-7
eBook: 978-1-3505-1357-0

Typeset by Deanta Global Publishing Services, Chennai, India
Printed and bound in Great Britain

To find out more about our authors and books visit www.bloomsbury.com and sign up for our newsletters.

To Léonard Vincent
for paving the way

Contents

Part IV   The Gold of the New Pharaohs

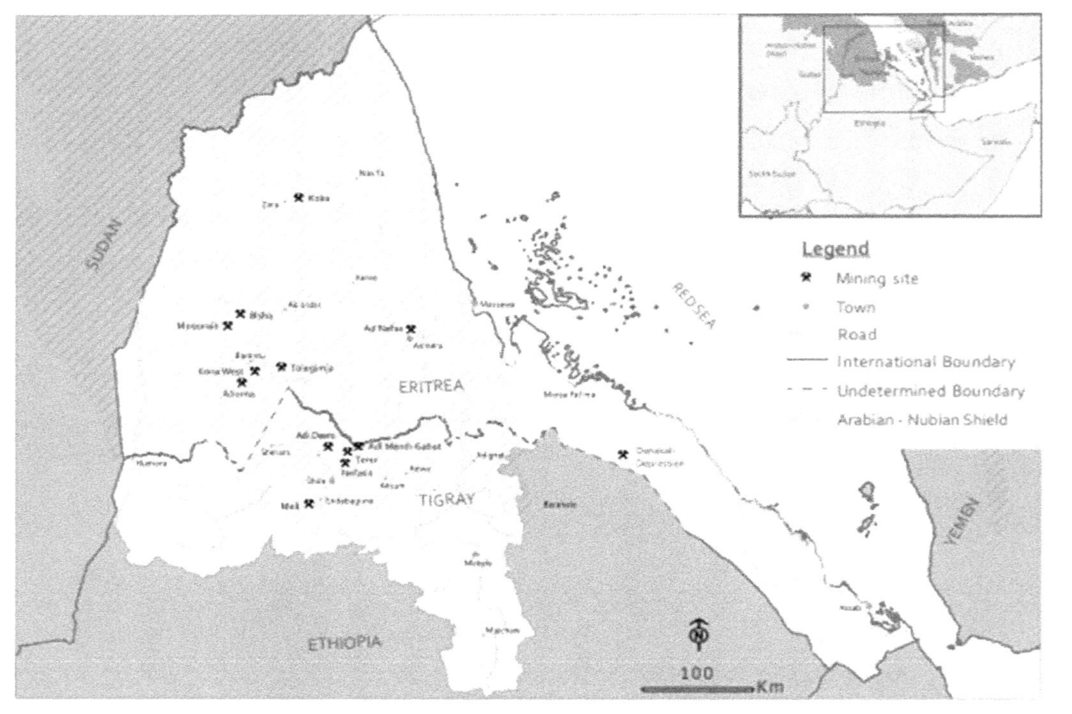

Map Main mining sites in Eritrea and Tigray(map)

List of Abbreviations

AES	Alliance of Sahel States
AFRIC	Association for Free Research and International Cooperation
AiM	accusation in a mirror
AML/CFT	Anti-Money Laundering and Combating the Financing of Terrorism
ANS	Arabian-Nubian Shield
BMSC	Bisha Mining Shareholders Corporation
BRICS	Brazil, Russia, India, China, South Africa
CAR	Central African Republic
CIRDI	Canadian International Resources and Development Institute
CSR	Corporate Social Responsibility
CUD	Coalition for Unity and Democracy
DIS	Defence Industries System
EDF	Eritrean Defence Forces
EFFORT	Endowment Fund for the Rehabilitation of Tigray
ENA	Ethiopia News Agency
ENAMCO	Eritrean National Mining Corporation

ENDF	Ethiopian National Defence Force
EOTC	Ethiopian Orthodox Tewahedo Church
EPLF	Eritrean People's Liberation Front
EPRDF	Ethiopian People's Revolutionary Democratic Front
ESAT TV	Ethiopian Satellite Television
GBV	gender-based violence
GERD	Grand Ethiopia Renaissance Dam
GNU	Government of National Unity
IMCTC	Islamic Military Counter Terrorism Coalition
INSA	(Ethiopian) Information Network Security Administration
KYC	Know you Customer
LNA	Libyan National Army
MIC	Military Industry Corporation
MLI	MacDonald-Laurier Institute
MoU	*Memorandum of Understanding*
NISA	(Somali) National Intelligence and Security Agency
OFAC	Office of Foreign Assets Control of the US Department of the Treasury
OHCHR	Office of the United Nations High Commissioner for Human Rights
PBoC	People's Bank of China
PFDJ	People's Front for Democracy and Justice

RSF	Rapid Support Forces
SAF	Sudan Armed Forces
SDIR	Subcommittee on International Human Rights of the Standing Committee on Foreign Affairs and International Development
SUMM	Supporting Ministry of Mines in Ethiopia
TDF	Tigray Defence Forces
TIA	Tigray Interim Administration
TPLF	Tigray People's Liberation Front
UAE	United Arab Emirates
VMS	Volcanogenic Massive Sulphide
2RP	Radio Révolution Panafricaine

Introduction

Nubia and the gold of the Black Pharaohs

If you discover our treasures, leave the gold to those who want to destroy themselves. After understanding the meaning of the characters that describe these things, you will gather all the riches in a short time; but if you limit yourself to taking the gold, you will destroy yourself, as a result of the envy of the kings who rule and that of all men.

Zosimus of Panopolis, *Letter to Theosebeia*, third century[1]

On 12 September 2012, I defended my PhD thesis in history at the Faculty of Letters and Humanities of the University of Neuchâtel in Switzerland, 'Purgatory in the Writings from Egypt and North Africa (Ist-/Vth Century AD)'.[2] As a young philologist with a passion for the languages and religions of the Nile Valley and the Horn of Africa, I chased after rare manuscripts in landscapes as sublime as they were inhospitable. The encounters were intense, from erudite monks to village militiamen and passionate, politicized students.

I had translated from ancient Greek and Coptic into French alchemical treatises never before published in modern languages, such as the *Letter to Theosebeia* and the *Authentic Memoirs* of Zosimus of Panopolis, a third-century author who had retired to Upper Egypt and whose work forms the core of the *Alchemical Corpus*. These texts reflect the syncretism prevalent in the region on both sides of the Red Sea at the time. Hermeticism, Greek Gnosticism, Judaism, Christianity and the Sabaean astral cult mingled and evolved in a highly plastic manner.

Far from medieval inflation, the texts forming the primitive core of the *Alchemical Corpus* contain nothing magical. The preoccupation was to purify one's soul to reach a level of clarity and incorruptibility symbolically compared to that of refined gold. This is what transmutation is all about: turning lead into gold. The processes described are allegorical. However, the descriptions are based on actual knowledge of the processes used by the miners and craftsmen of what modern geologists would call the Arabian-Nubian Shield. Even philosophers such as Zosimus may have played with crucibles, but they have given added meaning to these gestures so familiar to them. In another region, it would have been a different art, but around the Red Sea, it was gold that was worked.

Zosimus of Panopolis and his allegorical method are part of the Alexandrian theology of Philo, Clement of Alexandria and Origen. With them, it is possible to transcend the literal reading and move on to a figurative meaning. Thus, the apocalypses are not end-of-time wars, but allegorically represent the inner struggle that is taking place here and now in each and every one of us, just like the purification of metals. I write 'apocalypses' because from the last centuries before to the first centuries after the beginning of the current era, there are many apocalypses. It is only the process of canonization of the New Testament that will eliminate this diversity by selecting the sole Apocalypse of John. At the time, I was also particularly interested in the *Apocalypse of Peter*.[3] However, victim of a process of censorship by the Byzantine Church, this text was only preserved in Ge'ez, the language of the kingdom of Axum, which later became the liturgical language of the Ethiopian Orthodox Tewahedo Church (EOTC).

Axum, whose king Ezana converted to Christianity in 325, was the second Christian kingdom in history after Armenia and even before the Roman Empire. It did not undergo the same process of expurgation of biblical texts as the rest of Christendom and has preserved almost everything. Ge'ez literature is a philologist's paradise! That's how I began to learn Ge'ez and to give a scientific dimension to my passion to Ethiopian Christianity, and then by extension for the country and its varied populations.

War[4] and gold were metaphorical, spiritual. Little did I know that ten years later I would be caught up in one of the deadliest wars of this century, the Tigray war. I didn't suffer physically like the people of the Horn of Africa, but this war changed me, like purgatory fire. And gold had its part to play. Not the gold of philosophers, but the gold of foundries and central banks, the gold of the alchemists of death that transmutes into blood.

Having been born on the shores of Lake of Neuchâtel in Switzerland, I've known about gold since childhood. We were introduced to it on school outings or at open houses at the Banque Cantonale Neuchâteloise or the Metalor factory in Marin. We could touch the ingots and marvel at the weight of these veritable fortunes in bars. A 'Good Delivery' weighs an average of 400 ounce (12.4 kg). That's when I realized that an ingot was so dense that we couldn't lift them straight off (they are perfectly smooth and the slightly pyramid shape offers no grip), we had to slide them over the edge of the table. Incidentally, this puts into perspective the scenes in the movies where the thieves who have succeeded in opening the bank vault throw the ingots at each other before taking off with the loot.

I grew up with the Nazi gold affair and the unclaimed Jewish bank accounts, then awakened my political conscience with the death of banking secrecy in a Switzerland where a banking or financial scandal broke out every day. It was therefore quite natural for me to understand what was going on with the Nubian Shield gold.

As we shall see in this book, there are accusations of forced labour in gold mines operated by major Western companies, and then there are the links that can be uncovered between gold extraction and the financing of armed factions in Eritrea, Sudan, Ethiopia and Somalia; financing the Eritrean regime, one of the most secretive and repressive in the world, financing again a campaign of hatred that led to the genocide of the Tigrayans; and, finally, gold hoarding by the BRICS powers, led by China, in order to build up sufficient reserves to return to the gold standard and dispense with the dollar. And this is a revolution, the conscious and desired upheaval of the 'world order'.

All the major mines in Eritrea, initially commissioned by Canadian and Australian companies, have been sold to Chinese companies close to the government, which will use them to carry out its de-dollarization project. We may be witnessing the suicide of liberalism, a system that allows companies to sell themselves (and the resources they exploit, as well as the populations that depend on them) to illiberal regimes.

Gold production in the Nubian Shield is massive, thanks in particular to Sudan which, with almost 100 tonnes a year, is one of the biggest producers on the African continent. Ethiopia's gold production, although significant, has not yet reached the stage of systematic industrialization, but could equal that of Sudan. Despite or rather because of this underdevelopment, the sector is attracting a great deal of interest. So, by comparison, Eritrean production seems a little meagre, all the more so as the gold deposit at Bisha dried up as long ago as 2013, giving way to copper, zinc and silver. Other mines have certainly come into production or will do so very soon, but the most remarkable production at Bisha – remarkable in the sense of noticeable – is the corpus of arguments formalized in its defence and which will be put to use in the service of Putin's hybrid war in Africa, according to what is sometimes conveniently called the 'Gerasimov doctrine'.

The philosophical alchemists are far, far away.

A little history: From the Pharaohs to the Queen of Sheba

The gold mines of the Nubian Shield first appeared in history thanks to the Turin Mining Papyrus,[5] drawn between 1070 and 1060 BC by the scribe Amenakhte, but which probably records earlier traditions and observations. Discovered in Thebes, it describes a portion of the Ouadi Hammamat along the caravan route linking Coptos to the Red Sea. The aim was to map the region's mineral resources with a view to extracting rock for the monumental statues of Ramses IV. It is a kind of preparatory work with marginal notes. At the same time, the papyrus documents the gold mines of Faouakhir with its mining village active some two centuries earlier under Pharaoh Seti I. It was already in operation under Akhenathon, the pharaoh who tried to impose monotheism on Egypt around the sun god. Because of its colour, brilliance and incorruptibility, gold, associated with the sun, was particularly honoured in Egypt, even when Akhenaton's star was eclipsed. The Faouakhir mine was therefore abandoned, then reactivated under the Ptolemies and in the Roman period, at the time of alchemists such as Zosimus.

In the meantime, other gold mines, such as those in Nubia, had come into their own. Located in present-day Sudan, Nubia refers to the historical extent of the kingdoms of Napata and Meroe upstream from the Nile's first cataract. Long dominated by the Egyptians, the Nubians reversed the trend and wore the tiara of the pharaohs from 747 to 656 B.C. They formed the XXVth dynasty or Kushite dynasty, that of the 'Black Pharaohs'. After the sack of the capital Napata by the Egyptians, who regained control of the north, the Nubians withdrew and established their own kingdom at Meroe from the sixth century BC. The gold mines of Nubia and the land of Kush were famous in antiquity, but not only. Even today, the Wagner gold mines in Sudan, personally owned by the late Yevgeny Prigozhin, are called 'Meroe Gold'.

From the fifth century AD, the kingdom of Meroe declined in favour of the kingdom of Axum in present-day Tigray. Founded in the first century of the present era, the kingdom of Axum reached its apogee between the fourth and seventh centuries. A veritable empire stretching from present-day Ethiopia to Yemen, including Eritrea and eastern Sudan, Axum was the kingdom of the Queen of Sheba, whose dynasty is said to have descended from the love affair between the learned sovereign and the wealthy King Solomon. Another legend, that of King Solomon's mines, was born from this love story, sometimes located in Israel, sometimes in Africa.

The Ancient Testament makes numerous references to these African gold mines. Kush, Meroe and Axum are superimposed in the sources,[6] and the origins of the myth of the Queen of Sheba are lost in these confines. There are two competing traditions about the Queen of Sheba: one from the Arabian Peninsula about a white-skinned woman named Bilqis, and the other from Ethiopia about Makeda, a dark-skinned queen, the beloved of the Song of Songs. Her history was fixed in the early fourteenth century in the Ge'ez epic *Kebra Nagast* to glorify King Yekuno Amlak (who reigned from 1270 to 1285), Ethiopia's first Amhara sovereign who claimed Solomonic ancestry and, thus, legitimized the new dynasty.

It was partly in the name of this founding myth that the Tigray war broke out.

So much for the narrative. More concretely, excavations carried out in the Gash Barka,[7] thus Bisha's regions, show not only the economic dynamism of the Nubian Shield but also a certain material unity stimulated by trade routes from the Red Sea to Libya. Exactly the same routes are described in this book.

Nubian Shield nature and exploitation

The mines of the Nubian Shield were exploited for centuries by craftsmen. Proto-industrial mining began in the colonial period.

After Bonaparte's departure, Mamluks and Ottomans competed for Egypt. Taking advantage of the chaos, Mehemet Ali imposed himself and pushed southwards into Sudan and as far as Eritrea. Between 1860 and 1870, the Egyptians controlled the port of Massawa in present-day Eritrea but were finally defeated in 1882 after the Anglo-Egyptian War and eventually agreed a condominium in Sudan in 1892, while the Italians had established a colony in Eritrea in 1890. Ethiopia resists. In 1896, Negus' troops repelled the Italians at Adwa. Humiliated, the Italians were relentless in their attempts to make amends for this perceived affront, finally occupying Ethiopia in 1936. Each of the colonial powers present, whether Egyptian, British or Italian,[8] never ceased to want to exploit the mines of such a renowned region. After all, that's why they came in the first place!

Methods and equipment inspired by European industry were adapted and digging began to produce more than could be achieved by traditional gold panning. But the chaotic history of the century, from colonization to two world wars and then decolonization, did not allow for linear development of the industry, and many galleries were left abandoned until the 2000s. In Sudan, the revival was driven by Omar Al-Bashir, who has actively reinvested in the mining industry for personal gain and to place his relatives and allies in key positions such as Mohamed Hamdan Dagolo alias Hemedti, a businessman who built a fortune on the gold mines in Darfur. Hemedti is also a warlord who rose to prominence in the anarchy that followed the genocidal counterinsurgency in the same Darfur. Today, he is the cause of the new bloody conflict in Sudan, once again accused of war crimes.

While the Arabian-Nubian Shield (ANS) comprises Ethiopia, Eritrea, Sudan, Egypt and Saudi Arabia, the Nubian Shield is strictly speaking the African part. And if the Nubian Shield has fuelled legends, lust and violence, it's because it's a unique geomorphological region.

Formed at the end of the Neoproterozoic era (around 870 to 550 million years ago) during the formation of the supercontinent Gondwana,[9] the ANS is a combination of two geological formations: volcanogenic massive sulphide (VMS) deposits and orogenic deposits or orogenic gold deposits.

These two types of ore deposits form in distinct geological contexts but can sometimes be spatially associated due to their formation in geologically active environments, often in relation to tectonic and volcanic activity.

This association of deposits (VMS/orogenic) is a kind of holy grail for explorers and geologists looking for just this kind of overlap, promising maximization of resources in terms of quantity, quality and diversity (these are polymetallic deposits). VMS deposits contain base metals such as copper and zinc, more rarely silver and gold, but this is precisely the case in the ANS, as they couple with the orogenic gold deposits that are the source of most of the world's gold mines.

VMS deposits in the ANS are mainly associated with volcanic rock sequences formed in rift or submarine volcanic arc environments. Volcanic sequences containing VMS may have been subsequently deformed and metamorphosed, creating favourable conditions for the formation of orogenic deposits. The hydrothermal activity associated with VMS formation could also provide an initial source of metals for the subsequent formation of orogenic deposits, through remobilization of gold and metals during tectonic events.[10]

ANS mines have been exploited for centuries in a rather rudimentary manner, on the surface and therefore mainly for gold outcropping in quartz veins associated with shears. But for these deposits to reveal their full potential, digging is required. And polymetallism requires specific treatment to isolate the target metal.

But when the price of gold and metals like copper, strategic to the development of new technologies and the ecological transition, explodes, then the investment is well worth it for the very large international mining companies with sufficiently solid backgrounds and in search of risky investments, but with juicy profits. That's why the ANS, which has been described as the new El Dorado or, more specifically, the Nubian Shield, is so important. The political turmoil experienced by the countries south of the Red Sea (Egypt and Saudi Arabia being firmly under control) in the 1990s and 2000s made them ideal prey, especially when they were run by complacent leaders who knew how to take advantage of this new windfall without passing it on to the population. Such is the case of Eritrea and Sudan. Ethiopia has protected itself relatively well but is lagging behind.

Part I

Eritrea

An Open-Air Prison

1

National Service

Inferi, the Underworld

An open-air gold mine is a funnel of concentric circles. The image straight out of a medieval altarpiece of Dante's *Inferno*, the Pit of Hell with its grimacing figures, immediately springs to mind. *Inferi* is Latin for 'what lies beneath'. And underneath, there are ores. So, the link between the underworld and mining is almost a natural one, especially given the arduous nature of the miner's work, a real damned.

The history of mining is punctuated by rushes for gold and precious stones, synonymous with adventure and fortune, but also ruin, madness and death.

It also covers the history of slavery, from prehistory to the present day. In book titles and NGO reports, modern slavery is frequently associated with mining.

Whatever the sector, the professionals involved in mining seek to improve the industry from both a social and an environmental point of view, but there are also the bad apples.

So, when mining develops in a country where slavery is institutionalized, it takes on the same contours and the same worst aspects.

Welcome to mining hell in Eritrea

A life at the regime's disposal

Eritrea became de facto independent in 1991, then de jure in 1993. The Eritrean People's Liberation Front (EPLF), led by Isayas Afwerki, found it difficult to make the transition from guerrilla movement to government party. The EPLF became the People's Front for Democracy and Justice (PFDJ) in 1994, but Eritreans only saw democracy in name. No elections have ever been held, Isayas has ruled since 1991, and the promised constitution has remained a promise. Eritrean society has remained not only highly militarized[1] but also in a permanent state of war. It was against this background that the National Service Proclamation was issued on 23 October 1995.[2] The border conflict with Ethiopia, which broke out in 1998, confirmed this siege mentality.[3] However, there are two elements in the DNA of the PFDJ (and the EPLF before it) that need to be considered. First, it is a revolutionary party which, from its inception in the early 1970s, has sought to reform society and the individual and expects the latter to devote his/her entire life to the party and the revolution. Then, after taking power in Asmara, the party cadres, and Isayas Afwerki in particular, created instability and conflict in the Horn of Africa in order to maintain their hold on power. As a result, there is no prospect of demobilization.[4]

Until recently, it was in the hope of silencing the weapons and returning young people to civilian life that the peace agreement signed in 2018 with Ethiopia was welcomed. A fatal deception. It led to the deadliest conflict of the twenty-first century, with Eritrean soldiers accused of war crimes and crimes against humanity.[5]

Journalist Dan Connell, who has been able to follow the Eritrean adventure since the beginnings of the EPLF, recounts the enthusiasm aroused by these guerrillas, who wanted to educate the people and establish social justice,[6] from an exceptional point of view since he was able to accompany the movement for many years. But Connell's sincere enthusiasm waned with the disappointments and excesses of the EPLF and then of the PFDJ, particularly in 2002 after the Border War, when Isayas refused to implement the constitution that had been ratified in 1997. Connell's thinking followed a trajectory that must have been painful, but lucid and honest, as evidenced by his book published in 2005 *Conversations with Eritrean Political Prisoners.*[7] The journalist transcribed interviews with five officials who had been arrested for criticizing the dictator, who was now revealing his true colours. They had been Isayas' and Connell's companions in the quest to liberate the Eritrean people, but all ended up in Isayas' jails. At the time, their voices still expressed the hope of seeing democracy triumph after the revolutionary period, but in 2025, Eritrea still has no constitution, a free press does not exist, and terror still reigns. The revolutionary period was undoubtedly a heroic one, a generational quest for a utopia, but today, without a doubt, there is nothing positive in this regime. Eritrea is a totalitarian state in the truest sense of the word.[8]

The reader will also profitably discover or reread the work of Léonard Vincent, another (former) journalist who devoted a large part of his life not only to Eritrea, but to the Eritreans themselves in his texts,[9] but also by co-founding *Radio Erena* ('Our Eritrea'). Based in Paris, *Radio Erena,* the only free media capable of broadcasting in Asmara – as I write – is in danger of disappearing due to threats, hacking and lack of funding.

Mining and impoverishment

As a research team including Eritrean refugees outside the country's points out: 'The PFDJ, through the integration of education, National Service and the Warsay Yikaalo National Development Programme, controls the labour provided to enterprises operating in Eritrea, which are owned by individual PFDJ top officials or by PFDJ-controlled entities such as the Ministry of Defence and Red Sea Trading Corporation, which are all directly overseen by the President.'[10]

And to consolidate its monopoly, the PFDJ has also deliberately impoverished the population in order to keep it under its thumb.[11] The semblance of a private sector is in fact in the hands of PFDJ executives, who use the labour force of national service conscripts. It is therefore a case of forced labour and even state slavery.

Industry, tourism and services are virtually non-existent. Eritrea's only university was closed in 2006. The country is being depopulated, and the government in power is doing nothing to stop this haemorrhage; quite the contrary, since it is involved in the traffickers' business.[12]

Eritrea is essentially a rural country where pastoralism and breeding dominate. But even the livestock is now under the control of the PFDJ through the Crop and Livestock Corporation run by a military officer.[13]

Only one sector has developed since 1991: Mining
Although it can be a source of foreign currency, the mining industry as practised in Eritrea does not develop the economic fabric. It enriches the elite personally and predominantly feeds the president's warlike delirium. The country is literally falling into ruin.[14]

A path of servitude

From the age of sixteen, young people go to the Sawa military camp for their last year of school (grade 12), where they attend college, undergo military training and are subjected to all kinds of abuse (including sexual abuse). This is the educational programme known as Warsay Yikaalo.[15] Education in Eritrea is entirely militarized, as was clearly demonstrated in a Human Rights Watch report published in 2019 and eloquently entitled 'They Are Making Us into Slaves, Not Educating Us'.[16] The Warsay Yikaalo programme comes under the Ministry of Defence,[17] which says it all. Going through Sawa can already be considered conscription for minors. Then, at the age of eighteen, young adults begin National Service, which theoretically includes six months of military training and twelve months of civilian service. But everything is left to the discretion of the regime.[18] Therefore, Eritrea is known for its indefinite compulsory military service.

After the end of the open war with Ethiopia in the early 2000s, some of the recruits were demobilized, but what a surprise it was to find that they still had to serve, working against their will and for next to nothing (and sometimes nothing at all) for state construction companies.[19] This is exactly the case with Segen Construction Company, the subcontracting company employed from 2007 onwards by Nevsun and Sunridge to build infrastructure in Bisha and Zara mines, which will be attacked for forced labour by refugees.[20]

The National Service is so dreaded that the government must organize roundups called *giffas* to get the teenagers back.[21] And it is to escape these *giffas* that hundreds of young people prefer to go into exile, to cross the desert and the sea, with all the risks that this entails for them and their families back home. They are all de facto deserters, with all the legal consequences that may imply.

The NGO Eritrea Focus interviewed former Bisha mine workers in 2017.[22] Here are just two excerpts, two voices among thousands:

> **Ex-miner 2**: I was assigned to Gedem Construction Company as part of the national service programme after I left school. Whilst there, I tried to flee the country but I was caught and imprisoned for 11 months. [. . .] After release from the custody, in October 2011, I was assigned to Segen as a national service conscript. I had no other option but to accept the order of the gov't – otherwise I

would be detained. [. . .] I was assigned to Bisha Mine as part of the national service and against my free-will. [. . .] 12 hours a day, Monday to Saturday = 72 hours plus 6 hours on Sundays. A total of 78 hours a week. [. . .] As a result of heat exposure, chemical smells, combined with lack of adequate food and water, I suffered from H-pylori [stomach/intestine ulcers]. I was also repeatedly under stress, suffered from malaria. The national service clinic could not provide assistance beyond first-aid and I had to get treatment in Asmara at my familial expenses. [. . .] I fled from the Mine and the country in September 2015 because of the working conditions.

Ex-miner 3: After studying for three years in the technical school, I was assigned to Segen in 2009 by the gov't. [. . .] As a member of the national service I did not have a choice about my workplace – I had to oblige when I was assigned to Bisha Mine. [. . .] As a result of the lack of protective equipment, many of us sustained injuries. While working under a machine, some equipment fell off and I injured my small finger but I only received a first-aid [I had to go to Asmara to get a proper treatment at my own expenses]. I also witnessed others sustaining major injuries. A co-worker seriously injured his leg, and lost consciousness because of bleeding. [. . .] The food was extremely poor, and many were forced to cook privately in their rooms at their own expenses despite the meagre national service pay. The accommodation rooms for the national service had 10-12 beds with no facilities e.g. AC or refrigerators. We had to sleep outside because the heat was unbearable – reaching 42–43 degree Celsius at night. Because of the extremely hot weather and humidity I saw an Eritrean worker died of heatstroke. A three-year old child of a maid and a South African national also died of heatstroke whilst I was there. [. . .] I fled from conscription and the country in November 2015 because of the working conditions.

Similarly, Prof Mirjam van Reisen from Tilburg University and her research team, the organization Europe External Programme with Africa (EEPA)[23] and Research Advisors & Experts Europe (RAEE),[24] have meticulously documented the issue of forced labour in Eritrea, based on the testimonies of refugees who have fled the 'inferno'.

As an example, here is the testimony of interviewee 19 recorded in the Netherlands on 17 October 2019:

> I was a translator in the Bisha mine in Eritrea. I was payed [sic] 2,500 nakfa per month.[25] There was a lady who complained, but I had not done anything wrong. I then spent one year and six months in an underground prison, six months of which was in solitary confinement. I then changed prison; I was four years in prison in total. After four years I went back to the office in Bisha mine. I never had a lawyer. I had not done anything wrong. [. . .] The conditions in prison are atrocious: I was tortured for six months. I spent my time in the Barentu underground prison. We were allowed out once a day. We had a shower and washed our clothes once a month. I had no information from my family. Then I went to the prison in Karen. [. . .] My family came to see me there. In the underground prisons we were in chains, both legs and hands. I was on my own, alone in one prison room. We received one small piece of bread in the morning and sometimes food in the evening, but not always. We were very hungry. We received one small bottle of water. They beat me during those six months. They wanted information I did not have. They beat me, they electrocuted me, they gave me electric shocks, they hit me with plastic sticks. I walked to escape – I walked for seven days.[26]

Interviewee 19 then took the road to exile, using smugglers and traffickers. As soon as his defection became known, his wife was arrested in retaliation. She has since disappeared.

To defend the indefensible, a powerful lobbying campaign was deployed, with the aim of getting the following message across: 'It's bad in Eritrea, but not that bad.' Readers can judge the flippancy of the formula, but after a legal soap opera lasting several years, Nevsun was not condemned by the courts, thanks to a financial settlement.

Isayas Afwerki's regime on the brink of bankruptcy

Economy on its knees

Economic life in Eritrea is overseen by two major entities: the Red Sea Corporation, and the Hidri Trust. The former, headed by Hagos Ghebrehiwet W. Kidan, was created in 1984 to support the economic, military and social activities of the Eritrean People's Liberation Front (EPLF). The Hidri trust dates back to 1994,[1] the year in which the People's Front for Democracy and Justice (PFDJ), Eritrea's now single party, succeeded the historic EPLF.

Red Sea Corporation and Hidri Trist operate like nebulas, franchises that bring together, without any transparency, dozens of sub-entities ranging from the Red Sea Bottlers Share Company, which produces soft drinks, to the Dubai offshore funds.

The Hidri Trust is more of an umbrella that covers the multitude of activities of PFDJ executives and today includes the Red Sea Corporation. It manages most of PFDJ's international activities.[2] There is total porosity between the government, the party and the Hidri Trust.[3] Party cadres receive a sort of prebend that enriches them and guarantees their loyalty to the central power. This state micro-capitalism has gradually devitalized the private economic fabric. Even small and medium-sized businesses are run by PFDJ members. They benefit from many advantages, starting with the prestige induced by fear, but also from the free labour of National Service conscripts, which, beyond the ethical scandal it may raise, completely distorts the market.[4]

Another, more subtle, consequence is that foreign observers such as the chairman of the Australian mining company Danakali, Seamus Cornelius, claim, in good faith or not, that Eritrea is a corruption-free country.[5] It's true that, unlike some other countries, you don't have to pay baksheesh for everything in Eritrea. We can leave it at that. Or we can say that it's just the façade of a fundamentally corrupt system since all activity belongs to the PFDJ. First, no one would dare defraud the party without taking enormous risks, and second, the party doesn't need to extort anything, since everything belongs to it in the end. Corruption is institutionalized from the bottom to the top of society. The government doesn't need to take money from cab fares when the cab belongs to it.

In 2011, the UN monitoring group on Somalia and Eritrea distinguishes between the state economy controlled by the PFDJ and the informal economy controlled by the PFDJ.[6] The ruling party's omnipresence in the Eritrean economy, in terms of both industry and imports, has a direct impact on the cost of living in the country, which has become bloodless. The party has total control over what the population can and must consume, and at what price. In this context, it's a short step from importing to trafficking. Many foodstuffs are bought from neighbouring Tigray or Sudan and put on the market at prohibitive prices.[7] Since nothing escapes the party's notice, it's not hard to guess who's organizing the traffic and pocketing the profits. The trafficking of human beings does not escape the party either, whose prominent members are part of the criminal networks that kidnap and torture citizens fleeing the hell instituted by this same party.[8]

The war economy in which Eritrea has found itself since independence and the introduction of National Service have destroyed the traditional subsistence system of the various communities highly adapted to harsh climates and unique landscapes. Since 2000, everything has been organized by the state, often in an arbitrary manner. Even if the private sector is not formally abolished and the entire economy nationalized, it is nevertheless deliberately asphyxiated.[9] Government contracts are systematically awarded to Hidri Trust companies.

As reported in a 2006 telegram leaked by Wikileaks, US ambassador DeLisi posted in Asmara between 2004 and 2007, the Hidri Trust, whose accounts are completely opaque, secures money for off-the-books operations such as arms purchases.[10]

Despite the signature of the Algiers Agreements between Eritrea and Ethiopia on 12 December 2000, both countries started a cold war. They didn't demobilize, but the fighting has ceased overall. However, the weapons mentioned by Ambassador DeLisi in 2006 were not just for domestic use. This very year, Ethiopia became involved in Somalia in the context of the War on Terror. At the time, Somalia was a failed state dominated by warlords, pirates and Islamic Courts, soon to be eclipsed by Al-Shabaab.

Eritrean president Isayas Afwerki, who harboured a personal, even paranoid, hatred for Meles Zenawi, the Ethiopian prime minister from the Tigray People's Liberation Front (TPLF), funded all kinds of groups[11] that could harm the TPLF and the EPRDF, the multi-ethnic coalition led by the Tigrayan party at the head of Ethiopia, both at home and abroad. The most famous of these being undoubtedly the jihadist group Harakat Al-Shabaab Al-Mujahidin, now emerging in Somalia.[12] Nothing repels the Maoist-trained Isayas more than Islamists, but the end justified the means, namely weakening Ethiopia on its eastern flank. In Ethiopia itself, the PFDJ supported the Ogaden National Liberation Front, Oromo Liberation Front, Afar Liberation Front, Afar Revolutionary People's Democratic Front, Sidamo Liberation Front and Tigrayan People's Democratic Movement. The monitoring group on Somalia and Eritrea also mentions 'unidentified fighters from the Amhara and Gambella regions of Ethiopia'.[13] We now know the role played by the Amhara militias, particularly Ginbot 7, trained in Eritrea, in triggering the catastrophic Tigray war ten years later.

But supplying weapons and setting up training camps requires a great deal of funding, which the Hidri Trust and the Red Sea Corporation are unable to provide. Another major source of income is the diaspora. In February 2007, US ambassador DeLisi[14] reported that funds raised from the diaspora represented half of Eritrea's GDP, some $450 million. Irrespective of origin, remittance systems are extremely common between diasporas and their metropolis. Workers and merchants have always sent part of their income back to their families or, more broadly, to their communities. Letters of credit were developed with this in mind, but in the twenty-first century, remittance can take the form of wire transfers. Dematerialization is not only practical, it also guarantees a certain security, since no money or valuables are transported, but the exchange of cash still exists. In this case, the hawala is often used, or hybrid forms as we shall see.

Hawala and remittance from the diaspora

To transfer a sum of money from one country to another, you need to use the SWIFT system, the main standard for international money transfers, which requires you to go through the banking system. The sender deposits the sum to be transferred into an account, opened with a bank that has followed the 'Know you Customer' (KYC) procedure, and respects compliance, particularly in terms of 'Anti-Money Laundering and Combating the Financing of Terrorism' (AML/CFT).[15]

Money Gram, Western Union and other licensed operators allow you to send money deposited in cash to a person identified in another country, without opening an account. These official operators also comply with the traceability standard and always remain within the framework of an official banking system, passing through accounts. Identification will be required. Even at this stage, it is possible to produce forged documents. However, if the sums involved are too large, are paid frequently or are always sent to the same recipient, they will be monitored.

But when the sender is in an irregular situation in a country, has earned the money he wishes to send in a more or less honest or even downright illegal way or wishes to evade all forms of control and taxation, he will prefer to go through a similar, but informal and often communal, system, the hawala.[16]

A broker collects the cash and takes care of giving it a legal existence, either by means of false invoices or by drowning it in his official business (often in import-export). The equivalent will be handed over by a trusted person in the destination country in exchange for a code or a piece of paper. The transmission chain can be a long and complex series of cash compensations and even services rendered. Everything is based on trust and, above all, on the prestige of the boss. Money doesn't travel, it is compensated.

In pure hawala, there is no banking at all, and no paper trail, but in the twenty-first century, electronic transfers and telecommunications have joined the suitcases of cash.[17]

Eritrea emerged from open warfare (Liberation War, then Border War) in 2000, but its economy has never been able to take off. Income from domestic economic activity collapsed, and the Red Sea Corporation as well as the Hidri Trust doesn't bring in enough foreign currency to keep a newly independent country going. Since independence in 1991, the Eritrean government has established tax laws on the diaspora, until then introducing a compulsory levy of 2 per cent on the income of Eritreans abroad.[18] In exchange for basic consular services (passports, birth certificates, etc.) necessary to obtain asylum, Eritreans are registered and obliged to pay this tax. The process is tantamount to extortion. Financial flows remain mysterious. According to Ambassador DeLisi, PFDJ officials and diplomats travel with good old-fashioned suitcases of cash. The money may also be sent to accounts in their own names or those of front men, rather than state accounts. He quotes a *Financial Times* article from 4 January 2000, which mentions Eritrea 'in the top 10 for countries with the largest percentage growth in anonymous deposits in Swiss banks'.[19] In 2011, the monitoring group gained access to a Swiss account linked to a high-ranking general in the Eritrean army.[20] In a private discussion on 12 June 2024, Matt Bryden told me that the Swiss authorities had shown more but had not authorized publication. Indeed, banking secrecy had only just begun to crack, with the first breach opening timidly in 2009.

Even today, Hidmona offers remittance services all that is classic. The highly polished website is registered in Switzerland with offices in the main Swiss cities and a telephone number in the canton of Vaud (Lausanne area). But Hidmona also offers another face, that of shameless PFDJ propaganda. Indeed, the company's Facebook page and YouTube channel are not encumbered by political correctness. Hidmona organizes and promotes 'PFDJ cultural festivals', events that today see sometimes violent clashes between opponents and supporters of PFDJ. Hidmona also produces the video clips of Awel Said, apologist for the #NoMore movement[21] (see dedicated chapter) and champion of national service in Sawa. It doesn't take a vivid imagination to work out that Hidmona is, in fact, the channel through which the Eritrean government's international fundraising flows.

The operations we have just described are truly mafia-like. 'Eritrea is a personally owned political-business corporation.'[22] The country has no annual budget,[23] just as it has no constitution.[24] Everything is in the hands of one man and his associates. 'According to a former Deputy Minister of Finance (now in exile in Europe), "the entire economy of Eritrea is in the hands of the President with the support of three individuals; the Head of Economic Affairs, Head of Political Affairs and the Head of Cultural Affairs". The Country never publishes a budget, and there is a complete lack of accountability and transparency.'[25]

But are the 2 per cent of Eritreans' income in the diaspora, support festivals and a few troubled operations in the Gulf countries enough to feed a state with a GDP at ground level, in perpetual war and bolstering all kinds of arms-hungry groupuscules? The answer is loud and clear: not at all.

> Given the totalitarian nature of Eritrea's political and economic system, mining companies operating in the country are complicit in helping to maintain the regime, and thus its repression. There are two main aspects to this – their financial support to the state through mining taxes, and their complicity in the Eritrean state's use of forced labour in mine development projects. [. . .] Eritrea's economic growth is now being largely driven by mining. The World Bank states: 'Eritrea's Gross Domestic Product (GDP) growth was estimated at around 9% in the 2011–12 period (the latest point for which data is readily available), up from an estimated 2.2% in 2010. The growth was mainly stimulated by the mining sector (gold), the coming on stream of the Bisha mine in 2011 and the historically high gold price prevailing at that time were key drivers.'[26]

The economic sanctions imposed by the international community against Eritrea for its support of terrorist groups were aimed at stifling the government, provoking a popular uprising and regime change. The US ambassador's cables show this expectation and document the agony of the regime until the gold windfall fell.[27]

In 2008 and 2009, just as all observers were expecting Isayas Afwerki's Eritrea to fall to its knees, foreign currency began to flow back into the state coffers thanks to exploration licences. Indeed, the mining sector was not subject to sanctions. It's almost incomprehensible.

The regime saved by international mining companies

Back in 2003, several PFDJ executives, Isayas first among them, express their distrust of the rush by multinationals to invest in Eritrea's mining sector. The PFDJ, which emerged from the EPLF, is a Marxist-Leninist party. It therefore seems inconceivable to let companies embodying triumphant capitalism exploit Eritrea in the geological sense of the term. But Isayas shuns all systems ideology, all -isms[28] except that of pragmatism, even opportunism. The Eritrean government therefore created ENAMCO in 2004, the national agency that enables the PFDJ to acquire shares in the joint ventures that will manage the mining projects from 2007 onwards. One exploration project follows another, and all ideological and ethical scruples disappear. From 2014 onwards, Isayas even imposed a proactive policy to develop the sector, despite the publication of a report by the Monitoring Group on Somalia and Eritrea warning of the opacity of the mining sector in Eritrea and the potential financing of military activities in contravention of Resolution 1907 adopted in 2009.

Nevsun and the Eritrean government have been doing business since at least 2007, but this relationship turns into solidarity from 2009 and the international sanctions against Eritrea. In 2011 and 2012, according to calculations by engineer Philmon Yohannes based on Nevsun's results, the Eritrean government would have reaped at least $900 million in gold sales.[29] To these gains must be added taxes,

Nevsun being the only foreign company to pay taxes in Eritrea: $85 million in 2014 and a projected $14 billion over the next ten years, according to UN experts.[30]

> 'The complete lack of transparency is especially notable because mining is one of the most successful economic sectors in Eritrea and payments derived from mining activities are an important source of revenue for the Government'. [. . .] The Eritrean political system can only maintain itself largely through mining revenues. Much of Eritrea's foreign exchange income comes from foreign gold/copper mining company projects, in which the Eritrean Government holds a 40 per cent stake.[31]

In the same year, 2014, the union between the Eritrean government and Canadian mining company Nevsun Resources takes a new turn with the filing of a complaint by former Nevsun 'employees', accusing the Canadian company of complicity in forced labour and other degrading treatments at the Bisha mine. Nevsun's strategy will be relatively simple. The company lawyers and champions are not going to try to discredit the plaintiffs or deny the allegations, they will defend the Eritrean model. The argument could be summed up as follows: 'No, it's not forced labour, it's a new model of society, and those who oppose it, the defenders of human rights, have understood nothing to Eritrea, or worse, they are the playthings of Western imperialism.' Coming from a multinational company paying international mercenary lobbyists to sell this argument, it's not lacking in salt, but it's clever!

Nevsun will hire a lawyer and pay researchers to enhance its public relations and buy itself a positive image. In doing so, Nevsun will literally be paying for Isayas Afwerki's soft power. No wonder the former Maoist has changed sides and henceforth cherishes Canadian and Australian mining companies.

Part II

The Sun Constellation

3

Nevsun, Sunridge, Sun Peak

Canadian mining in Eritrea and Tigray

On 7 February 2024, Vancouver-based Sun Peak Metal Corp issued an eye-catching press release[1] to reassure investors that the mining company would soon resume exploration and drilling for gold and copper near Shire, in the Tigray region of northern Ethiopia. Tigray has just emerged from two years of devastating war against the troops of Ethiopian prime minister Abiy Ahmed and his Eritrean ally Isayas Afwerki. All economic and industrial activity came to a standstill.

The Shire Project comprises five main licences: Adi Dairo, Adi Mendi, Nefasit, Terer and Meli. The first three sites are operated solely by Sun Peak, the last two in a joint venture called Axum Metals with Ezana Mining Development PLC, an Ethiopian company.[2]

The Sun Peak team is proud of the affiliation with Nevsun Resources Ltd and Sunridge Gold Corp and insists on the geological continuity of the Nubian Shield, presented as a region without borders.[3] According to the brochure, the Shire Project should be a replica of the Eritrean mining success story. Doesn't 'the team' have twenty years' experience? Indeed, the team cut its teeth from 2003 with Nevsun discovering the Bisha mine, then from 2005 to 2016 with Sunridge until its sale to a Chinese company. In 2018, it will also be Nevsun's turn to become Chinese. Freed, the Canadian team landed further south, in Tigray, with a wealth of experience and capital. All this at a time when the invasion of Tigray is already being prepared by Eritrea,[4] which owes so much to Nevsun. Can Shire's mines be considered as war prizes? Let's take a look back at an odyssey lasting almost twenty years.

Gold rush in red soil

The resources of the Nubian Shield have long attracted geologists, and in Eritrea, they were already there when the country gained independence in 1993. In 1995, Tesfai Ghebreselassie Sebhatu, the minister of Energy and Mines, promulgated the young state's mining code. Mining was a hopeful prospect. It could be a long-awaited source of foreign currency for the country's development, and in the same year, the Ministry of Energy and Mines published a booklet for investors entitled *Mineral Prospects of the State of Eritrea*. I must admit that there's something touching about reading the few pages summarizing the history of mining in colonial times and presenting the geology of Eritrea. In impeccable English, the brochure explains the efforts made and how the system for granting licences to international investors works. Everything was still possible; the future was opening up for an independent Eritrea. That was before the authoritarianism of the PFDJ and its leader became obvious. That was before the disastrous Border War with Ethiopia. During the latter, from 1998 to 2000, all investments were de facto suspended. But from 2003, when the security situation seemed to improve, there was a veritable gold rush. Eritrea and the Nubian Shield were the New Frontier of mining, an unexplored and untapped region where the promises of enrichment were as tantalizing as the risks are real. One after another, international companies were trying to obtain prospecting and exploration licences for the Eritrean subsoil, and this was no mean feat. For one thing, the security situation remained very tense. Despite the cessation of open fighting with neighbouring Ethiopia, skirmishes were still frequent and armed factions practiced banditry. So much so that British geologist Timothy Nutt, working for Nevsun, was murdered on 12 April 2003.[5] He was found with his throat cut and his hands and feet bound. His death could be attributed to the Eritrean Islamist Jihadists, a group based in Sudan.[6]

Then there were the regime's ideological reservations. Heir to the EPLF, the PFDJ claims to be rooted in Marxism-Leninism and the struggle for decolonization. From his personal experience in China, Isayas Afwerki is strongly influenced by Maoism. All these currents of thought defend the idea that the country's natural resources should benefit the people. The EPLF, the party founded by Isayas in 1972, is above all a nationalist party.[7] It therefore seems contradictory that the PFDJ, which emerged from this party and established its control over all spheres of Eritrean society in the name of popular revolution, should allow what could be seen as predatory multinationals to operate. It was to resolve this contradiction that the Eritrean government suspended all prospecting activities on 2 September 2004,[8] in the face of an influx of licence applications.

According to internal sources, Isayas was initially rather hostile to the development of the mining sector and lost interest in it for a long time. He delegated. Minister Tesfai Ghebreselassie Sebhatu finally took charge of overhauling the mining code and in 2006[9] created the Eritrean National Mining Corporation (ENAMCO). This new national agency was initially intended to enable the Eritrean government to acquire a stake in Bisha Mining Share Co, a joint venture in which ENAMCO owned 40 per cent and Nevsun 60 per cent. The Eritrean government will subsequently impose the form of the joint venture with ENAMCO to all international companies developing mining projects in the country.

According to article 9 of the proclamation law, the five-person board of ENAMCO is appointed to President Isayas. The chairperson is appointed by President Isayas. To date, ENAMCO has never published a proper balance sheet. The agency is supposed to report to the Ministry of Mines, but it has been finally attached directly to the President Isayas. So, he made it a personal business.

In a March 2006 press release,[10] the minister of Mines expressed his desire to see knowledge of the country's geology grow and become more systematic. The idea was that, to stand up to the multinationals, Eritrea needed to train its own professionals and build up a solid body of scientific knowledge. Training geologists should have been the mission of the University of Asmara, but true to the totalitarian model, Isayas Afwerki's regime closed the country's only university the same year, in September 2006, for fear of dissent.

But not everyone is a geologist. Eritrean scientists cannot train either in the country or by traveling, which is forbidden. This growing lack of knowledge is precisely what puts the country at risk. In the industry, it is said that Nevsun has had to bear the brunt of ENAMCO's ignorance and amateurism, and has shown a great deal of patience, but in return, the company has been able to make the most of it. It always pays to do business when you have the advantage.

During the early years of the regime, it seems that the mining sector and its potential to bring in foreign currency, incomparable with any other in Eritrea, was the subject of a tug-of-war among PFDJ executives. There was clearly a tension between those in favour of developing the mining sector and a force holding them back. In a cable dated 7 October 2007, Melinda Tabler-Stone, Deputy Chief of Mission at the American Embassy in Asmara, provides an interesting analysis: a group of senior Eritrean government officials are allegedly taking advantage of the President's lack of interest in the mining industry to deliberately keep him at arm's length and prevent any deleterious decisions on his part affecting a sector vital to the regime's survival.[11] But after the imposition of international sanctions and the start of production at Bisha, Isayas understood what he owed to the mines and was never going to interfere – quite the contrary. He will leave Todd Romaine and his lawyers, who work so well for him, to their own devices.

The major mining projects that have come to fruition in Eritrea are all interconnected. The initial competition between the Canadian and Australian companies disappears over the years and turns into complicity. A handful of individuals (geologists, businessmen, lawyers) move from one company to another. Nevsun, Sunridge, Sun Peak, on the Canadian side, they carry the solar metaphor. All around the world gold is frequently associated with the sun for its brightness, but I cannot help but think of the alchemical Corpus and the prophetical dreams of Zosimos. In the alchemical corpus, gold is the metal of the 7th heaven, the sphere of the sun, that of enlightenment.

The Bisha mine

Most of Eritrea's mining projects have come to nothing. Don't let the hype fool you. There are three types of licences: prospecting, exploration and finally exploitation. In the 1990s and 2000s, many international companies expressed their intention to prospect in the fledgling state located in the Nubian Shield, on the shores of the Red Sea, whose political regime was not yet known. The PFDJ could still be seen as more approachable than Omar Al-Bashir's Sudan, and above all as completely inexperienced in the art of raw material negotiation. Of all the companies that attempted to obtain prospecting and exploration licences in Eritrea, only a handful did obtain any, but never proceeded to the exploitation stage. Nevsun and the Bisha mine were to change the history of Eritrea, the Horn of Africa and perhaps beyond.

Bisha is located in the Gash Barka region, famous for its subsoil, some 150 kilometres west of Asmara. The deposit is characterized by an upper layer of gold, mined first. Next come copper and silver, followed by zinc. As is the case throughout the Nubian Shield, local people know that gold can be found and are familiar with certain veins. Traditional gold panning exists in Eritrea, but the type of deposits at Bisha produce few nuggets. Gold must therefore be separated from other minerals and amalgamated. After colonization, the Italians did collect metals at Mdre-Zien, Adi Shmagle, Gala and Awgaro, but these were always surface operations. A confidential telegram from Ambassador McMullen reveals that a Chinese company called Eritrea-China Exploration and Mining Company (ECEM) has been trying since 2007 to rehabilitate the Awgaro site, which was opened during Egyptian colonization and abandoned by the Italians in 1930.[12] The mine is located 30 kilometres west of Badme, which was the bone of contention between Eritrea and Ethiopia and the trigger for the 1998 war.[13] But the mine was not profitable. Surface gold panning and the simple refurbishment of colonial mines were not enough. To be profitable, you must dig, as they did at Bisha. The Chinese have understood this and also covet the mother of Eritrean mines.

Indeed, the same diplomatic cable, dated August 2008, refers to rumours circulated by Australians about a possible Chinese takeover of their Canadian competitor Nevsun. Nevsun has been operating in Eritrea since the end of the twentieth century[14] and is undercapitalized, causing chronic cash-flow problems to advance work. Three Chinese companies are already in the running. The telegram concludes: 'Should Nevsun sell Bisha to a Chinese mining company it could delay the start of production and would result in substantial profits accruing to Beijing or Shanghai, as opposed to British Columbia. End Comment.'[15]

The sale didn't go ahead, and Bisha went into production in February 2011, generating $548 million in the first year for gold alone. In 2012, Nevsun was able to acquire the Mogoraib site, 15 kilometres from Bisha, from the Canadian company Sanu Resources Ltd. The mine also produces copper and zinc, for $566 million in 2012 and $466 million in 2013, mainly for copper.

With ENAMCO owning a 40 per cent stake in the Bisha mine, theoretically $365 million should have gone to the Eritrean state coffers in the first year of production. But this brilliant success conceals a darker reality. The veil was torn as early as 2014, when Eritrean refugees filed a complaint against the Canadian mining company for complicity in forced labour, crimes against humanity, slavery and torture.

In its defence, Nevsun embarked on an energetic whitewashing campaign. From twists and turns to appeals, the case lasts until 2020. A financial settlement was finally reached with the plaintiffs. Nevsun will therefore not be condemned.

In the meantime, Ambassador McMullen's fear has become reality: at the end of 2018, Nevsun sells its shares in the Bisha mine to Zijin Mining Group, one of the main Chinese companies specializing in precious metals.

Sunridge and the Asmara Project

Slightly more modest than Bisha, the Asmara Project comprises licences for the Emba Derho, Adi Nefas, Gupo and Debarwa sites, polymetallic open-pit mines containing gold, copper, zinc and silver.[16] The Asmara Project was developed in 2003 by the Australian company Sub-Sahara Resources NL, which at this time was also exploring in the Koka region with the Zara Mining Company. Sunridge Gold Corp soon acquired a stake in Asmara Mining Share Company. Based in Vancouver, Sunridge is a sister company of Nevsun, a lineage that is verified throughout the decade that follows. Who is who? Here is a page from the Social Register of the mining sector in Eritrea, which perfectly illustrates this proximity. Nevsun founder and ex-CEO Craig Angus co-founded Sunridge. David Daoud who had been working for Nevsun since 2003 became Sunridge's exploration manager in 2005,[17] and Greg Davis, Nevsun's country manager and vice-president for exploration from 2004 to 2011, became Sunridge's Business Development manager in 2011. Both will be co-founders of Sun Peak in Tigray in 2018. Scott Ansell, Nevsun's former project manager, became Vice President of Sunridge in 2010, and Chris Attwood, Nevsun's former mining manager, was recruited by Sunridge in 2013.[18] The boundary between Nevsun Resources Ltd and Sunridge Resources Ltd is therefore completely porous.

From 2005 onwards, when Daoud joined the project, Sub-Sahara was gradually pushed out of the Asmara Project, and in 2006 Sunridge (and therefore Nevsun) regained full control of it at the behest of the Eritrean government.[19]

In June 2008, David Daoud confided to the consular officer of the American embassy in Eritrea that he did not believe the Eritrean government would take more shares in the Asmara Mining Share Company joint venture between Sunridge and ENAMCO than the 10 per cent free under the mining code. According to the geologist, ENAMCO had taken a substantial stake in Bisha because it was the first mining operation in Eritrea. The government had wanted to impose itself for the sake of honour and prestige but will probably not repeat the operation.[20] And yet Daoud was wrong, since ENAMCO ended up taking a 40 per cent stake in the Asmara Mining joint venture.

Sunridge finally agreed to sell its 60 per cent stake to Sichuan Road & Bridge Mining Investment Development Corp. Ltd in November 2015, a purchase that will be effective on 26 April 2016[21] in the midst of a lawsuit against arms broker Delizia. At the very moment when, boosted by the publication of the feasibility study and its new mining licence (and not just exploration licence),[22] the Asmara project was about to become profitable.

Sun Peak Metals Corp

As soon as the Asmara project was wound up, the Sunridge board split between Alpha (Michael Hopley) in Eritrea and Sun Peak (David Daoud, Greg Davis, Scott Ansell and Doris Meyer)[23] in Tigray, Ethiopia. Sun Peak is headquartered in Vancouver and listed on the Toronto Stock Exchange.

The Shire site where the Sun Peak concessions are located is indeed in Ethiopia, but only 170 kilometres from the Asmara project (Debarwa and Emba Derho) and 180 kilometres from Bisha,[24] both in Eritrea. The team is well acquainted with the site's mineralization, characteristic of the Arabian-Nubia Shield, consisting of Volcanogenic Massive Sulphide (VMS) gold-copper-zinc deposits and orogenic gold more on the surface, which have been the subject of artisanal mining.[25]

'We are very excited to be conducting mineral exploration in Ethiopia on the same Nubian Shield geology as we did in Eritrea at Bisha and the Asmara projects,' Daoud tells *Northern Miner*.[26] 'When we first visited the Shire project area, we saw the same tremendous mineral potential for discovery of large high-grade VMS deposits.' And Davis confirms, 'The geology is the same as both Bisha and Asmara. It's the same trend that comes from the north and crosses the border.' The region is devoid of modern mining infrastructure, and Davis is also counting on a drastic drop in energy prices over the next few years, thanks to the commissioning of the Grand Ethiopia Renaissance Dam (GERD).

The Shire mines project comprises five licenses: Nefasit, Terer, Adi Mendi-Gabat, Adi Dairo and Meli. The latter two are operated under a joint venture between Sun Peak and Ezana Mining Development

PLC called Axum Metals. Ezana is a subsidiary of the Endowment Fund for the Rehabilitation of Tigray (EFFORT), a powerful trust active in all areas of industry and agriculture which enabled the development of Tigray and Ethiopia when the EPRDF was in power in Ethiopia.

Its director, Fisseha Meresa, is also head of the Tigray Mining Bureau, that is, in charge of the official licensing process. This dual role raises questions about potential conflicts of interest, and in fact the company has gained a monopolistic position, with the role of draining gold, including from small-scale operations, not only from Tigray, but also from other regions to the National Bank of Ethiopia.

Two whistle-blowers contacted me in March 2024 to explain that deliveries have not been made in recent years, with the gold evaporating into parallel channels for the benefit of a handful of Ezana officials, members of the old TPLF guard. What's more, many of the senior civil servants currently working in the Ethiopian Ministry of Mines, even though they are not Tigrayans, were trained by Ezana executives, fostering a culture of clientelism and increasing the risk of corruption.[27] A secret meeting had been held in November 2023, they told me, to resolve the problem of gold deliveries to the National Bank of Ethiopia, in preparation for the reforms demanded by the International Monetary Fund and the World Bank to release billions in financial aid for the country. Tensions rose, and suddenly gold reappeared.

The Tigray Interim Administration (TIA), chaired by Getachew Reda, is well aware of the problem and has ordered the closure of mining sites (including Sun Peak's) until further notice, in order to clarify the interests at stake and provide Tigray with new mining legislation. But both the TIA and the TPLF are facing internal challenges, notably from some of the TPLF's historical leaders. Bringing order to mining means confronting them directly.

As I write, there is a tug-of-war going on in Tigray, and mining is suspended until the sector is reformed.

Sun Peak does not communicate on the closure of its sites simply because this would affect the price of its shares on the stock market. This is the opposite effect of what the brochure with which I opened this chapter was published for. Communicating about the discovery of a vein, the granting of a licence or the resumption of activity raises the price, and this is how the companies finance themselves.

Summer 2018, peace, sun and gold!

Following the sale of Sunridge's shares in 2016 and Nevsun's in 2018 in their respective joint ventures with ENAMCO to Chinese companies, Canadian mining teams are immediately reorganizing. Alpha Exploration Ltd and Sun Peak Metals Corp are the latest avatars. Moreover, the old rivalry between Canadian and Australian companies is over.

In 2018, Nevsun and Danakali Limited (the Australian potash producer) are joining forces. In March 2018, Nevsun's Todd Romaine and Danakali's Seamus Cornelius co-hosted an event at the United Nations headquarters in Geneva entitled 'Demystifying Eritrea: The Ground Reality, Mining and Human Rights',[28] echoing the 'it's not that bad in Eritrea' argument.[29] While Nevsun and Danakali have been pinpointed by several human rights organizations,[30] the two champions explain that the problem is a perception of ground reality distorted by the 'current media'. They intend to provide a more balanced perspective and 'lay the foundations for more constructive approach'. The 'constructive' approach is language borrowed directly from Nevsun's lobbyists,[31] as is the denigration of the mainstream media as a source of misinformation. The event is organized in partnership with the Eritrean Consulate in Geneva and Eritrea's Permanent Mission to the United Nations. The consulate is known for collecting the 2 per cent income tax on nationals abroad, tracking down opponents, organizing fundraising events and propaganda festivals for the regime. At the time, the mission was headed by diplomat Adem Osman, a dashing representative of the regime. 'When Eritrea was once again pilloried in the Human Rights Council, he listened stoically. Only to then say that everything was completely different, that Eritrea is making great progress in terms of human rights – reports to the contrary are Western lies and should be rejected, according to the regime's prominent mouthpiece,'[32] reports the Swiss daily *Neue Zürcher Zeitung*. Exactly the line of the Nevsun and Danakali event. It is not uninteresting to note that Adem Osman disappeared in September 2023. He defected and sought political asylum in Switzerland. He is undoubtedly one of the best informed about the horrors of the regime he is now fleeing and why he is in hiding.

The other highlight of 2018 for mining companies in Eritrea is the move across the border to benefit the rapprochement between Ethiopia and Eritrea. In fact, the Nubian Shield knows no borders, and deposits of gold, copper and potash stretch indiscriminately across Eritrea, Ethiopia and Sudan. Cornelius' presentation at the Geneva seminar, intended to set the record straight regarding the perception of Eritrea, includes a map showing potash deposits included in a zone known as the potash development project,[33] most of which is located in Ethiopia. The two speakers, Seamus Cornelius and Todd Romaine (the latter will join the former at Danakali less than ten months later), have cross-border ambitions. What exactly do they know?

Their UN seminar takes place on 8 March 2018. Ethiopian prime minister Hailemariam Desalegn has just resigned on 27 February and Abiy Ahmed is to be elected head of the EPRDF on 27 March following an internal process. There are no elections by universal suffrage for the head of government in Ethiopia. On 2 April, he was approved as the new prime minister by the Ethiopian parliament.

Given the Eritrean regime's support for factions backing Abiy Ahmed, one can only wonder at the anticipation of the Nevsun and Danakali leaders. Similarly, Nevsun's management accepted Zijin's takeover offer just one week before the signing of the Jeddah Agreement on 16 September 2018. They really do have an excellent flair for business or very good information.

The summer of 2018 was intense in negotiations between the Ethiopian prime minister and the Eritrean president which culminated with the signing of the so-called Jeddah Agreement which put an end to twenty years of more or less open war, more or less cold depending on the period, but which at strongest of the fighting was extremely lethal.

The peace agreement includes many secret closes, among others on the destruction of the TPLF and, as far as we're concerned here, access to the Red Sea.[34] All these underhand negotiations were accessible in 2018 only to a minority of insiders. The talks took place under the patronage of António Guterres, between the Eritrean and Ethiopian governments and Amhara leaders.

On 8 July 2018, Abiy Ahmed visits Asmara. Isayas explicitly asks Abiy to intervene upon his return with the UN Secretary General to have the sanctions against Eritrea lifted.[35] Guterres immediately jumps on a plane to Addis Ababa, where he meets the Ethiopian prime minister. Without any hindsight, he declared to the press the same day that the sanctions against Eritrea were now 'obsolete'.[36] Two weeks later, on 24 July 2018, Danakali Limited was listed on the London Stock Exchange.

The peace agreement has not yet been officially signed, but the Australian mining company's management is clearly counting on it and the lifting of UN sanctions against Eritrea. Otherwise, why register on the stock market? Which investors would bet on a mine in a country under sanction and embargo? What do the board know? Are they aware that the question of Eritrean ports on the Red Sea is at the heart of this agreement (because it is, in return for the destruction of the TPLF)?

In any case, there was a great deal of coordination. Alem Kibreab, director-general of mines in the Ministry of Energy and Mines of Eritrea, has announced the possible construction of a port-to-port facility at Anfile Bay,[37] just 75 kilometres from the Colluli mine operated by Danakali, itself 75 kilometres from the Ethiopian border, to export minerals and possibly other commodities from Ethiopia. Seamus Cornelius speaks out on this occasion in an article published by Bloomberg on 23 August 2018, and on 20 September he gives a conference at a networking forum in London. His presentation published by Danakali include a map showing the Colluli mine, the ports available and the cross-border deposit.[38]

In this document intended for investors, the management of Danakali chooses to include under the headline 'Eritrea is a Mining Friendly Jurisdiction'[39] a photograph of Isayas Afwerki shaking the hand of Abiy Ahmed all smiles during the signing of the Agreement in Jeddah four days earlier. And next in quote, the Bloomberg headline 'Nevsun Finds a White Knight in Zijin with $1.41 Billion Deal'.[40] Indeed, on 5 September (three weeks before the Jeddah Agreement), the Nevsun board advised its shareholders to accept Zijin Mining's offer and sell the Bisha mine to the Chinese company. Through this quote and the mention of this colossal sum, the management of Danakali hopes to arouse the desire of investors.

The same day, namely 5 September 2018, Isayas Afwerki, Abiy Ahmed and Mohamed Abdullahi Mohamed nicknamed 'Farmaajo', the Somali president, are laying the foundations of the Tripartite Agreement,[41] a military alliance whose sole achievement is the sending of joint troops to Tigray. They visit the port of Massawa together and admire the 'Ethiopian vessel that contested for first time & won bid for shipment of zinc produced by Bisha Mine',[42] in the words of

Yemane Ghebremeskel, Eritrea's powerful Minister of Information. Great communication operation!

What excitement in the two months preceding the Jeddah Agreement concluded in the presence and under the patronage of António Guterres, the Secretary General of the UN. In the process, carried by the ambient enthusiasm, the United Nations commissioned two consultants to write a report on the potential of Colluli to develop Eritrea.[43] It's a real red carpet that unfolds in front of Danakali after its listing on the London Stock Exchange.

Red carpet and river of blood, because the invasion of Tigray was also part of the 'peace' plan of the Jeddah Agreement. Considering that the team of lobbyists led by Todd Romaine for Nevsun was perfectly retrained in the promotion of the Tigray war, one can wonder if the minerals from Tigray (transported through Eritrean ports) were not one of the driving forces of this war.

Nevsun management asks its shareholders to accept the buyout proposal at the beginning of September 2018, the climax of an intense year. Once the deal was finalized, Todd Romaine joined Seamus Cornelius at Danakali, with whom he had begun this promotional year. Was this already on the agenda when they defended Eritrea's mining industry together in Geneva? In any case, the game of musical chairs is in full swing!

Alpha Exploration Ltd, border crossing

On 18 January 2018, Alpha received the concession for Kerkasha, a gold and copper mine located in the Gash Barka region southeast of Bisha, not far from the Ethiopian border. On 13 September 2018, three days before the signing of the Jeddah Agreement, the concession was expanded.[44] Alpha's founder and chief executive is Alasdair Smith,[45] the former director of Sub-Sahara involved in the Asmara and Zara Projects before the Australian miner was ousted by Sunridge. But in 2018, as I have already emphasized several times, competition between Canadians and Australians is no longer appropriate. Indeed, Alpha is co-directed by Michael Hopley, former head of Sunridge from 2004 to 2016 and who in 2008 wanted to develop in Colluli potash with his subsidiary Crescent Resources Corp.[46] He also directed Sun Peak. John Clarke, non-executive director of Alpha, was the president and CEO of Nevsun from 1997 to 2008. Tewelde Haile, exploration manager of Alpha, also worked for the Zara Project, as well as in Ethiopia.[47] Registered in Switzerland and the British Virgin Islands, Alpha is however de facto Canadian, listed on the Toronto Stock Exchange from September 2021 on.[48]

Quoted in an article in the *Mining Journal* from January 2022, which is more of a promotional leaflet, Michael Hopley takes up all the language elements of Nevsun and Danakali on the good atmosphere in Eritrea, the mining code, the stability of the region and so on. He declares that he was not at all disturbed by the 'political noise in the neighbourhood',[49] that is to say the war in Tigray. It's true, after all, it was only a mouse scratch, just political noise.

War in peace: A false opportunity

As for most economic actors in the Horn of Africa, the 2018 peace between Ethiopia and Eritrea was to represent an exceptional opportunity, the promise of the opening of the border between the two countries and therefore the easier access to the sea for landlocked Ethiopia and the lifting of international sanctions against Eritrea. Investors would be reassured.

But one of the clauses of the peace agreement was the destruction of the TPLF, which constituted the elected government of Tigray. A new war was therefore not only inevitable but, above all, desired and prepared by the two governments.

It is impossible to say with certainty what information was available to mining companies in Eritrea and Ethiopia. But it is clear that there was an upsurge in their activity in 2018 and even an expansion on the eve of the invasion of Tigray by the Eritrean armed forces allied with the Ethiopian army.

In August 2020, at a time when the Ethiopian prime minister had already adopted Isayas' phrase 'Game is over',[50] that is to say that war is imminent, Abiy Ahmed appointed the former mayor of Addis Ababa Takele Uma Banti as minister of Mines. At the end of October (while the troops are already positioning themselves around Tigray), he unveiled the new Mineral Policy developed by consultants from the Canadian International Resources and Development Institute (CIRDI) as part of the Supporting Ministry of Mines in Ethiopia (SUMM) project.[51] The text is subject to public consultation for around ten days,[52] knowing that the Tigray war breaks out on 4 November 2020.

But ultimately it is not so much the actual exploitation of resources that is at stake as the publicity stunts. A Tigrayan geologist assured me that no one had actually seen the Sun Peak teams working. They only come to take a few photos for the investors and that's it. In fact, he explains to me, what matters is to reassure the markets and create buzz through press releases. 'A new vein of gold discovered!' and shares take off; 'The war stops, activity resumes!' new jump on the Toronto Stock Exchange; 'The potash which must feed the world will be able to be transported', and it is the London Stock Exchange which is celebrating. This is how Western companies make their money, not by developing resources, he told me. Pure speculation.

The costs and income of exploitation are the Chinese's lot, since all the companies active in Eritrea and followed in this book have been sold to them.

Alpha Exploration Ltd and Sun Peak Metals Corp are the last sparks of the Nevsun sub-fragmentation. But the peace fizzled out.

The Tigray war was contained in the Jeddah Agreement so awaited by mining companies. Were their management team aware of this? Still, their hopes of abolished borders and shared infrastructure have been dashed. The break between Abiy Ahmed's Ethiopia and Isayas Afwerki's Eritrea is once again complete.

The question of ports and access to the Red Sea, which had rightly aroused enthusiasm, is at the heart of the new quarrel which is once again throwing the triangle of Ethiopia, Eritrea and Somalia into the whirlwind of inflammatory declarations and demonstrations of force.

The Nevsun Trials

The Nevsun Trials

On 20 November 2014, Gize Yebeyo Araya, Kesete Teklemariam Rekemariam and Mihretab Semere Gebremedhin, three Eritrean refugees, filed a claim in the Supreme Court of British Columbia in Vancouver, Canada, against Nevsun Resources Ltd. They argued that, in the name of National Service, they had been forced to work in the Bisha mine and subjected to 'cruel, inhuman and degrading treatment'.[1]

Although the Bisha mine has been producing gold since 2011, and copper since 2012, operations at the site began in 2008. The mine is operated by a joint venture, the Bisha Mining Shareholders Corporation (BMSC), 60 per cent owned by Nevsun and 40 per cent by the Eritrea National Mining Corporation (ENAMCO). BMSC subcontracts various services to state-owned companies, the main one being Segen Construction Company.[2] For skilled jobs, Segen hires contractors who work as part of their national service, and for unskilled jobs, there is not even a contract, the conscripts simply being made available to Segen by the army,[3] and therefore to BMSC and ultimately to Nevsun. The plaintiffs believe that Nevsun knew or should have known that their subcontractor was using forced labour.

Back in January 2013, Human Rights Watch highlighted the problem and denounced human rights violations at Bisha.[4] Nevsun's management defended itself by pleading ignorance and that the use of national service labour had ceased.

Yet again in 2015, the OHCHR-mandated Commission of Inquiry on Human Rights in Eritrea established in its report that forced labour was indeed real and institutionalized in Bisha.[5] The commissioners report deprivation of rest, torture, with conscript workers regularly punished, tied to trees at night so as not to encroach on their working hours[6] or detained at the Bisha National Security Prison.[7]

In October 2016, the Supreme Court of British Columbia confirmed that the proceedings should take their course in Canada, as the plaintiffs were not entitled to a fair trial in Eritrea. Nevsun appealed, a legal move rejected by the British Columbia Court of Appeal in November 2017. The court upheld the following charges against Nevsun: crimes against humanity, slavery, forced labour and torture. The trial was due to take place on 23 January 2019, but in the meantime, Nevsun turned once again to the Supreme Court of British Columbia, requesting leave to appeal the 2017 decision, which was granted on 14 June 2018. Nevsun points to the inadmissibility of the complaint in Canada.[8]

The judges of the Supreme Court of Canada rule on 28 February 2020. They recognize the serious human rights violations at Bisha, but do not rule on Nevsun's direct responsibility. The issue before them is whether the British Columbia courts have jurisdiction to hear the case under customary international law, as the plaintiffs contend. Nevsun, on the other hand, argues that under the 'act of state doctrine', Canadian courts cannot try a case under the jurisdiction of another country. The majority of the Supreme Court of Canada rejected this argument, as the 'act of state doctrine' is not part of Canadian law.[9]

Here we see the clash between a universalist conception of human rights, which is more Western, and the sovereignty ardently defended by Russia, China and Eritrea.

In 2020, no fewer than fifty-seven plaintiffs brought proceedings against Nevsun. On 3 March, the Supreme Court of British Columbia confirmed that all complaints would be dealt with in a single trial.[10] The legal world and the press were already announcing a landmark ruling on corporate criminal liability,[11] but a financial settlement with the plaintiffs was finally reached in early October 2020,[12] the amount of which was not disclosed. Nevsun will therefore never be convicted.

At the end of 2018, Nevsun had been acquired for C$1.41 billion[13] (around US$1 billion) by Zijin Mining Group Co. Ltd, one of China's leading mining companies. This sum is divided between the shareholders. Nevsun remains a legal entity, its assets and liabilities, including cash and financial reserves, passing under Zijin's ownership. The financial agreement with the Eritrean plaintiffs is concluded in the name of Nevsun, but it is, in fact, Zijin that pays for the extinction of the legal proceedings.

Happy ending for Nevsun management and shareholders

Nevsun's defence

As soon as the Human Rights Watch press release appeared in January 2013, Nevsun's management took full measure of the damage to the company's image. Todd Romaine was appointed vice president, Corporate Social Responsibility, and took charge of a veritable charm offensive that will have global geopolitical repercussions. Romaine's strategy is a shrewd one. He knows that for Western opinion, which sees thousands of Eritrean refugees arrive every year, the Isayas regime is unacceptable. He's not going to try to deny or pretend that Nevsun has no links with the Eritrean government; everyone knows that you can't do business in Eritrea without going through its helmsman. Nevsun is now in solidarity with the Asmara regime. The company's strategy is to support this latter and to undermine the defenders of human rights. Isayas becomes the hero of a new world painted in the colours of alter-globalism, while the advocates of democracy and human rights are the henchmen of American imperialism. All this is quite comical coming from a person working for a firm listed on the international stock market (Toronto and New York stock exchanges) and which prospers by exploiting the resources of the African continent. Ultra-capitalism to the rescue of Maoism, the better to save its own skin. It was a daring move.

Todd Romaine is going to hire Ruby Sandhu, a British lawyer who claims to specialize in business and human rights.

On her website RS Collaboration (the initials of Resilient System not to be confused with Ruby Sandhu apparently) where she claims to have been working since May 2013, she is the only employee under the tab 'our team'. She cites dozens of countries where she says to have worked with 'diverse range of clients including Governments, Multinationals, iNGOs, charities, individuals and HNW around the world',[14] but her LinkedIn page features only articles on Eritrea and comments on veganism.

Of Indian origin, Sandhu seeks to embody a discourse close to that of the non-aligned leaders: human rights were invented by the Europeans and their descendants and have nothing to do with the anthropology of the South, which does not value the individual, but the collective.[15] Consequently, those who complain about forced labour in Eritrea are intoxicated by Western individualism. They would be nothing more than egotistical navel-gazers who have understood nothing about the project for a new society and a new world towards which the PFDJ is heading. They would be the agents of the American conspiracy, whose sanctions would be solely responsible for the misery of the Eritrean people.

Justice takes its time. Nevsun's defence was then organized outside the courts, in an active lobbying campaign with unsuspected ramifications.[16] And so we shall meet Ruby Sandhu again in the next chapter.

Delizia, the arms broker

In parallel with proceedings launched by former Eritrean workers, the arms broker Delizia Limited launches another lawsuit against Nevsun and Sunridge. The dispute dates back to 2003. At the time, Delizia had supplied equipment for combat aircraft to the Eritrean army and therefore to the Eritrean state, which was never paid for in full. The joint venture model between ENAMCO and the mining companies provides for the Eritrean agency to claim a certain percentage of the capital of the Bisha Mining Shareholders Corporation as well as of the Asmara Mining Share Company. According to Delizia's lawyers, these shares are considered to be a debt owed by Nevsun and Sunridge to the Eritrean state, itself a creditor of Delizia. As a result, Delizia takes direct legal action against these two companies in the Canadian federal court in 2013, but the case is finally dismissed on appeal on 29 March 2018 by the Supreme Court of Canada.[17]

Delizia Limited is an interesting company in its own right. Based in Larnaka on the island of Cyprus, it was then run by Alexander Volfovich.[18] In 2005, it was taken over by Cycompserv Limited.[19] Also based in Larnaka, this company is known for its financial advice on opening accounts in Switzerland or the Virgin Islands, and for providing 'Cyprus Golden Visas'. This system, specific to the Mediterranean island, enables citizens who are not nationals of the European Union, the European Economic Area or Switzerland to obtain a long-term visa in Cyprus and thus in the European Union, facilitating access to European citizenship in exchange for investments or setting up a business on the island. Many Russian oligarchs have benefited from this scheme. On 1 February 2023, OFAC announced sanctions against the 'Zimenkov network', of which Alexander Volfovich was a key player.[20] This network was said to have supplied arms and 'technological gadgets' to Russia even after the invasion of Ukraine on 24 February 2022. Volfovich is also recognized as a notorious arms trafficker to Africa, exploiting the Golden Visa system.[21]

Information about Delizia Limited was hard to find, so I contacted the lawyer Robert Cooper who filed the application for leave to appeal on behalf of Sunridge Gold Corp against Delizia. After an affable introductory e-mail, all communication was then cut off. I received no information.

In these two sets of proceedings, it is already clear that Nevsun and its little sister Sunridge stand shoulder to shoulder. Solidarity between them, but above all in solidarity with the Eritrean regime. In both cases, the plaintiffs turned against Nevsun and Sunridge, but it was the Eritrean government and its policies that were targeted (irregular arms purchases, forced labour as part of National Service).

But the two mining companies, Nevsun being the more powerful and exposed of the two, made a rod to be beaten by building a relationship with the PFDJ that goes beyond the distribution of shares in a joint venture.

The first lobbying campaign to defend Nevsun and Isayas Afwerki

Romaine, the face of Nevsun

In 2014, three Eritrean refugees filed a complaint against Nevsun for complicity in forced labour. This marked the start of a lengthy trial. From all the cases brought against Nevsun and its satellite, the image of a close relationship takes shape, a de iure and de facto solidarity between the Canadian mining companies and Eritrea National Mining Corporation (ENAMCO). To defend the company that then employs him, Todd Romaine, Nevsun's vice president, Corporate Social Responsibility, chooses not to deny outright both forced labour and solidarity with the Eritrean government, which is after all obvious, but devises a strategy to clear the Eritrean regime and the Nevsun galaxy in the same move.

To help him in his plans, he hires the British lawyer Ruby Sandhu. Together they give lectures and conferences. They even plan a series of meetings in the House of Lords, British Parliament, in June 2015. Their narrative is to subvert the arguments of human rights defenders by accusing them of being reactionary and in the pay of international capitalism, which seeks to keep developing countries in poverty. According to them, Eritrea, led by its visionary leader, is a courageous bastion offering an alternative model where there are hardly any forced labourers, but soldiers fighting to establish a new order in which the individual disappears. This is the polished version of the Maoist revolutionary discourse that Isayas Afwerki has been proposing for nearly forty years, since his training in China during the Cultural Revolution. It must, however, be recognized that Isayas' ideological background has fluctuated a lot, from the China of his youth to the Eritrean maquis surrounded by Marxist-Leninist companions; he developed a nationalist doctrine, aiming at the modernization of his country through a brutal and opportunistic state-collectivism. He reminds me of the Albanian leader Enver Hoxha.

As we shall see, the PFDJ's defenders often come from the far left,[1] blinded by their anti-capitalist ideology, and paradoxically aided in this by dollars. Ruby Sandhu is a militant vegan and alter-globalization. She defends the idea of being innovative, 'constructive', not politicizing human rights, and not making them a priority. 'If I have to choose between an election and the food and the belly, I choose the food and the belly,'[2] she declares during a public panel when the question of democracy in Eritrea and the stolen constitution arose. It seems audacious, to say the least, to make such a statement by asking a rhetorical question, since the Eritrean people have no choice. It's a mining company making millions in cahoots with an autocratic regime that chooses for the Eritreans, not them. She raves about the exotic cliché of the good savage: 'Eritreans speak directly, simply and have a value system yet untainted by western consumption and consumerism – however I doubt whether they will be able to stop the floodgates of consumerism which the internet and social media has already facilitated – the western dream.'[3] In a burst of uninhibited paternalism, she asserts it is therefore normal to limit and monitor the internet to 'preserve' these brave Eritreans. She adds without seeing the contradiction, that speech is free in Eritrea, that there is a feeling of security (we call it a military regime) and that education is of high quality and free. In fact, all sixteen-year-olds pass through the Sawa barracks to 'graduate'. Abuses, including sexual slavery, are constant, and this is common knowledge as reported by the Office of the United Nations High Commissioner for Human Rights in its report covering 2015. Just one example among thousands: 'A male soldier in Sawa also provided the following explanation: "We watched sexual abuses. Systematically, they forced girls to obey their instructions; to have a relationship with them. If she doesn't obey, they find any kind of military punishment".[4] This is the free, high-quality education Ruby Sandhu stands for.

In August 2015, Ruby Sandhu and Todd Romaine appeared in Las Vegas on stage at the eleventh Young PFDJ festival, the youth of the Eritrean regime. These events are notorious for being great moments of propaganda flirting with legality (young people can be seen miming war scenes or calling for hatred against opponents or Ethiopians and in particular Tigrayans) and have since been cancelled several times in different host countries. These festivals also serve to raise funds for the party. So in 2015, with Nevsun already in the crosshairs of the judiciary and the UN, Todd Romaine and Ruby Sandhu found it judicious to display themselves in a completely uninhibited way under the banner of the single party of one of the world's worst dictatorships.[5] In fact, on 21 September 2015, the Eritrean Ministry of Information published a strange interview with Todd Romaine in which it's hard to know who's speaking, Todd Romaine or Yemane Ghebremeskel, the PFDJ's evergreen herald, the Minister of Information and advisor to the Eritrean President.[6] In the interview Todd Romaine says about the UN commission of inquiry into human rights violations in Eritrea:

> To date, well over 180 interviews have been conducted by an independent human rights lawyer [Ruby Sandhu] inside Eritrea which one would think would be significant and worthy of consideration amongst the UN COI Commissioners.
>
> This is especially true given the UN COI frequently complains that they cannot get access into the country. If such exclusions

of relevant information can be made with respect to the Bisha Mine, one can only assume other selective and arguably biased methodological approaches were applied in a similar manner to other aspects of this report.

The reality is that other nation states and organizations have or will be making misinformed policy choices negatively affecting Eritrea and Eritreans.

They will be doing this reflective of a questionable report that discriminately seeks to limit balanced information from within Eritrea. It is most ethical to take an approach of inclusion of all stakeholders inside and outside Eritrea in order to disseminate enough well-balanced information to enable other countries and organizations to make more informed, optimal decisions with respect to their policy choices.

It is believed that several individuals are deliberately using hurtful misinformation campaigns as a mechanism for their own political or financial self-interests and are strategically targeting the mining sector.

The sad irony is that those that champion 'human rights' or are the collectors of these 'allegations' are more preoccupied with deliberate attempts of economic sabotage that would negatively impact the human rights of all Eritreans. [. . .] This prevailing narrative is influenced by deliberate misinformation and the multiplier effect and this has helped contribute to the current distorted portrayal of the country.

The whole arsenal of Eritrean propaganda is present, with its paranoid litany about other states (i.e. Ethiopia and the United States) and organizations (TPLF, Human Rights Watch, Amnesty International, etc.) that have a grudge against Eritrea for enrichment. The 'sad irony', I think, lies rather in his sentence, uttered by the head of a mining company who most probably doesn't work for free. Noticeable is also the strange technique of using the voluntary closure of the country to explain that investigators can only tell fables. But if access to the country is restricted, whose fault is that? That in itself constitutes a crime against humanity. This argument will be reused with great cynicism by Ann Fitz-Gerald during the Tigray war, when the region will be subjected to a siege by Eritrean and Ethiopian troops: there is no free information, but what transpires is catastrophic. Don't listen to this! We who support the oppressor, we will give you the true independent version and so on.

The team is formed: Bronwyn Bruton and Herman J. Cohen

But back to the podium at the PFDJ youth festival in Las Vegas. Alongside Todd Romaine and Ruby Sandhu is a high-profile guest, Bronwyn Bruton, researcher and vice-director of the Atlantic Council's African Center. It's quite a stunt, as Bruton seems to be the PFDJ's entry into the world of American think tanks and academia. But nothing is free, for, as French journalist Léonard Vincent has shown, in 2015 Nevsun contributed between $100,000 and $249,000 to the Atlantic Council:

> Nevsun made a contribution to the Atlantic Council last year because we were impressed by their ongoing constructive work on Eritrea.[7]

The word 'constructive work' is not uninteresting. Roughly equivalent to 'pragmatism' or 'real politics' in international relations, it's a way of announcing that we're going to dance with the devil. The adjective is used several times by Todd Romaine during his intervention before the Canadian House of Commons on 5 June 2014, when he was grilled by the Subcommittee on International Human Rights shortly after the Eritrean workers filed their complaint. Among other things,

Mr. Romaine states in his conclusion that Nevsun engages in 'constructive dialogue' with all stakeholders.[8]

'Constructive' is taken up like a mantra by Ruby Sandhu[9] in April 2016 and by Bronwyn Bruton, notably during her hearing before the House Committee on Foreign Affairs, Subcommittee on Africa, Global Health, Global Human Rights, and International Organizations in Washington on 14 September 2016.[10] She pleaded for a change in relations between the United States and Eritrea, which should resume on a 'constructive footing', notably by lifting sanctions. It's worth remembering that the difficulty international companies active in Eritrea have in finding investors stems from their fear of financing projects in a sanctioned country that has been banned from the world, with the insecurity and image risks that this can entail. This is undoubtedly the kind of message Nevsun would seek to convey if they had to support someone to do so.

Bruton would almost suggest that the expression 'constructive footing' comes from Isayas: 'But my own dialogue with Asmara over the past 18 months leads me to believe that President Isaias would very much like to put his relations with Washington on a more constructive footing.' Eighteen months brings us to the beginning of 2015, shortly after the complaint against Nevsun was filed, when it was necessary to find 'advocates'. It is not difficult to understand who provides the language elements, since 'constructive' is in fact the tagline of the Atlantic Council. 'The Atlantic Council promotes constructive leadership and engagement in international affairs' is the first line of their website and appears at the end of their reports, including Bruton's in 2016.

On 23 June 2016, Bronwyn Bruton published an opinion piece in the *New York Times* entitled 'It's Bad in Eritrea, but Not That Bad',[11] and this 'not that bad' became a subject of tragic joke among opponents of the regime and human rights defenders.

In this campaign to defend Nevsun and the Eritrean government, Ruby Sandhu and Bronwyn Bruton do not completely deny the facts, but: (a) claim to change the way narrow-minded Westerners look at this regime: it is not violence, it is education, it is not a crime, it is a necessary evil, it is not slavery, it is collectivism; (b) reduce testimonies of crimes against humanity to anecdotes. Both women say they went in Eritrea and found nothing shocking. Everyone knows what guided tours are worth for foreigners in dictatorships, these trips embarked with the army and the secret services. Sandhu and Bruton contrast an impression with cohort studies. When the UN or Human Rights Watch publish reports, they rely on dozens or even hundreds of cases. The EEPA team around Mirjam van Reisen (University of Tilburg and Leiden) is also doing systematic scientific work. And without claiming to be exhaustive, I have spoken with a very large number of refugees who report consistent accounts of torture and deprivation of liberty in their native countries. I do not know, and I will never know because I do not search hearts if Ruby Sandhu and Bronwyn Bruton are sincere but fooled by the situation of the Eritrean people or if it is cynicism, a blindness caused by money or ambition.

Bruton also uses whataboutism. During the hearing before the House Committee on Foreign Affairs she stated, 'My research has convinced me that there is no serious opposition inside Eritrea to President Isaias or his government.'[12] Then instead of dealing frankly with the situation in Eritrea, she lists the failings in other countries in the Horn of Africa, each time emphasizing the EPRDF's Ethiopia. She bases her entire argument on a difference in treatment between Eritrea and Ethiopia by the United States. In short, we observe a childish game consisting of saying that the Ethiopians are naughty and yet they are not under sanction. So, what is this way of reasoning? Yes, Ethiopia did not respect certain commitments towards Eritrea, yes there was a repression of the Oromo movements in Ethiopia from 2015, but that in no way washes away Isayas, in particular the crimes committed against his own people. It is possible to denounce both. Unless you have a precise agenda aimed at subtly disseminate the world view of the Eritrean president, a bias which makes it impossible for you to be complex. If you are not with him then you are against, a polarization that extends to all international relations and which bursts into the face of world opinion in July 2023 during the Russia-Africa Summit, when Isayas lends allegiance to Vladimir Putin as leader in building the new world order against the West and its allies. No room for grey in the black-and-white vision of Isayas and his thurifers.

But if in 2016, Isayas' policy and his alliance with Moscow are already in place behind the scenes, Bruton claims that Isayas is ready for a rapprochement with the United States. She hammers home almost like a threat that without him the entire Horn will be destabilized and that we must bet on the helmsman of Asmara. Basically, Eritrea is not that bad.

In fact, the archaeology of words can go back a little further. Bruton's article is entitled 'Eritrea: Coming in from the Cold', a direct reference to 'Time to Bring Eritrea in from the Cold' published on 16 December 2013, in *African Arguments*[13] by Herman J. Cohen, former US Assistant Secretary of State for African Affairs and then President of Cohen and Woods International, an international affairs consultancy. Only a note leaked on the opposition media *Asmarino* on 8 July 2015, and written by Eritrean diplomat Berhane Gebrehiwet, Chargé d'Affaires to the United States, reveals that Ambassador Cohen would have been overseen by Asmara to publish his paper and find contacts to bend US policy in favour of Isayas Afwerki's government.[14] A mission that bears a striking resemblance to that of Bronwyn Bruton.

Herman 'Hank' Cohen worked for the Department of State between 1989 and 1993, the exact period when the Derg collapsed in Ethiopia and Eritrea gained independence. The PFDJ was still called the EPLF, and Cohen's approach was to ally himself with the Eritrean party against the USSR-backed Derg.[15] A friendship that obviously lasts!

Cohen explains the haemorrhage of young Eritreans fleeing at the risk of their lives by the Border War with Ethiopia. According to Cohen, the reason for Eritrean militarization and indefinite conscription is to resist the Ethiopians.

It's hardly surprising that in the interval between their two articles, Herman Cohen and Bronwyn Bruton found themselves at a roundtable on Eritrean refugees scheduled by the Atlantic Council on 10 December 2015.[16]

So, from 2013 onwards, the Eritrean government seeks support in the West through its network of embassies and consulates, and is ready to pay for it. From 2014 and the complaint filed against Nevsun, the Canadian mining company has in any case paid part of the campaign costs. Todd Romaine has very good relations with the Eritrean embassies or at least does not hesitate to appear in their events. In return, their press officers are also actively seeking to contribute to the effort and are looking for people to buy from 360 degrees. For example, French reporter Pierre Monégier, who shot in 2016 a documentary entitled *Érythrée, la Terre des Évadés* ('Eritrea, the land of escapees') for the famous 'Envoyé Special' series, was offered €15,000 and a vacation in New York or Tokyo if he avoided mentioning 'dictatorship' in his report. He refused. 'I'd never seen anything like it,'[17] he says.

It is quite remarkable that Nevsun Resources LTD's proven lobbyists have been heard at such a high level as Canada's House of Commons, the US Congress or the British Parliament's House of Lords.

In the Ethiopian diaspora

The example of Ambassador Cohen shows that beyond financial opportunism, friendship networks and ancient strategies still guide the course of events, right up to the heart of current affairs, as we shall see with the Tigray war lobbyists.

So, let's take a quick dip into history. Sister movements in the 1970s, the Eritrean People's Liberation Front (EPLF), already led by Isayas Afwerki, who renamed his party PFDJ in 1994 after Eritrea's independence, and the Tigray People's Liberation Front (TPLF) joined forces in the 1980s to overthrow the Derg regime in power in Ethiopia, led by Mengistu Hailemariam, infamous for being responsible for the Red Terror and famine of 1984–5. For the EPLF, the fight against the central power in Addis Ababa is coupled with a struggle for autonomy and even independence since Eritrea was annexed to Ethiopia in 1962.

The Tigrayans are very close to the Eritreans of the high plateaus in language, culture, religion and so on, but the two populations were separated by Italian colonization in the late nineteenth century and followed different paths. Nonetheless, the ties between them endure, from fraternity to fratricide. On 24 May 1991, the EPLF liberated Eritrean territory and supported the TPLF and its allies in the capture of Addis Ababa. This coalition of Ethiopian parties became known as the Ethiopian People's Revolutionary Democratic Front (EPRDF) and lasted until its dissolution by Ethiopian prime minister Abiy Ahmed in November 2019.

The Eritreans were quick to demand independence, which was endorsed by a referendum in 1993. But several grievances would persist and grow in intensity between the EPLF (soon to be PFDJ) of Isayas Afwerki, now president of Eritrea, and the EPRDF led by the Ethiopian prime minister of Tigrayan descent, Meles Zenawi. Armed conflict broke out on 6 May 1998. This was the Ethiopia–Eritrea Border War. The high-intensity conflict lasted two years, from May 1998 to July 2000. This was followed by the Algiers Agreements signed on 12 December 2000, and the establishment of the Border Commission, whose recommendations Ethiopia did not respect. A cold, or at least lukewarm, war ensued until 2018.

Playing the proxy war card, Isayas allies himself with and encourages all opponents of the EPRDF. In his anti-Meles delirium, Isayas is ready to support the Somali Islamists of the Islamic Courts, then to train Al-Shabaab fighters, despite the fact that he persecutes all religious groups at home, including jihadists from Sudan, as soon as they appear in Eritrea. But Somali Islamists are also nationalists and threaten Ethiopian territorial integrity. They are therefore very useful for distracting Ethiopia on its eastern flank. In fact, Ethiopia is the target of a call for Holy War issued by the Islamic Courts on 9 October 2006. Although troops were already present on Somali territory, Meles Zenawi announces that Ethiopia was officially at war with the Somali Islamists. A major offensive is launched on 21 December 2006.

Always in the vein of 'the enemies of my enemies are my friends', Isayas is ready for any contradiction, such as joining forces with those nostalgic for the Ethiopian empire, the ultra-nationalist Amharas, even though he dedicated his entire youth and twenty years of guerrilla warfare to smashing that empire!

For nearly a millennium, Ethiopia was an empire ruled by an emperor from the Amhara ethnic group.[18] The predominance of the Amharas was maintained under the Derg leading to an overlap or even an identification between Ethiopia and Amhara culture. It was this domination that ended in 1991, when the EPLF and the TPLF, surrounded by its multi-ethnic coalition of the EPRDF, put an end to centralized power around Addis Ababa. The EPRDF then implemented its ethno-federalism programme according to the democratic constitution of 1995. Ethiopia is a mosaic of peoples and nations, generally installed on a well-defined territory. The federated regional states are then delimited according to mainly linguistic criteria with a large autonomy but attached to the federal government whose head is the prime minister. The first was therefore the Tigrayan Meles Zenawi.

Ethiopian democracy does have its flaws. Many opponents were silenced, which led, for example, to the formation of the opposition movement Ginbot 7 after the contested elections of 2005. Those of 2010, won by 99.6 per cent by the EPRDF, were contested by many international observers.[19]

Most of the opponents of the EPRDF and those dissatisfied with the ethno-federalist system went into exile, somewhat in Europe, but mainly in the United States and Canada. The Amhara diaspora is very present there. Politicians, intellectuals and activists are developing media (ESAT TV) almost entirely dedicated to the self-celebration of their ethnic group and to the hatred of the TPLF, then outright of the Tigrayans. These media will prove to be powerful relays of hatred[20] before and during the Tigray war.

The PFDJ very early on approached certain Amhara nationalists in an alliance that could be described as crazy if it did not turn out to be deadly.

The Nevsun lobbyists who were already used to blaming the TPLF for all of Eritrea's ills will gradually also show their sympathy for the enemies of the TPLF in exile.

They follow the logic of 'alliance against' practiced for a long time by Isayas Afwerki and which will culminate in the so-called peace agreement between Eritrea and Ethiopia, signed on 16 September 2018, in Jeddah. Peace only has the name, because it is indeed a 'war agreement' which was sealed between Isayas and Abiy Ahmed Ali, the new strong man in Ethiopia. Supporter of a One and centralized Ethiopia, of Amhara and Oromo ancestry, Abiy Ahmed would restore the imagination of imperial Ethiopia by destroying the ethno-federalism established by the EPRDF (and behind it the TPLF). Immediately, it is the honeymoon in Canada and the United States between the Amhara nationalists in America and the supporters of the PFDJ.

With the ideological matrix developed by and for the Eritrean regime, new actors will emerge and bring this hitherto fairly marginal rhetoric out of its small revolutionary world to give it an almost global dimension. Attention, Ethiopia is entering the game! It is not only an African giant in size, demographics and economy, but also a symbolic giant, the only country on the continent not to have been colonized. '*Aethiopia*' the land of return for slaves, the empire of Haile Selassie 'Ras Tafari', the beacon of Pan-Africanists and Non-Aligned.

Part III

#NoMore

#NoMore, the Eritrean-Ethiopian opinion campaign

Ginbot 7 and ESAT

On 15 May 2005, Ethiopia's general elections were held and the ruling EPRDF party won. A protest movement arose to denounce irregularities, which was put down in blood by the government. Three years later, in 2008, Andargachew Tsige and Berhanu Nega founded Ginbot 7 (Ginbot Sabat or G7), an opposition Amahara-based party whose name literally means '7 May', corresponding to the date of the disputed elections in the Ethiopian calendar (15 May in the Gregorian calendar). The party quickly developed into an armed faction aimed at overthrowing the government in Addis Ababa. As the EPRDF was founded around the TPLF, the main Tigrayan party, Ginbot 7's opposition gradually came down to a fight to the death against the TPLF, and then against Tigrayans in the broad sense.

Andargachew Tsige went into exile in England in the 1970s as a refugee. Having married, he obtained British nationality and renounced his Ethiopian passport. So he was living in England when Ginbot 7 was created. Nor was Berhanu Nega physically in Ethiopia, as he was living in the United States at the time. In 2009, both were sentenced to death by an Ethiopian court in abstentia.

In 2010, Ginbot 7 executives set up ESAT (Ethiopian Satellite Television), based in the Netherlands, around Fasil Yenealem, the redactor-in-chief. Offices were then set up in London and Washington. In 2013, a recording leaked in which Berhanu Nega can be heard declaring that Ginbot 7 is financed by the Eritrean government. He talks about an instalment of half a million dollars, $200,000 of which is earmarked for ESAT. In *The Horn Affairs*, Daniel Berhane wonders where these funds ultimately come from, given that Eritrea is bankrupt. He wonders about Libya, Egypt or Qatar, but rejects all three hypotheses.[1] The source is perhaps to be found at the bottom of a gold mine since mining has become almost the sole source of foreign currency in Eritrea. Andargachew Tsige publicly acknowledged the Eritrean funding in 2022.[2]

Ginbot 7 has become a paramilitary armed group trained and equipped on Eritrean soil. On 23 June 2014, Andargachew Tsige, then secretary general of Ginbot 7, was arrested in Sanaa, Yemen, by the Ethiopian secret service while in transit returning from Dubai to Asmara. He had already been living in Asmara for two years.[3] Similarly, Berhanu Nega, the chairman of Ginbot 7, was also resident in Eritrea.[4]

After Abiy Ahmed came to power in 2018, several ESAT journalists returned from exile and Andargachew Tsige was released on 29 May. In his own words on the BBC Hardtalk show on 14 June 2018, he acted as an intermediary between Abiy Ahmed and Isayas Afwerki in what was to become the peace agreement, known as the Jeddha Agreement, between Ethiopia and Eritrea, but also the death warrant against the TPLF and Tigrayans in general.

In May 2019, Ginbot 7 is dissolved into a new party (Ezema) which includes other extreme Amhara nationalists, and in 2020, Andargachew Tsige becomes the CEO of ESAT. As Sarah Vaughan, a specialist in Ethiopian politics, notes, 'In the final four to five months before the [Tigray] war began, a number of ESAT broadcasts included more specific calls, prefiguring with remarkable accuracy the strategies of the war. [. . .] Its discussants called for "fraternal" joint military activity by Ethiopia and Eritrea against the TPLF.'[5]

Andargachew Tsige feels like a warlord. A few days after the launch of the #NoMore campaign (see below) following a year of war in Tigray, a video emerged of him, in uniform, haranguing ENDF soldiers or Amhara militiamen, urging them to use 'the most savage of cruelties', and he insisted: 'I tell you, you must not hesitate from resorting to the most barbaric of cruelties when you face them [the Tigrayans]. [. . .] You must be merciless, you must act beyond what our Amhara or Ethiopian cultural values permit.'[6]

The beginnings of the war in Tigray

In March 2018, Abiy Ahmed came into power within the EPRDF, the party that has been governing Ethiopia since the fall of the Marxist Derg regime in 1991. Of Oromo and Amhara descent, he quickly set about dismantling the coalition party. His programme was to destroy the ethno-federalism that was the hallmark of the EPRFD (and thus TPLF) and return to centralized power around Addis Ababa. He passed himself off as a young, modern, liberal democrat who would at last speak for the Oromos, but as soon as he came to power, he dismissed his fellow comrades from the Oromo Qeeroo movement and got enrolled by the Amhara nationalists. His plan and his instrument of power was to set up an (almost) single party in 2019, the Prosperity Party. To achieve this, he proclaimed an amnesty and brought back from exile the most fervent opponents of the TPLF, including the Ginbot 7 cadres, who thus facilitated the rapprochement between their protector – the old Eritrean despot – and the new Ethiopian Prime Minister.

Yesterday's enemy was celebrated as a hero. To complete his dream of 'One Ethiopia', the restoration of a homogenic empire of which he would be the seventh king,[7] Abiy Ahmed needs to subdue the Tigrayans, and to do this, he needs the help of Isayas Afwerki. But the PFDJ leader's return to favour involved a reversal of the narrative in Ethiopia. The unbelievable happened, and the Eritrean propaganda that Isayas had been harping on about for nearly thirty years, and which Nevsun's lobbyists had put down to paper, became the official discourse in Ethiopia too. All the problems in the Horn of Africa would henceforth be due to the 'Woyane'. This expression is used to designate the TPLF as a political party and to pretend not to attack civilians, whereas all Ethiopian and Eritrean listeners know that this expression confuses the two and applies from infants to the elderly.[8] 'Woyane' historically refers to the Tigrayan revolt against the centralization of power crushed in 1943 by Emperor Haile Selassie. The term finally came back as a reference to the spirit of independence of the Tigrayans, who claim it with pride. For other Ethiopians, particularly the Amharas, it is an insult.

Unsurprisingly, members of the TPLF refused to join the Prosperity Party, which was seen as an act of sedition. Tensions grew between the federal government and the Tigrayan authorities; one borderline statement followed another. Thus, when in April 2020, Abiy Ahmed's government declared that the general elections due to be held in August would be postponed indefinitely due the Covid-19 pandemic, discontent rose even higher. With the government's term due to end in September, the opposition saw the postponement as a way for Abiy Ahmed and the Prosperity Party to retain power unconstitutionally. The TPLF has already announced that elections will nevertheless be held in Tigray. Both parties accuse each other of trying to seize power in an irregular manner. Abiy Ahmed declares, 'Young people should not die, mothers should not cry and houses should not be demolished just so politicians can take power,'[9] which barely conceals the threat of war in the event of disobedience. Then he became very explicit, declaring that measures would be taken against what he would consider another seditious act.

On 9 September 2020, the Tigray regional state nevertheless held its elections, which were declared illegal by the federal government.

The Tigray war officially began on 4 November 2020, when Tigrayan forces attacked the headquarters of Northern Command, a federal base not far from Mekele, on the night of 3 to 4 November. This assault is undeniable. On the Tigrayan side, it was presented as a pre-emptive attack. Confidential documents and money were intercepted by Tigrayan intelligence. A commando unit was to arrest and eliminate a list of some fifty TPLF figures within two days, as a prelude to a massive attack on the region to take control of it. The federal government and its allies were caught off guard, but forces had already been pre-positioned. 'Troops' movement and redeployment before that day is an open secret',[10] confirms a former Eritrean diplomat. In fact, a few hours after the Northern Command attack, a large-scale combined arms offensive was launched against Tigray, which could not be organized at short notice. Fighting began on seven fronts, but the entry of federal troops into Tigrayan territory was only possible thanks to the support of the Eritrean army attacking from the north. Here too nothing had been left to chance; even the veterans had been recalled leading the assault. War did break out on the morning of the 4th, but without the element of surprise. The Tigrayan armed forces were able to withstand three weeks of resistance before withdrawing into the bush. It was then that the Tigray Defence Forces (TDF) were formed.

I was able to speak to several pilots at the Debre Zeit base near Addis Ababa, who confirmed that the operation had been well prepared and that the attack on Northern Command was just the pretext they had been waiting for. Antonovs had been transporting troops towards the Tigray border and the region had been surrounded since the end of October.

On the morning of 4 November, it was party time in Debre Zeit, one of them told me. The colleagues were jubilant: 'We can take off now!' The Tigrayan transport pilots and employees were arrested. The Tigrayan combat pilots ('the elite') were locked in their rooms. They protested that they were part of the Ethiopian National Defence Force. If there is a threat to the country, they must go, just like the others.[11] Therefore, the offensive that is beginning is not a targeted operation to neutralise the TPLF; it is an ethnic war aimed at Tigrayans wherever they are. All the Tigrayans in Debre Zeit, whatever their rank, were eventually deported to concentration camps. A tiny handful of men managed to escape, but many died.

Gebremeskel Kassa, a Tigrayan politician and a member of the Prosperity Party, who was appointed to the interim government set up just after the offensive by the Prime Minister and who therefore took part in meetings with Abiy Ahmed, confirms that the war was announced several months before 4 November 2020.[12] Similarly, a diplomat based in Moscow told me that an Ethiopian military delegation had travelled to Russia at the end of October 2020 to 'announce' the war.[13]

'Tigray war started immediately after Abiy assumed power', said Ambassador Wondimu Asemnew, a senior Tigrayan diplomat and negotiator. The war was not immediately military, but it already existed. On 20 June 2018, during the annual commemoration of the Martyrs Day in Eritrea, Isayas Afwerki pronounced a speech in which he repeated an expression he has just coined 'Game over' Woyane,[14] referring to 'the TPLF clique, and other vultures'[15] as he said. He already had an agreement with Abiy Ahmed. 'There was nothing in writing, but Abiy was very generous about handing over the border territories, and well beyond, as far as Shire [A/N the mining region]. Everyone made promises. Isayas offered access to the Red Sea.' But promises only bind those who believe in them![16]

Still in 2018 the Ethiopian and Eritrean governments and Amhara leaders already published a press statement about the dismantlement of Tigray.[17] Abiy Ahmed's high-profile visits to Asmara in the summer of 2018 were almost weekly. They continued, but more discretely, as the world entered the Covid-19 pandemic. Eritrea took drastic measures to prevent any movement, but this did not prevent Abiy Ahmed from visiting Sawa in June 2020. He is the first head of state to have set foot in this military base. Witnesses in Eritrea also claim to have seen buses carrying Ethiopian soldiers on the border with Tigray, again in contravention of anti-Covid measures.

In their respective books, Tom Gardner, Sarah Vaughan and Martin Plaut give a perfect account of the approach to war before the attack on Northern Command.[18]

Open-source observers of Ethiopian politics have above all seen the rise of hate speech in the media in Ethiopia, in the diasporas and on social networks from 2018 onwards, and then exponentially. In the American diaspora, and then worldwide, ESAT has played a crucial role in disseminating dehumanizing hate messages and calls for the murder of Tigrayans. The level of online violence during the Tigray war reached unprecedented proportions, which would have fallen within the scope of the law for incitement to hatred and murder against a targeted group, had the regulatory bodies for the media and internet platforms done their job. But what is most shocking is that this violence was expressed in the real world. Tigrayans have been molested, reported, arrested and even killed by their neighbours. A legal action against Meta was launched by the son of a Tigrayan professor murdered by a mob on the way from his university in Bahr Dar (capital of the Amhara region) to his home.[19] The policy of Facebook and Meta has been changed forever, proving that this hate campaign sets a precedent.

The classic defence of the haters was that they were not attacking Tigrayans as a whole, but the TPLF. This is one of the language elements directly produced by Abiy Ahmed's Prosperity Party. Moreover, according to this line, there was no Tigray war, but a law enforcement operation to arrest TPLF cadres, an operation which resulted in the deaths of more than half a million civilians, tens of thousands of women raped and the destruction of the region's agricultural[20] and industrial production facilities, with the result that famine[21] is still rife in 2024.[22] This is not a targeted action limited to one political party.

The haters, who are not bothered about legal or sociological rigour, are quick to take the plunge, accusing all civilians of being TPLF members. The party certainly has a strong popular base in Tigray, but it is an abuse to say that everyone, from children to the elderly, are 'junta', 'Woyane' or hostage victims of the TPLF.

#NoMore

On 2 November 2021, after a year of war and with the TDF (the coalition forces defending Tigray, as distinct from the TPLF) gaining ground and threatening Ethiopia's federal capital Addis Ababa, journalist Hermela Aregawi launched the #NoMore campaign, meaning: no more TPLF, no more foreign interference, no more imperialism. She asked people to take photographs of themselves with a sheet of paper inscribed '#NoMore' on a purple background and to post the pictures on social networks, then to spread the hashtag for each related publication. Hermela appeared on Twitter, the Horn of Africa Hub, her own YouTube channel HermelaTV and, of course, ESAT.

'No More' is in fact a pun to hijack the word 'Yakl', meaning 'no more, enough is enough' in Tigrigna, used by Eritrean opponents to denounce the PFDJ regime. Launched in 2019 in the Eritrean diaspora, this movement aims to establish democracy in the country.[23] Its recuperation and the almost sarcastic misappropriation of 'Yakl' in favour of #NoMore clearly indicate the Eritrean origin of the hashtag.

The campaign took off immediately, reaching half a million retweets in the days that followed. However, the power of this campaign does not seem 'natural', as we shall see. On the other side, the Tigrayan diaspora is also extremely active on social networks, and especially on Twitter with the hashtag #TigrayGenocide.

The Canadian researcher and journalist Claire Wilmot followed the behaviour of the two campaigns, Amhara and Tigrayan respectively.[24] The pro-Tigrayan #TigrayGenocide campaign is showing strong mobilization but at the same time remaining organic. The waves hardly exceed 150,000 tweets a day and have remained at this cruising speed for several months. By contrast, #NoMore started from scratch and immediately grew to several hundred thousand tweets, most of them from Eritrean accounts.[25] Given that the internet is almost non-existent in Eritrea, this suggests the campaign is supported by troll farms.

The #NoMore slogans – 'no more foreign interference, no more imperialism' – are particularly popular with Russian and Chinese diplomats, who are using the hashtag in their own tweets. For example, the Russian Permanent Mission to the UN Office in Geneva posted a Twitter thread on 17 December 2021 explaining why Russia was supporting the Ethiopian government in its war in Tigray in the name of national sovereignty (some fourteen months before Russia invaded a sovereign country, Ukraine): 'Russia reaffirms its commitment to the sovereignty, independence and territorial integrity of Ethiopia'. 'Russia consistently opposes politicisation of the situation in Ethiopia at the Human Right Council [. . .] Russia adheres to the postulate: "African Solutions to African problems"' and finishes with a final theatrical tweet: '#NoMore'.[26]

It is completely inappropriate to talk about sovereignty and territorial integrity in relation to the Tigray war. The only foreign forces to intervened are Eritrean troops and a Somali battalion trained in Eritrea, all invited by the Ethiopian government. The Tigray war is in no way a secession war, except in the Eritrean propaganda, which is consistent with its logic of accusatory inversion. This version is endorsed and broadcast by official Ethiopian and Russian channels.[27] In a sleight of hand that only the best disinformation campaigns can produce, #NoMore becomes a pan-Africanist motto. Tigrayans are called 'enemies of Africa' in the pay of the West and the Tigray war became Africa's war against Western imperialism. #NoMore brings together Eritrea's first lobbying campaign and Russia's soft power offensive in Africa, particularly in the Sahel.

On 27 November 2021, Ethiopian News Agency (ENA), the official agency of Abiy Ahmed's government, publishes an article entitled '#No More Campaign Should Be Amplified' with a photograph showing a crowd wearing Ethiopian colours with a central sign reading 'No More U.S. intervention'. The campaign is presented as follows: 'Its central objective is to oppose the ongoing Western media disinformation campaign, economic warfare, diplomatic propaganda and military interventions in Africa in general, and the Horn of Africa in particular'.[28] The article then continues, rather strangely, with an interview with Kassoum Coulibaly, presented as the president and CEO of the African Development Group. This name is in fact the literal translation of 'Groupe du Développement de l'Afrique', based in Bamako, and shouldn't be confused with the group that oversees the African Development Bank in Abidjan, Côte d'Ivoire. Kassoum Coulibaly plays the Ethiopianism card to the full, one of the currents that gave birth to pan-Africanism and made Ethiopia, the only country not to have been colonised, the lighthouse of Africa. 'Now I am supporting Prime Minister Abiy Ahmed as our prime minister. [. . .] This campaign [i.e. #NoMore] is not only for Ethiopia but also for Mali, western African countries, central African countries, and other regions in the Africa.'

Kassoum Coulibaly adds: 'This campaign should be amplified. We need media, including TV, radio, websites, and so on, from Ethiopia to be open to us. We need to have different languages like French, Arabic, Spanish, and Portuguese to come together from Africa.'

This press agency for Africa could be Sputnik! Less than a year after this article published by the Ethiopian News Agency (ENA) and the launch of #NoMore, ENA formalized its relationship with Sputnik, the Russian news agency considered to be the voice of the Kremlin and banned in the European Union, by signing an MoU.[29] Or BRICS TV, founded in August 2023 in Johannesburg on the sidelines of the BRICS summit at which the extension of the alliance to Ethiopia was announced.

It is not uninteresting to note that since 2013 Kassoum Coulibaly has been the de facto president of the African Mining Alliance based in Mali, a country that has seen one of the strongest Russian campaigns against France, with mining at stake. Wagner's Russian mercenaries have profited greatly from this, but what is less well known is that Canadian mining companies have been rushing to Mali since 2019.[30]

The return of the Canadians

In the chapter dedicated to the first lobbying campaign in support of the PFDJ regime, the single party in power in Eritrea since 1991, if not to whitewash its leader President Isayas Afwerki, we followed the work of Ruby Sandhu, Bronwyn Bruton and Ambassador Herman J. Cohen. While one is a lawyer, the second a researcher and the last a diplomat, all have been directly or indirectly paid for their services.

Todd Romaine, then vice-president for corporate social responsibility at Nevsun, openly occupied the stage with Ruby Sandhu and Bronwyn Bruton at a meeting of the PFDJ, among other advocacy events. As a lawyer, Sandhu defends people or institutions for a fee. It is her profession. Although Ambassador Cohen and Bronwyn Bruton have devoted their careers to the geopolitics of Africa, they remain generalists of sorts. But with the Tigray war, a newcomer has entered the lobbying game, Ann Fitz-Gerald, who is a specialist in Ethiopia and Eritrea.

A Canadian, daughter of a doctor who was deployed to Ethiopia, a country she discovered as a child, Ann Fitz-Gerald is known for her academic career in the field of security studies. In particular, she directed a programme funded by the British Ministry of Defence for senior officers in the Ethiopian army (ENDF). She was married to a British Army officer at the time. It was during this period that she developed an important network in Ethiopian military and political circles. As a well-informed expert, she also worked on a project with the World Peace Foundation, Tufts University, in direct contact with Professors Alex de Waal and Mulugeta Gebrehiwot Berhe in 2015. So when war broke out between the Ethiopian federal government and the government of Tigray, Ann Fitz-Gerald's violent statements, her adoption of the arguments of the #NoMore movement and all the propaganda of the Ethiopian and Eritrean governments were particularly disturbing, especially when expressed in contributions that were supposed to be scientific.

Let's look back at a series of enlightening events. In October 2021, Ethiopian prime minister Abiy Ahmed congratulated the Ethiopian diaspora and in particular associations such as the Amhara Association of America, the Ethio-American Development Council and the Ethio-Canadian Network for Advocacy and Support for their efforts, and invited them to raise funds to pay lobbyists to 'silence the noise', that is, the so-called Western propaganda of those who simply denounced the war crimes committed during this conflict, such as mass rape.

On 2 November 2021, the #NoMore campaign was launched on Twitter, promoted in particular by journalist Hermela Aregawi. On 4 November 2021, Hermela hosted Ann Fitz-Gerald in a show for Adebabay Media, 'a venue of news and views about or related to Ethiopia and the Ethiopian Orthodox Tewahedo Church', which is used to relaying the most violent speeches of the Amhara clergy. Together they spoke of the importance of leading a campaign to denounce what they called 'lies' in the Western media and what they described as the complicity of Western governments in legitimizing the crimes of the TPLF through a so-called inversion of murderers and victims, an argument which in turn can be overturned.

On 5 December 2021, Ann Fitz-Gerald and Jeff Pearce, a Canadian writer very proud to defend the myth of One Ethiopia according to the Ethiopianist vulgate and a fervent supporter of the #NoMore movement, were awarded a Crystal Mine (which is rather ironic given the role of mining companies in these lobbying campaigns) 'for their work in advocating and writing for the truth in Ethiopia',[31] as complacently reported by the Ethiopian News Agency.[32]

On 28 December 2021, Ann Fitz-Gerald published a joint article with Bronwyn Bruton of the Atlantic Council, one of the spearheads of the first lobbying campaign by Nevsun Resources Ltd, the Canadian mining company operating in Eritrea. Nevsun's funding of the Atlantic Council was aimed at working the American government and public opinion in favour of the Eritrean government to lift sanctions. The joint article by Bruton and Fitz-Gerald is entitled 'To End Ethiopia's War, Biden Needs to Correct Course'.[33] Once again, the intention is to 'silence the noise' and influence American foreign policy (literally 'correct course'). In essence, according to them, the terrible war in Tigray was entirely the fault of the TPLF and the Biden administration that covered up for them. On 31 December, Bruton drove the point home on ESAT TV's Insight programme, entitled 'US Policy: One Sided?'[34]

On 28 April 2022, Ann Fitz-Gerald published a report for the Ottawa-based think tank MacDonald-Laurier Institute (MLI) entitled 'The Frontline Voices. Tigrayans Speak on the Realities of Life under an Insurgency Regime'. The MLI promoted the report on Twitter as follows: 'News: As the Tigray war unfolds, Ann Fitz-Gerald warns that "the narrative echoed by TPLF supporters living outside of Ethiopia does not align with the voice of the Tigrayan communities on the ground". The report has now been removed from the MLI website. The basic idea was to show that the oppression of Tigrayans did not come from the Ethiopian federal government and its allies, the Eritrean and Amhara governments, but from the TPLF.

However, with Ann Fitz-Gerald being a Canadian, a small group of researchers and journalists remembered the importance of the Canadian mining company Nevsun in the first round of whitewashing of the Eritrean government. Tom Gardner, then correspondent for the British weekly *The Economist*, contacted the Macdonald Laurier Institute to find out about their sources of funding and whether there might be any conflicts of interest or bias, having in mind the example of the Atlantic Council. There was an outcry in the Amhara diaspora, and their champions, notably Jeff Pearce, launched a smear campaign.[35] Gardner finally had his accreditation withdrawn and had to leave Addis Ababa in a hurry. In the midst of the turmoil, in collaboration with Léonard Vincent, who had already revealed the scandal of Nevsun's funding of the Atlantic Council, we were able to show that the Canadian Mining Association was funding the MacDonald Laurier Institute.[36] At the time, I was the main editorial writer for the *Ethiopia Cable*[37] of Sahan Research, a think tank based in Nairobi, and I wrote a page highlighting some interesting connections.[38]

I continued to work on the mining companies in the Nubian Shield and gradually the idea of a book took shape. Discussing the progress of my work with Matthew Chandler de Waal, the editor of Sahan and Alex de Waal, this latter drew my attention to a troubling episode.

As the Tigray war officially began on 4 November 2020, Professor Mulugeta Gebrehiwot Berhe of the World Peace Foundation was in Mekele. As he saw the genocidal intent of the war, he joined his former Tigrayan comrades in arms in forming the TDF. On 27 January 2021, he managed to call his colleague Alex de Waal in Boston by satellite link and gave the first insight of the situation on the ground. De Waal recorded and published the call.[39] Mulugeta explains the first weeks of fighting, the asymmetry of forces and how the EDF, ENDF and special forces destroyed everything in the region, including crops and food stocks, which were set on fire. He also mentions the intervention of the United Arab Emirates with their drones, which disarmed the Tigrayan forces by pulverizing tanks, howitzers and ammunition, then igniting the fuel. He says that the Eritrean troops are the fiercest and intend to stay on Tigrayan territory.

Since 4 November, Tigray had been under a complete blockade of electricity, telecommunications, and the internet. As we can see from the #NoMore movement and the dissemination of hate speech on social networks, the war in Tigray is also an information war. So, Professor Mulugeta's direct testimony is very disturbing, for several reasons. First of all, he has succeeded in making his voice heard and telling what the Ethiopian government wants to hide from the world. But what's more, his criticism of the Tigrayan authorities, namely speaking of the TPLF, explodes the official vulgate, which would have the world believe that the war in Tigray is simply a police operation against the 'TPLF rebels'.[40] It is a total war targeting civilians. Even people who don't support the authorities are affected.

For the Ethiopian government and general staff, Mulugeta had spoken, and he must be silenced. Ann Fitz-Gerald was going to offer them a solution on a silver platter. Or so she thought.

Professor Fitz-Gerald had worked with Tufts University, and she had the mobile phone number of her colleague Mulugeta. They knew each other well, even when Ann was teaching in Addis Ababa.

I learned from an employee of the Ethiopian Ministry of Foreign Affairs that the Ethiopian Embassy in Canada was actively recruiting lobbyists to defend the Prosperity Party's discourse. This person told me how Ann Fitz-Gerald had enthusiastically taken part in the campaign.

Ambassador Aster Mamo really wanted to please Abiy Ahmed and to show the commitment of her diplomatic mission. The employee recalls that, at the beginning, things didn't take off and that they had to recruit second fiddles like Jeff Pearce. The person also testifies that the staff used to proofread Ann Fitz-Gerald's texts. And one day it went even further: the Canadian academic gave Mulugeta Gebrehiwot's mobile phone number to the ambassador. The employee claims to have heard Ann Fitz-Gerald say: 'You can locate him by triangulation.'

Did she understand the significance of this sentence? Indeed, although all telecommunications were cut off in Tigray, it was possible to connect to the Amhara region's relay antennae from time to time when at the border, and Ethiopian intelligence knew this perfectly well. This information was going to be used for targeting. They also assumed that General Tsadkan Gebretensae and other key Tigrayan figures would also be in the same area. The ENDF forces were thus able to identify the GPS position of Professor Mulugeta, General Tsadkan and their colleagues and target them in an aerial attack. Mulugeta remembers two incidents on 25 May and 11 June 2021, when fighter planes of the Ethiopian Airforce dropped their payload near a location where Mulugeta and his colleagues were convening a meeting but fortunately not in a sufficiently surgical manner. Ann Fitz-Gerald then called Alex de Waal to offer her condolences on what she believed to be the death of Tsadkan. Apart from the incredible cynicism of the move, it proves that she had privileged military information channels. But her haste played tricks on her because neither Professor Mulugeta nor General Tsadkan was affected.

Ana Gomes

While Bronwyn Bruton did not hesitate to appear at events organized by the PFDJ, Isayas Afwerki's party, Ann Fitz-Gerald makes no secret of the fact that she is close to the Amhara nationalists and the ENDF. For both, the technique is the same, questioning the conclusions of human rights defenders, turning the argument on its head, accusing the TPLF and the United States of all the ills of Ethiopia and Eritrea, and finally considering all their detractors as Trojan horses of Western imperialism (and of the TPLF, it's obsessive).

This line is shared by Ambassador Ana Gomes, a Portuguese diplomat and politician, who loathes the TPLF and the very memory of Meles Zenawi. So, it came as no surprise when, on 30 April 2022, she republished on Twitter Ann Fitz-Gerald's controversial report 'Tigrayans Fleeing the TPLF: Their Opinions Ignored with Today's Most Misunderstood War', expressing her full support for the author. Like Fitz-Gerald the Canadian and Bruton the American, Gomes the European spoke out on ESAT TV before being picked up by the Eritrean media controlled by the PFDJ.

A law student at Lisbon University and a member of the Portuguese Communist Party at the time of the Carnation Revolution in 1974, Ana Gomes was a political comrade of António Guterres and José Manuel Durão Barroso.

The Carnation Revolution was initiated in 1972 by members of the military (wearing the famous red carnation) who rejected Portugal's colonial wars. This opposition was quickly followed by civilians, who developed it into a veritable political and social overhaul to the left, culminating in 1974 in the end of the regime established in 1933 by António de Oliveira Salazar. Several leading figures in the Portuguese Socialist Party forged their political convictions in this revolutionary melting pot, which was widely connected throughout the world with the decolonisation and pan-Africanist movements.[41] For the record, between 1972 and 1974, Ethiopia saw the birth of the PFDJ and the TPLF, as well as the military coup against the last emperor, Haile Selassie.

In 2000, Ana Gomes was appointed ambassador to Indonesia on the proposal of António Guterres, then prime minister of Portugal, to settle the issue of the decolonization of East Timor. She was then elected Member of the European Parliament in 2004 when José Manuel Durão Barroso was president of the European Commission (not without having succeeded António Guterres as prime minister of Portugal between 2002 and 2004). In 2005, Ana Gomes was appointed Chief of the European Union Election Observation Mission (EU-EOM) in Ethiopia. As she herself confided in an interview for the ESAT Insight programme on 26 July 2018, she was chosen because she knew nothing about Ethiopia. As soon as she arrived in Ethiopia in April 2005 and therefore even before the elections were held, she found herself snapped up by the Coalition for Unity and Democracy (CUD), the opposition party whose vice-president at the time was none other than Berhanu Nega and who would give birth to Ginbot 7. According to an observer who approached her the day after the elections, when the opposition was claiming victory, she seemed overwhelmed by events. She repeatedly and rightly denounced irregularities, but her preliminary report gave the opposition the winner even before the final vote count. She concluded that the EPRDF was finished. The Ethiopian prime minister (and historic leader of the TPLF) Meles Zenawi replied to her personally on 31 August 2005 in the *Ethiopian Herald*. Ana Gomes then displayed a personal hostility towards Meles Zenawi, and more broadly towards the TPLF. She undoubtedly went one step too far by becoming clearly partisan and showing her friendship for the members of Ginbot 7. On 25 June 2008, for example, she invited her parliamentary colleagues in Strasbourg to a meeting with Berhanu Nega, an invitation she repeated on 15 December 2017, even though it is well known that he is the leader of an armed movement trained by Eritrea, a country under international sanctions. As for Andargachew Tsige, the other leader of Ginbot 7 intercepted between Dubai and Asmara by the Ethiopian authorities, and who had long been granted British nationality, on 3 July 2014 she sent a letter as a member of the European Parliament to the UK Secretary of State for Foreign Affairs William Hague asking him to work towards Andargachew Tsige's release.[42]

Ana Gomes was also a member of the committee in charge of the European Development Fund for Eritrea, which had released 122 million euros for the Isayas regime until the latter stood on his dignity in November 2011 and refused the funds in the name of his entire country and his fellow citizens.[43] He thus took the opportunity to develop his rhetoric of the small African state that manages without Western charity. It should be remembered, however, that in 2011 the Bisha mine went into production[44] thanks to a multinational and (forced) national service workers.

For a decade Ana Gomes commented on politics in Ethiopia and Eritrea. Like Bronwyn Bruton, she focused on the Oromo uprisings from 2015 onwards. The repression was excessive and reprehensible, but there was an over-excitement of the enemies of the EPRDF (and *a fortiori* of the TPLF), which she describes as 'totalitarian forces' and which became responsible for all the misfortunes of Ethiopians and Eritreans, despite significant progress, particularly in economic, agricultural and educational terms. She therefore welcomes the advent of Abiy Ahmed in 2018, driven by the joint enthusiasm of the Oromos and Amharas, who will create the Prosperity Party to wipe out the legacy of the EPRDF. She is also delighted at the rapprochement between Ethiopia and Eritrea, including and especially if the condition for this peace is the destruction of the TPLF. She returns triumphantly to Addis Ababa and takes part in a spectacular event on 16 February 2019 (broadcast by ESAT, of course).

The much-celebrated peace agreement between Ethiopia and Eritrea was sponsored by António Guterres himself, advised by Ana Gomes. She had introduced her friends from Ginbot 7 and ESAT to the UN Secretary General. On 8 July 2018, the Ethiopian prime minister is in Asmara for his historic rapprochement visit. He signed an agreement that served as a prelude to the September peace agreement. The Eritrean president then asked him to intervene officially to lift the sanctions against Eritrea.[45] On the very next day, 9 July, the journalist Fasil Yenealem, the founder of ESAT in Amsterdam and a member of Ginbot 7, which has been sentenced by the Ethiopian Federal High Court to life imprisonment in abstentia for terrorism, publishes an article recalling the links between himself, his fellow fighters and the two Portuguese. Ana Gomes and António Guterres clearly identified the Carnation Revolution with the Amharas' struggle against the Tigrayans. 'They advised us to fight hard by bringing up their own youth struggle experience. "Many people have died in Portugal's transition to democracy. Making a difference is not easy. Continue in the way you started. There will be change in your country, you will win".'[46]

Fasil Yenealem has been calling for the extermination of Tigrayans since at least 2016.[47] He and his accomplices 'continue[d] in the way [they] started' and it ended in a genocide.

Andargachew Tsige, founder of Ginbot 7, CEO of ESAT and friend of Ana Gomes, boasted of having brought Abiy Ahmed and Isayas Afwerki together for this peace agreement sponsored by António Guterres. It is difficult to think the General Secretary was completely unaware of the clauses about the invasion of Tigray. His silence about the war crimes especially the use of rape as a weapon of war in Tigray was deafening and well heard by all parties.

During the #NoMore campaign, an aggressive relay of Prosperity Party propaganda, under the name of George Bolton, stood out on Twitter with António Guterres' face as its profile picture. 'Bolton's tweets in support of the Ethiopian government were picked up by a former ESAT journalist before making their way to multiple Ethiopian state-affiliated media outlets.'[48] The account, which was obviously not maintained by the UN secretary general, was eventually closed, but it's interesting to wonder who (at ESAT?) wanted to pay tribute to him.

Danakali Limited, Australia, China and Russia

Sub-Sahara and Chalice, the temptation of Zara's gold

The Koka region in northern Eritrea, 165 kilometres northwest of Asmara, has long been known for its gold outcropping in parallel veins of quartz, relatively easy to collect for artisanal miners.[1] In 1998, the Australian company Dragon Mining Limited, associated with Genesis Mining, both based in Perth, Australia, as well as the Hong Kong investment group Africa World Wide Resources, was granted a prospecting licence called 'Zara' named after the nearby river in this region south of the Nubian Shield still neglected by investors.[2] From the start it was agreed that these three companies would share the exploration costs, but that other parties (meaning the ruling party) would receive 5 per cent profit sharing in the event of a profit.[3]

Against all expectations, prospecting was certainly slowed down a little, but not compromised by the war between Eritrea and Ethiopia which began precisely in 1998. The Koka region was outside the conflict zone.[4]

In September 1999, Dragon Mining bought Genesis'[5] shares, and in 2003 the company created a joint venture called Zara Mining Share Company with Sub-Sahara Resources NL,[6] a company also based in Perth. This latter took over the management of drilling operations from 2005 on.[7] As for Dragon Mining, it no longer takes an active part in operations in the Nubian Shield, although it remains a shareholder, but will focus on Northern Europe, mainly Finland and Sweden.

Sub-Sahara is not completely new to the Nubian Shield, since in 2001 it had already taken over the licence from Normandy Mining Limited based in Adelaide, owner since 1998 of the company LaSource which operated in Adi Nefas, not far away from Asmara. On 21 August 2003, Sub-Sahara signed a letter of intent with the Canadian Sunridge Gold Corp announcing participation in a joint venture, Sub-Sahara remaining the operator of the Asmara Project until 2 September 2004, when operations were suspended by decree of the Eritrean government.[8] They will resume at the beginning of 2005, but it is Sunridge which takes the reins. In 2006, after a conflicting procedure, all shares returned to Sunridge Gold Corp according to the wishes of the Eritrean government.[9] Sunridge is part of the Nevsun galaxy.

But coming back to the Zara Project in Koka, in February 2008, Sub-Sahara Resources announced that it had identified a gold deposit of 1.04 million ounces of gold worth a billion dollars.[10] The value of the deposit is similar to that of Bisha, but exploitation is much easier. The deposit is monometallic unlike Bisha or Adi Nefas (Asmara Project) that do produce gold, but also silver, copper and cobalt, which complicates extraction. Furthermore, in Koka, gold is found on the surface, which is why the site was already known to artisanal miners. But Sub-Sahara carried out drilling work to measure the importance of the deep deposit. Regarding artisanal miners, Ambassador McMullen wrote this strange sentence in a confidential telegram in 2008: 'They [artisanal miners] bag the gold-rich powder and sell it to nearby Eritrean military units. The Eritrean Defense Force [sic] provides "protectors and minders" for Sub-Sahara Resources and the artisanal miners [. . .] The country manager said Sub-Sahara Resources has unusually good relations with the artisanal miners, who "often show us where the gold is".[11] I am not trying to overinterpret this sentence from Ambassador McMullen, but when picturing the scene in reality, it looks like mafia behaviour. The EDF soldiers are trafficking gold and provide 'protection' for ransom. One can also question the benevolence of artisanal miners towards the gigantic competition represented by a huge multinational. Wouldn't they be a little frightened by these 'protectors' who work with the big Australian company?

2008 was a year of global recession, including for mining companies[12] that had to find investors, these latter having become overcautious. The reason of the strongest prevails, and on 3 April 2009, Chalice Gold Mines Limited (also based in Perth) bought Sub-Sahara Resources. The aim of the operation is to combine 'Chalice's strong cash position with Sub-Sahara's 69 per cent interest in the high-grade Zara Gold Project'.[13]

At the same time, the security situation hardly improved and, despite the protective measures mentioned by Ambassador McMullen, a Chalice vehicle is attacked with machine guns on 4 October 2009. The three passengers (Eritrean employees and contractors) are killed, and the driver injured.[14] As usual, the Eritrean government does not comment, so as not to give the impression that the situation is beyond its control and not to discourage investors, but rumours are circulating which attribute the assault either to an Islamist group (by repeating the same version as for the murder of a Nevsun employee in 2003) or to an Ethiopian commando (an obsession of the Eritrean government).[15] But according to David Daoud, who is obviously everywhere (the only witness to the 2003 murder or assassination while he worked for Nevsun, Sunridge geologist during the 2009 shooting and today in Tigray), it is the local miners who would be the perpetrators of the gunshots,[16] those who were supposed to get along well with the Australians. This attack, which will spell the end of the

Australian presence in Eritrea's gold sector, leaving the field to the Canadians, still raises many questions.

As Ambassador McMullen indicates, there is competition between the Canadians (Nevsun and Sunridge) and the Australians (Sub-Sahara, Chalice). And tensions may be heightened by sentiment that Canadians are clearing, and Australians are harvesting. Indeed, the latter can benefit from the pioneering work of Canadians in Bisha, particularly in the education of the very young ENAMCO.[17] In addition, the exploitation of the Koka deposits by the Australians is much easier, which seems to give them a head start over the Canadians.

End then, last twist in 2010, Chalice buys the shares of Dragon Mining, then ENAMCO takes possession of 40 per cent of the shares in Zara in 2011[18] and on 26 December of the same year a head of terms is concluded with Shanghai Construction (Hong Kong) Limited and China SFECO Group, two subsidiaries of Shanghai Construction Group Co Ltd. The agreement (the SFECO Transaction) is approved four months later in April 2012 by the shareholders, and Chalice sells its 60 per cent.[19] One of the reasons given is the announcement of the strengthening of sanctions by the United Nations against the Eritrean government for its support of various terrorist groups, notably Al-Shabaab in Somalia and for the occupation of disputed territories on the Djiboutian border. The Chinese don't seem to mind.

ENAMCO still owed Chalice $34 million for its stake in the Zara Gold Project.[20] SFECO is then responsible for paying off ENAMCO's debts. The Koka mine (Zara Project) finally enters production in 2016.

The Zara Mining Share Company is still today entirely in the hands of the Eritrean government (by ENAMCO) and a Chinese company.

But the Eritrean adventure of Australian miners does not stop. They will find their niche, that of fertilizers.

Colluli potash

In 2001, Australian businessman Liam Cornelius founded South Boulder Mines Ltd. Initially active in gold and nickel, it acquired concessions in Western Australia (Pilbara) which allowed it to familiarize itself with the market for potassium sulphate or sulphate of potash (SoP), commonly known as potash.[21] This is the introduction to the brochure published in 2014 by South Boulder Mines LTD entitled 'Potash for Product. The Colluli Project, an equal joint venture between South Boulder Mines and the Eritrean National Mining Company (ENAMCO) is a unique potash resource that will help feed the world.' Everything is said. First, the legal form that we know well now, namely the joint venture with ENAMCO and then this ambition to feed the world in which the leaders of South Boulder, then of Danakali, wrapped themselves for almost twenty years. Unlike other players in the sector (notably Todd Romaine and David Daoud of Nevsun) who are guided solely by pragmatism, the Cornelius family also seems to toy with some political ideas.

As of 2008, Canadians and Australians are still competing for potash, as the Vancouver-based company Crescent Resources Corp led by Michael Hopley and Don Halliday, CEO and vice-president of Sunridge, has also applied for a licence in Eritrea.[22] But as we have seen, the Canadians will ultimately focus on gold, leaving the fertilizer to the Australians.

South Boulder Mines therefore received its exploration licence at Colluli in the Danakil Depression in 2009. All gold and nickel assets are brought together in a new entity called Duketon Mining Limited and South Boulder Mines is now entirely dedicated to the exploitation of sulfate of potash (SoP) in Colluli.

The deposit is located a little more than 170 kilometres southeast of Asmara. The Danakil Depression, which extends south of the Red

Sea to Ethiopia, is located below sea level. Formerly submerged, it offers salt outcrops, some of which are rich in potassium, as is the case at Colluli. The mine is open pit, reputed to be one of the largest SoP reserves in the world, it is also famous for the simplicity of exploitation which would make it extremely profitable. The only downside: the geopolitical situation in Eritrea.

And this one weighs like a ball and chain on the destiny of this mine, because investors and banks remain cautious when it comes to investing in the country, despite the potential of the deposit. In 2014, South Boulder was unable to borrow the $700 million needed to develop the project.[23] Less than a year later, South Boulder Mines was renamed Danakali Limited, and the project was reformatted at $442 million. The directors inject new funds, the shareholders also put their hands in the wallet and the Colluli project is back on track.[24]

This new dynamic can be credited to Seamus Cornelius, Liam's brother who joined him on board. He is a business lawyer who worked for twenty-five years in China. Together they expanded the capital of the company, and in 2017, Liam left the ship, leaving the entire place to Seamus who greeted him in a press release dated November 20, 2017: 'While [Liam] is well known for his unorthodox approach he should be better known for his moments of inspiration and insight. He passionately believes that Colluli is an asset that will bring tremendous benefits to global agriculture, Danakali shareholders, our joint venture partners ENAMCO, Eritrea generally and the local communities in particular. His final, typically unorthodox act as a director is to voluntarily resign from the Board so that people with skills and experience more relevant to the company's current needs can drive the company forward.' It is worth noting Seamus' insistence on the iconoclastic character of his brother; so much he seems to be alluding to some stormy affairs.

This rather unbrotherly sentence especially gives the impression that Liam Cornelius has been closeted. The people whose skills align more with the company now are himself, Seamus, and, as we will soon see, Todd Romaine from Nevsun!

Seamus Cornelius is a discreet, complex and in some ways sulphurous character. Open supporter of the Eritrean government, slayer of the West, admirer of Julian Assange and the new 'world order' led by China and Russia. Smart, he knows how to perfectly take care of his image and that of Danakali. He keeps a low profile on social networks and only publishes politically correct comments or business-related posts, but the 'likes' thread on his X account is infinitely informative and smacks of conspiracy. Once the reins of Danakali were firmly in his hands, he lists the company on the London Stock Exchange on 24 July 2018. That same year he is very active and showed his support for the Eritrean government about which he is full of praise. With his impeccable, yet casual, shirts and fancy glasses, he appears in several videos, outlining his positive experience of ENAMCO and Eritrean lifestyle. He promotes the country, normalizing its image and even making it trendy. Incidentally, it is a strategy that has also been put to the test at pro-PFDJ festivals, which in recent years have featured fashionable singers and musicians to say that conscription is so cool!

Seamus Cornelius also appears with Todd Romaine from Nevsun. Both are key speakers at a conference at the UN Palais des Nations in Geneva under the auspices of the Eritrean embassy. And when on 5 September 2018, Nevsun announced that it was selling its shares to Zijin Mining Group, it was already agreed that Romaine would join Danakali as Chief Sustainability Officer, the same position he held at Nevsun during the trial, when he developed the pro-PFDJ and anti-Western lobbying campaign.

The marketing slogan of 'constructive work' that had been the hallmark of Nevsun's lobbying campaign is shifting to 'sustainability'. We find it in the job title of Todd Romaine, as well as in the title of the report commissioned by the UN following the rapprochement between Eritrea and Ethiopia and which praises the Colluli project.[25] Product of a long chain of events and sympathy,[26] 'Analysis of the Potential Contributions of Colluli Potash Project to Sustainable Development Goals in Eritrea' was released just after the company entered the London Stock Exchange. A nice gift from the UN for the Danakali rating.

In promotional videos that have since been removed from the Danakali website, Seamus Cornelius explains that the Colluli project is a paragon of sustainability, that Eritrea is a corruption-free country, that people are enthusiastic about their government and that Asmara is so safe and clean that he brought his son with him.[27] On this last point, he is probably not wrong, it is often the same in great dictatorships, so Pyongyang is clean and safe for the regime's guests!

As for corruption, it is simply systemic and therefore omnipresent, which undoubtedly makes it invisible, as one Eritrean national explains: 'The near-complete control over the economy and economic actors by the PFDJ, without any accountability, creates deep corruption and fungibility: "It looks as if it is legal, you get receipts and all that, but it is used for personal benefit. It is not to generate income for the PFDJ at the party level, but it benefits the individuals in the PFDJ directly. It is a system of the winner takes all. There is no law, it is divide and rule. Because there is no law, two generals will not agree. Without the law, there is just corruption. Anyone who can do it, will go and do it".[28]

It is important to bear in mind that there are no budget or official accounts in Eritrea.[29] It is therefore impossible to speak of good governance, or even governance at all. So the dividends paid to ENAMCO are lost in various pockets.

Russia and China are eyeing fertilizers

Seamus Cornelius also proudly describes the partnership between Danakali and Eurochem Trading GmbH, 'a Swiss company' as he puts it, which will distribute the entire Colluli SoP via its infrastructure in the Red Sea port of Massawa.

In reality, EuroChem is owned by Andrey Melnichenko, a Russian citizen under sanction from the European Union, Great Britain and the United States since 2022. Melnichenko had relocated his company, a fertilizer production giant, to Zug in Switzerland in 2015 (following the annexation of Crimea), a canton known for granting privileged tax status to large foreign companies, in order to escape international sanctions. Faced with global food demand, the fertilizer crisis places Eurochem in a strategic position, as does Colluli, which is considered one of the most profitable potash mines on the planet.

According to the Russian ranking of *Forbes*, Melnichenko is the richest man in Russia in 2023 with a fortune amounting to $25.2 billion[30] (it was 'only' $15.5 billion in 2018,[31] during the deal with Danakali).

Coming back to Danakali, as we have seen, Todd Romaine joined the company immediately after Nevsun sold the Bisha mine to Zijin Mining Group, a Chinese company. On 3 October 2022, his new company in turn sells its shares in the Colluli mine to a Chinese company, Sichuan Road and Bridge Group Co, whose subsidiary Sichuan Road & Bridge Mining Investment Development Corp. Ltd had already acquired Sunridge's shares in the gold and copper mine of Asmara. In the meantime, Colluli has moved further upmarket with the production of high-quality rock salt (sodium chloride) for the development of sodium ion batteries.[32] China, which has placed emphasis on this technology which allows energy to be stored and which is the subject of bitter rivalry with the United States, announced in May 2024 the commissioning of a giant factory in Guanxi,[33] the first in the world.

The pattern is always the same for all major mines in Eritrea: (Bisha, Zara, Asmara, Colluli): a Canadian or Australian mining company prospected in the 2000s, set up a joint venture with ENAMCO then sold its shares to a Chinese company at a time when the site is productive in strategic minerals.

Connection with the anti-French discourse in the Sahel

A 'rape culture in Tigray'?

On 17 April 2021, the activist website Radio Révolution Panafricaine (2RP) published an article entitled 'Rape Culture in Tigray region of Ethiopia'.[1] Based in West Africa,[2] the medium normally publishes in French. It is therefore highly likely that this article comes from an exceptional contributor. A clue may be found in the second paragraph: 'Yet, today, [UN agencies and many European countries] pretend [rape crisis in Tigray] is an issue that is related to the law enforcement operations by the central government. Worse, they point fingers at Eritrea, a nation where rape is practically non-existent.' If the contributor is not Eritrean in any case, he/she is a person who loves this country enough to be blinded. He/she uses the expression 'law enforcement operations' to describe the Tigray war, which is a piece of language directly borrowed from the Ethiopian and Eritrean governments.

By the end of 2020, I was already aware of cases of rape of Tigrayan women by Eritrean and Ethiopian soldiers as well as Amhara militiamen. Along with fellow researchers and activists, we began to share our information, which was hardly trickling in because of the blockade. At the beginning of 2021, there was still no significant media coverage on the issue of wartime rape in Tigray.

It was Ethiopian journalist Lucy Kassa who brought it to the fore in the international press with an article in the *Los Angeles Times*[3] in February, followed by Al Jazeera on 21 April 2021.[4] For my part, I began negotiations to take legal action in defence of victims of weaponized rape in Tigray. But all this was still relatively confidential. Nothing like the outcry generated by the Amnesty International report in August 2021. Radio Révolution Panafricaine's article, which is intended to be defensive, is, in fact, rather preventive, and does not respond to media pressure. It sets the stage for a verbal war to come and seems to have been teleguided from Asmara. It uses the same codes, notably the accusation in a mirror (AiM)[5] and the characterization of all those who denounce the crimes of the Eritrean regime as 'TPLF apologists'.

The 2RP article published in April 2021 appears to be the draft of a larger report published on 9 May 2021, by the New Africa Institute, a puppet think tank with only one employee, Simon Tesfamariam, an Eritrean born in the United States, but close to the PFDJ, whose conventions he runs.[6] His argument consists of blaming the TPLF for everything, from the outbreak of war to the internationalization of the conflict, with conspiracy overtones since, he maintains, everything said in the press is nothing but a propaganda campaign to smear Eritrea, relayed by the Western media. In the chapter devoted to the wartime rapes attributed to Eritrean soldiers, he directly attacks Lucy Kassa because rape is 'virtually unheard of in Eritrea'.[7]

The 2RP article was published four days before Lucy Kassa's for Al Jazeera, so it can hardly speak about it. Simon Tesfamariam's report, published eighteen days later, simply serves as an expansion of the 2RP article with a rebuttal to Lucy Kassa's, both *addendum* and *corrigendum*. The rhetorical basis of the TPLF/Occident conspiracy is identical to the 2RP article.

Two days later, Yemane Ghebremeskel himself, Eritrea's powerful Minister of Communication, tweeted[8] a link to an abridged version of the report hosted by the African Media Council, a media organization based in Equatorial Guinea like 2RP and now defunct.

The article by Radio Révolution Panafricaine and the report by Simon Tesfamariam defend the idea that it is not the invading troops (Eritrean and Ethiopian) who have committed the rapes, but the Tigrayans themselves, or rather the TPLF, as this is clearly an obsession. Rape is said to be rampant in the region and even socially accepted. Simon then quotes a 2019 tweet by Meaza Gidey Gebremedhin,[9] a leading figure in the defence of victims of weaponized rape in Tigray, where the Tigrayan feminist activist denounces the impunity of rapists in Tigrayan society.

This argument was taken up word for word by Hermela Aregawi at the very start of the #NoMore campaign. In a tweet dated 8 November 2021,[10] she denounced the 'TPLF and allies' for ignoring the pre-existing rape culture in Tigray. She too echoes Meaza's tweet. This latter tweet exists and was perfectly legitimate in 2019, but Hermela's process is doubly fallacious. First, it compares completely different situations in peacetime and wartime. Second, Tigrayan society is certainly patriarchal and perfectible from the point of view of gender equality, but no more or less so than other regions of Ethiopia and even the Horn of Africa. However, as I and other colleagues have seen, Tigrayan society was in a state of exceptional ferment in the ten years leading up to the war. It was because feminist associations (such as Meaza's) were formed and were able to express themselves that GBV was denounced, not because it was part of a so-called rape culture specific to Tigray. This is the exact opposite of Eritrea. Radio Révolution Panafricaine claims, that 'rape is practically non-existent' in Eritrea, but it should be written that 'rape is virtually unheard of' in Eritrea, simply because no one has an ounce of freedom to denounce institutionalized rape, harassment or sexual slavery.

Moreover, in a tweet dated 1 April 2022, which has since been deleted, Hermela Aregawi declared that she understood Meaza's concern about the issue, having herself been born of rape. So much for this lady's style and ethics.

Pan-Africanism with a Russian twist

So why this campaign, so early and so vehement, as if it had been prepared? In fact, it's part of a wider campaign.

Radio Révolution Panafricaine is close to the NGO AFRIC (Association for Free Research and International Cooperation),[11] headed by Yulia Afanasieva, an associate of the late Yevgeny Prigozhin and sanctioned in 2021 by the US Treasury as part of the investigation into interference in the 2020 elections.[12] 2RP is a conduit between Moscow and pan-Africanist activists and collaborates with Black supremacist leader Kemi Seba.[13]

Born in Strasbourg, France, of Beninese origin, Kemi Seba has been convicted on several occasions of incitement to racial hatred and was stripped of his French nationality on 8 July 2024.[14] Known for his outbursts (he burned his French passport) and his rants against France and the West, he was financed by Yevgeny Prigozhin to lead a hate campaign against France in French-speaking Africa. His action is an extension of that of Nevsun's lobbyists.

Before the collapse of the Eastern bloc, the USSR had supported the Derg, which the PFDJ, then allied with the TPLF, overthrew in 1991. PFDJ executives therefore had no personal links with Russian figures who might have survived the Soviet period. What's more, Yeltsin's chaotic Russia had lost its ideological and pragmatic allies. It no longer had the aura of the Red Empire, the bulwark against Western capitalist imperialism. Above all, it no longer had the means to buy friends. The young Eritrean state led by the PFDJ certainly had more contact with the Russians than with the Americans, but no privileged links until the anti-Western turn of the master of the Kremlin.

Vladimir Putin and Isayas Afwerki's interests converged. In the bride and groom's basket, Isayas deposited a well-stocked rhetorical toolbox for almost universal use, but above all against France as part of the deployment of Russian influence on the African continent.

The Kremlin's armed wing on the continent was Yevgeny Prigozhin, whose interests and networks are closely interwoven with those of Isayas Afwerki, particularly in Sudan. Gold is once again crucial. Wagner, Prigozhin's organization which feeds off mining resources in the countries where it deploys its mercenaries, has been present in Africa (Libya) since 2014, the year of the Nevsun trial and therefore of the development of the first lobbying campaign.

The same rhetoric has been recycled in the 'Projet Kemi',[15] also an anti-Western conspiracy lobbying campaign using pan-Africanist symbolism, named after above-mentioned Kemi Seba, a pseudonym of Stellio Gilles Robert Capo Chichi. Kemi Seba, literally 'the black star' in 'ancient Egyptian', sometimes claims to belong to Islam, sometimes to Kemitism, an 'African' religion inspired by ancient Egypt, and defends the segregation between Black and 'leucoderms' (whites, as he calls them) people, which hasn't prevented him from frequenting the Kremlin since 2017. Kemi Seba admitted in 2020 that he had been invited to Russia, Libya and Sudan by Prigozhin.[16] It is proven that Seba received funds from Prigozhin in 2018 and 2019, as evidenced by internal documents at Wagner.[17]

Seba is in the sights of US authorities as 'Russia's hidden hand' alongside Nathalie Yamb.[18] Seba and Yamb are among the most influential political personalities on social networks in French-speaking Africa. In July 2024, Seba had 1.3 million subscribers on Facebook, 272,800 on X, 306,000 on Instagram and Nathalie Yamb had 716,000 subscribers on Facebook, 439,000 on X, 438,000 on YouTube, 88,700 on Instagram, 70,000 on Tik Tok.

Nathalie Yamb, who dreams of being France's nightmare, is also close to the NGO AFRIC,[19] like 2RP, which published the pro-Eritrean article on rape culture in Tigray. Resident in Zug in Switzerland (just like Andrey Melnichenko), a small canton renowned for its advantageous tax system, and owning a shell company in Delaware,[20] Nathalie Yamb is also said to be funded by Moscow. Publicly, she denies this, as she did in March 2023 in a Swiss radio and television documentary but adds that she would have no qualms about receiving Prigozhin's money.[21] Yamb has been known as the 'Lady of Sochi' since her memorable speech at the first Russia-Africa Summit of 2019 in Sochi.[22]

Her hobbyhorses are the abandonment of the CFA franc or ECO,[23] the withdrawal of French troops from Africa or the economic emergence of Africa thanks to Russia, citing the example of the Central African Republic. In the latter case, the 'win-win' exchange turned into a catastrophe, with Wagner terrorizing civilian populations and plundering gold resources.[24]

Nathalie Yamb is Kemi Seba's 'big sister of struggle and heart'. And in this context of violent pan-Africanism, Black supremacism and hatred of the West, as reflected in the #NoMore campaign, it is interesting to listen to Kemi Seba's speech on Ethiopia.

On 7 August 2020, when the Prosperity Party was galvanized in Ethiopia and the war in Tigray had already been announced, Kemi Seba published a video in French as part of his weekly *Afro Pertinent* program on his YouTube channel (230,000 subscribers),[25] using all the codes of Amhara nationalism and Ethiopianism.

He announces his intention to analyse the situation in Ethiopia in the summer of 2020 from a global pan-Africanist perspective, opening with praise for the man he calls 'His Majesty': Haile Selassie. The emperor is presented as a 'diplomatic genius', challenger of the West and symbol of Africa. Referring to the 1973 famine, when hunger was used as a political tool against rebel regions, Seba starts excusing the emperor. The polemist states that the famine was due to climatic conditions, that Haile Selassie would have done his best and that communications were not as developed as they are today. These external factors would explain why the ruler was unaware of the catastrophe that would precipitate his downfall. Somewhat contradictorily, the influencer suggests that the Negus prophesied the chaos that was to follow his deposition. Chaos necessary for the purging of elements contrary to the country's unity, and the prelude to rebirth through the advent of Haile Selassie's (spiritual) successor: Abiy Ahmed, of whom he makes an almost messianic figure. He evokes the periods in between, that is to say the Derg (rogue Marxists) and the 'reign' of Meles Zenawi, 'the perfect soldier of Western oligarchy on the African continent'. He goes on to denounce the 'm'as-tu vu of the Tigrayan caste' (this expression is extremely pejorative in French). The Tigrayans have become the 'new bourgeois, but that doesn't make them nobles', alluding to Haile Selassie and the Amharas, who are the nobility of Ethiopia. Nobility with which Abiy Ahmed is reconnecting, according to Kemi Seba. In a messianic tone, he adds that the prime minister is a living synthesis of Ethiopian unity, since his father is Oromo, a Muslim, and his mother Amhara, a Christian. It's like reading the Prosperity Party's program. Seba concludes: 'We hope he can continue to pacify the country, because Ethiopia's stability will be Africa's stability, as Haile Selassie intended.'

Seba's demonstration, exalting Haile Selassie and saluting a certain idea of Ethiopian greatness, could perfectly do without Tigrayan-bashing. The French-speaking world knows nothing about Tigrayans, and all the more so in 2020, before the war. Its sources are to be found in PFDJ and Ginbot 7, the great inspirers of #NoMore. I noted the intervention of Malian Kassoun Coulibali, president of the African Mining Alliance, at the very start of the campaign. There's nothing anecdotal about this, and it's not surprising that Coulibaly called for support for the 'No More' motto when it first appeared. He added in November 2021: 'I am supporting Prime Minister Abiy Ahmed as our prime minister. Our proud leader has been doing great job to bring peace and reconciliation. So, we support him'.[26]

There is a real junction between Eritrean and then Amhara propagandists and the hard core of French-speaking pan-Africanists. They have all been linked to the late Yevgeny Prigozhin or the Kremlin and funded by the mining industry. They hate the West and use Tigrayans as scapegoats.

Radio Révolution Panafricaine, which relayed the abject article on rape culture in Tigray, also frequently publishes on the West's war against the Sahel states. For example, an article written by Mikhail Gamandiy-Egorov, a prolific contributor to 2RP and one of the major players in Russian propaganda in the French-speaking world, nicknamed 'l'Ambassadeur' by his African contacts,[27] opens with these lines:

> The interaction between the member countries of the Alliance of Sahel States (AES) and Russia continues to grow in strength, and is already an inspiring and successful example for many other nations on the African continent. If the enemies of Africa, Russia and the international multipolar order observe the processes underway with not only a rage that's no longer even veiled, the essential thing is that the logical march of the contemporary world will continue to make its way.[28]

The article is illustrated by a large map in which Eritrea and Sudan are counted among the Sahelian states.

The 'Gerasimov Doctrine'

On 27 February 2013, Russian General Valery Gerasimov, Chief of the General Staff of the Russian Federation Armed Forces, published an article in *Military-Industrial Kurier*, the Russian weekly that also frequently serves as a platform for military experts and defence sector executives.

He begins by analysing the new forms of conflict and the shift in violence towards non-military actors, drawing on the example of the Arab Spring. For him, these 'conflicts' are real wars, and that's how war should be viewed from now on. Henceforth, it will be hybrid and asymmetrical.

> The very 'rules of war' have changed. The role of nonmilitary means of achieving political and strategic goals has grown, and, in many cases, they have exceeded the power of force of weapons in their effectiveness. The focus of applied methods of conflict has altered in the direction of the broad use of political, economic, informational, humanitarian, and other nonmilitary measures – applied in coordination with the protest potential of the population. [...]
>
> Asymmetrical actions have come into widespread use, enabling the nullification of an enemy's advantages in armed conflict. Among such actions are the use of special operations forces and internal opposition to create a permanently operating front through the entire territory of the enemy state, as well as informational actions, devices, and means that are constantly being perfected.[29]

In short, to win the wars of the future, one must rely on destabilization through disinformation and support for the opposition either in enemy countries, or in countries where the enemy has interests, or by proxy by playing on the enemy's public opinion. Military action by a regular army only completes the job. Gerasimov notes that these methods have already been used by the major powers, notably the United States during *Operation Desert Storm* in Iraq in 1991. The Russian army needs to get to grips with them as soon as possible, and Russian military science needs to develop its skills in this field through its researchers.

When analysed by Western thinkers, General Gerasimov's words caught on, and the myth of a 'Gerasimov Doctrine'[30] coined by Prof. Mark Galeotti quickly spread. Galeotti, a British historian specializing in the Russian world, and in particular in security studies and transnational crime, was the first to deplore the distortion of his words and the essentialization of this famous 'doctrine'.[31] Indeed, colleagues have noted that disinformation and cunning are as old as war itself is documented. Homer and Sun Tzu bear this out. So, there would be nothing new or exclusive about it. But the Russian general, far from draping himself in history, calls on new technologies.

While Western analysts do what they do so well, building up concepts and then deconstructing them, it is clear that even if the 'Gerasimov Doctrine' does not form a fixed corpus, it nonetheless reflects a very real strategy deployed by Russia on the African continent from 2013 onwards.

The grievances of Africans against France and the West in general are perfectly justified, and the activists raise real questions about the CFA franc and the domination of the dollar. These demands are ancient, much older than the creation of Wagner or even Vladimir Putin's rise to power. They were at the heart of the decolonization struggles that also gave rise to Eritrea's independence.

Vladimir Putin and his entourage have exploited a legitimate anger[32] whose rhetoric was inspired by Isayas Afwerki, one of the last guerrilla fighters of the twentieth century. Both have perverted a noble fringe of the pan-Africanist movement, whose heralds have become propagandists for Moscow and its predatory subsidiaries.

This chapter is not a criticism of the pan-African movement in all its rich multiplicity – quite the contrary – but rather an exposure of the deviancies of a few haters paid to sell the continent.

Part IV

The Gold of the New Pharaohs

Isayas Afwerki, Hemedti, Haftar

Traffic routes

Gold and human trafficking

Since coming to power in 1991, Isayas Afwerki has interfered in the affairs of neighbouring countries. Sudan is hardly an exception. Over the years, he has perfectly played out alliances in the complex mosaic of interests and loyalties of the various geopolitical players on his doorstep, as well as far away.

Isayas Afwerki has maintained a fluctuating relationship with Omar Al-Bashir, president of Sudan for almost thirty years. The latter was overthrown in 2019, and a transitional government was put in place. The head of state is then a military officer, General Abdel Fattah Al-Burhan, but Prime Minister Abdallah Hamdok is responsible for leading the country towards a civilian democracy. His government was, however, overthrown by the army on 25 October 2021. Al-Burhan remained the head of state, but Mohamed Hamdan Dagolo, known as 'Hemedti', was then appointed vice-president of the Transitional Sovereignty Council of the Republic of Sudan.

Hemedti is a businessman who made his fortune in gold mining. He is the leader of the Rapid Support Forces (RSF) militia, reputed to have committed war crimes in Darfur. The agreement between the president and his vice-president quickly turned sour. On 15 April

2023, Hemedti launched an offensive against several bases in Sudan, plunging the country into a new civil war. It soon became apparent that the warlord had the support of Yevgeny Prigozhin, Wagner's Russian mercenary leader,[1] who had also made a fortune from the gold mines in the Sudanese part of Nubian Shield through the Meroe Gold entity. Hemedti had prepared himself for support: on 24 February 2022, on the very day that Russian troops invaded Ukraine, Hemedti was in Moscow during a trip organized by Wagner,[2] and his last foreign visit before launching his own offensive was to Isayas in Asmara on 13 March 2023.[3]

Indeed, Hemedti was close to Isayas at the time. Trafficking and shared enmities linked the two men. The eastern part of Sudan, bordering the Red Sea, Ethiopia and Eritrea, is a thriving trade area. Alliances come and go according to the profits to be made by clan and faction leaders. By April 2023, Hemedti's RSF and the SAF (Sudan Armed Forces), Al-Burhan's regular army, were not yet in open conflict even if rivalries could create occasional tensions, and everyone was profiting.

Human trafficking is the most sordid side of the business that develops in this area, stretching as far as Egypt and Libya. The entire PFDJ apparatus in Eritrea is involved in the trafficking of Eritreans attempting to flee this very regime. This is one of the party's sources of income.[4] All Eritrean citizens over the age of five are forbidden to leave the country. Young people aged sixteen must do their military service, but this is precisely what most Eritreans want to avoid, including by paying smugglers and most of the time traffickers. The party knows this and cynically organizes the traffic. Human trafficking is institutionalized in Eritrea. Fugitives then pass from hand to hand through Sudan, via the areas of influence of Hemedti's RSF. There are several routes, but they all end up in Libya, particularly in Marshal Haftar's Cyrenaica. Agents of the Eritrean government operate there.[5] For a long time, Haftar, Hemedti and Isayas have also been involved in the same system of alliances headed by the United Arab Emirates, where arms, gold and mercenaries are exchanged to fight the Houthis in Yemen.[6]

When the conflict between the RSF and the SAF of Al-Burhan broke out in Sudan, Isayas was naturally on the side of the RSF, especially as the SAF, who controlled the Al-Fashaga triangle, were in conflict with the Ethiopian Amharas, Isayas' allies and protégés.

The Al-Fashaga Triangle is a portion of territory allocated to Sudan in 1902 by the Anglo-Ethiopian Treaty but contested ever since. A compromise was signed in 2008 allowing Ethiopian farmers to crop there. The region is fertile and rich in gold. With the rise of Amhara nationalism in Ethiopia, the area has begun to be claimed as part of an expansion strategy that also includes the annexation of Western Tigray to the Amhara region. But in 2020, during the Tigray war, the SAF drove out the Amharas, leading to armed fighting.

The border area with Amhara-occupied Western Tigray came under SAF control. It also serves as a rear base for the Tigray Defence Forces to retake the Western Tigray to the Amharas, and as a refuge for thousands of Tigrayans fleeing the atrocities committed by the Amhara militias and the Eritrean and Ethiopian armies.

Ethiopian prime minister Abiy Ahmed was well aware of this, and had pre-emptively asked General Abdel Fattah Al-Burhan, on a diplomatic visit to Addis Ababa on 1 November 2020 – two days before the launch of the 'law enforcement operation' – to close his border with Tigray.[7] The border has become harder to cross, but a degree of porosity has remained.

The occupation of Western Tigray

The Western Tigray or Mi'irabawi Zone is the area west of the Tekeze River in relation to the rest of the Tigray region, and south of the same river when it marks the border with Eritrea. To the west lies the border with Sudan, and to the south with the Amhara region. Western Tigray accounts for almost a third of Tigray's territory, with its most fertile lands.

The history of this region is eventful, but part of it, notably Wolkait, was annexed to Begemder in 1941 under Haile Selassie, while his own son Asfa Wossen administered the region around his capital Gondar. Then, under the 1995 constitution promulgated by the EPRDF, Begemder was divided, with the north joining Tigray and the rest becoming the Amhara region. Today, Western Tigray is claimed by both Tigrayans and Amharas, who call it Wolkait by synecdoche. But although the latter was administratively under Amhara control for a long period, 92 per cent of its inhabitants are Tigrayans according to the official 2007 census.

Some Amhara leaders wish to erase the entire period of the EPRDF, the coalition in power in Ethiopia since the fall of Mengistu and therefore since the end of the Derg, in which the TPLF played a predominant role. On the principle that 'the enemies of my enemies are my friends', they allied themselves with the Eritrean president, who has a visceral hatred of the TPLF and Tigrayans in general.

During the summer of 2018, Ethiopian prime minister Abiy Ahmed and Eritrean president Isayas Afwerki have been courting each other assiduously. On 16 September, they signed a peace agreement between their two countries in Jeddah, but on 5 September, Isayas Afwerki, Abiy Ahmed and Mohammed Abdullahi 'Farmaajo', president of Somalia, had already signed a Joint Declaration of Comprehensive Cooperation in Asmara,[8] marking the birth of the Tripartite Agreement.

On 9 and 10 November, the three leaders of the Horn of Africa met in Gondar, hosted by Gedu Andargachew, president of the Amhara region, to 'advance' this cooperation. In the days that follow, the Ethiopian parliament considers the annexation of part of Western Tigray (Wolkait and Tsedege) to the Amhara region, which corresponds to the reconstruction of Begemder. A debate welcomed by the Eritrean news agency in a 21 December 2018 post entitled 'Gondar May Border Eritrea Soon', which stresses: 'the regions of Humera, Tsegede, Wolkait and other territories found to the west of River Tekeze up to the Sudan border may go back to the "original" administrator of Gondar region. These areas were awarded to Tigray region by EPRDF. Before that, they were part of Begemedir/Gonder province.'[9]

It's becoming clear that the famous peace agreement between Abiy and Isayas, crowned with a Nobel Prize, was in fact just the latest round in the Eritrea–Ethiopia war that was to result in the removal of Tigray.

Behind the historical pretensions and nationalist posturing lay a real expansion plan by the Amhara leaders to capture agricultural[10] and gold-bearing land and lay their hands on extremely lucrative resources – gold, cereals, and sesame[11] – bound for the Gulf states via Eritrea. By annexing Western Tigray, the Amharas would control the entire border between Ethiopia and Sudan, as well as linking up with Eritrea.

The friendship between Isayas and the Amhara leaders went over the Ethiopian prime minister's head. They quickly dispensed with him, as the training of Amharas militias on Eritrean soil is a long-standing practice.[12] In fact, Amharas militiamen and Eritrean soldiers sometimes operate together in mixed battalions or in complementary roles,[13] but they mainly divide up Tigrayan territory between themselves: the Amharas occupy Western Tigray, where they carry out a veritable ethnic cleansing, while the Eritreans are deployed in the central and western regions. At the time of writing, these troops are still present on Tigrayan territory, even though their withdrawal was one of the promises that prompted the Tigrayan delegation to sign the Cessation of Hostilities Agreement on 2 November 2022.

The gold circuits

The occupation of Western Tigray has precipitated the informalization of the sesame circuit, a crucial business in the area, to the benefit of the Amharas and the RSF, to whom they have turned since the SAF expelled them from Al-Fashaga.[14] This rerouting was not complicated, since the RSF are already accustomed to what could be described as a 'grey economy', or even trafficking, if not banditry.

While the sesame ('white gold') goes to several Gulf countries, the gold goes specifically to Dubai. At this point, it should be remembered that the United Arab Emirates are the main sponsors of the RSF, but also of the Ethiopian government allied with the Amharas. They are also the backyard of Eritrean business, since the Red Sea Corporation is based in Dubai.

Dubai is also home to the headquarters of the Kaloti Group, founded in 1988 by Munir Ragheb Mousa Al Kaloti and comprising a dozen companies all linked to precious metals.[15] The Swiss Secrets Leaks database of the Organized Crime and Corruption Reporting Project describes it as follows: 'Kaloti Jewelry Group, a Dubai-based conglomerate that is one of the world's largest gold traders and refiners, as well as a key player in the dirty gold trade. According to U.S. authorities, Kaloti was buying precious metals from sellers suspected of laundering money for drug traffickers and criminal groups.'[16]

Gold is fusible, gold is fluid, unlike diamonds it is impossible to trace it once refined. And there are refineries in Sudan, Dubai and Switzerland.

So, while the RSF are inextricably linked to the gold trade by their very history, the SAF are not to be outdone. Each group has its own trust: the Military Industry Corporation (MIC), also known as the Defence Industries System (DIS), a state-owned company linked to the powers in place in Khartoum, in this case Al-Burhan and the SAF, and Al-Junaid Multi Activities Co Ltd, the Dagolo family business run by Hemedti and his brother on the RSF side. Both Al-Junaid and DIS are subject to OFAC sanctions.[17]

Sudanese gold extracted from SAF-controlled territory is refined directly in Sudan under the auspices of the Al-Burhan-controlled Central Bank before being shipped to Dubai, legally but mostly illegally. Indeed, the overwhelming majority of production is diverted.[18] Gold from the RSF and Al Junaid is sent directly to Dubai. Kaloti has a refinery in Sharjah. Artisanal and/or trafficked gold is also collected from Kaloti's offices in the Dubai souk. It must be remembered that regulation in Dubai is very lax. It is perfectly legal to transport raw gold in your hand luggage,[19] tax free. Whether refined before shipment or raw and refined in Dubai, all this gold is centralized by Kaloti and then shipped to Switzerland, mainly to Valcambi SA.[20] The small Central European country is the hub of the world's gold trade, refining and trading. But going through Valcambi is not just a question of commercial and logistical opportunity. The Ticino-based company is registered with the London Bullion Market Association. This means it can have its gold certified, which then enters the very official circuit of the world's central banks. This is far from being the case for Kaloti.

Switzerland was also the primary destination for Eritrean gold. In 2009, two years before the Bisha mine in Eritrea went into production, the American ambassador in Asmara Ronald K. McMullen, no doubt well-informed, estimated that the gold from Bisha would be flown directly from the mine, then smelted in Switzerland.[21] And indeed, from 2011 onwards, raw gold ingots were transported by Nevsun to Switzerland, to Metalor's plant in Marin in the canton of Neuchâtel, transported from Asmara via Frankfurt by Lufthansa flights. Twenty-two tons of raw gold from Bisha were refined in Switzerland.[22]

I myself was born in the canton of Neuchâtel, and as a child I had the opportunity to visit the Metalor Technologies SA factory. This plant as well as its employees and management is part of the local social fabric. On the strength of this proximity, I contacted Metalor to find out if they were aware of the conditions under which this gold was extracted. After an initial response, I have not heard from them since.

Like Valcambi, Metalor is registered with the London Bullion Market Association and can have Nevsun's bullion certified. The gold vein was exhausted in Bisha from 2013 onwards, and mining has shifted predominantly to copper, a conductive metal that has become strategic with the development of new technologies and green energies based on electricity. The collaboration between Nevsun and Metalor has thus come to an end.

Wagner and Russia

Hemedti, the leader of the RSF, hails from Darfur in western Sudan. Initially known as a 'businessman', he built up an empire thanks to the gold mines in his native region. Born into an Arab tribe, he rallied around him the Janjaweed, who remain infamous for their atrocities against the Black population of Darfur from February 2003 onwards. He created Al-Junaid in 2009, and in 2013, Omar Al-Bashir, wishing to integrate the Janjaweed into the country's security architecture, renamed them Rapid Support Forces. In fact, Al-Bashir distrusted his own army and overruled the objections of his army chief of staff General Imad Addawi. Moreover, rumours were circulating about a possible coup prepared by the latter. It was therefore largely to bypass Addawi that Al-Bashir created the RSF. Consequently, Hemedti will partly hand over the reins of Al-Junaid to his brother Abdelrahim Hamdan Dagolo to concentrate on his paramilitary activities.

Hemedti has been in business with the late Yevgeny Prigozhin since at least 2017. This is explained by the type of business the two men are involved in (gold, weapons, mercenaries) and the geographical position of Hemedti's stronghold, Darfur. This latter lies on the road to eastern Libya, held by General Haftar, and borders the Central African Republic, the strongest bastion of Wagner. The Russian SMP has become President Faustin-Archange Touadera's Praetorian Guard since 2017, and in its usual pattern, Wagner thrives on the country's mining resources.[23] Convoys circulate between CAR and Sudan[24] via Hemedti's Darfur region.

That same year, 2017, Wagner weaves his web in Sudan, while Omar Al-Bashir is still in power. The intermediary is Mikhail Potepkine. He runs Meroe Gold, a daughter company of M Invest, which is owned by Yevgeny Prigozhin.[25] Potepkine pretends he has no connection with Prigozhin, but in 2017, he did represent M Invest at a meeting between Dmitri Medvedev and Omar Al-Bashir. Potepkine is said to belong to Russian 'conservative' groups, linked to the neo-Nazi far right.[26] He is familiar with the ideologue Aleksandr Dugin with whom he appears in photographs, this latter being also close to Kemi Seba. This circle of influence is definitely very tight. Potepkine also appears in the Russian interference operation in the 2016 US elections.[27] His role is to promote violent Black supremacism in the United States and in Africa, with Sudan and Ethiopia among the priority countries.[28] From 2017 onwards, Meroe Gold receives substantial support from Prigozhin-linked companies, in funding and equipment, including helicopters and airplanes.[29] Meroe's core business is gold mining, and its nerve centre is Al-Ibaidiya, in the Nile River State in the east of the country. Russian planes then take off loaded with gold from Khartoum or Port Sudan bound for Russia to finance preparations for the invasion of Ukraine and the war effort.[30]

After the fall of Al-Bashir, Russia supported the military regime that took power in 2021, led by both Al-Burhan and Hemedti. When conflict broke out between these two on 15 April 2023, Russia armed both sides, seeking only its own interests. And this interest does not lie in the democratic transition in Sudan, which, according to Anna Evstigneeva, Deputy Permanent Representative of the Russian Federation to the United Nations, is at the root of the current crisis 'largely caused by an external interference in Sudanese sovereign affairs, attempts at forced political engineering in the country and imposing democratic recipes on it'.[31] Russia needs the chaos that will then see the emergence of an authoritarian, militarized regime.[32] Wagner maintained a privileged relationship with Hemedti, but Prigozhin's death on 23 August 2023 and the Kremlin's takeover of SMP's activities weakened ties. Moreover, Russia wants its naval base on the Red Sea, and Port Sudan is the best candidate. The port city being held by Al-Burhan, the Kremlin is going to favour him, regardless of Prighozin's former friendship. What's more, Al-Burhan is still the legitimate (albeit coup-derived) leader of Sudan. As Russia always asserts its sovereigntist line in international relations, it makes sense for it to ally itself with the recognized, 'sovereign' leader, whatever the internal unrest and power struggles. Russia now seems to be upsetting the delicate equilibrium and tilting the balance in favour of Al-Burhan and SAF.

Isayas Afwerki took the same turn. As late as 2023, Hemedti was in favour in Asmara. Indeed, a month before launching his offensive and plunging Sudan back into the hell of civil war, the RSF leader had made one last visit abroad, and that honour went to Eritrean president Isayas Afwerki, whom the warlord met on 13 March 2023, in Asmara.[33]

In fact, if Hemedti and Isayas were close for a time, it was essentially for economic reasons. The region covered by the Arabian-Nubian Shield, that of the wider Red Sea, sees a superposition of sometimes contradictory geo-strategic alliances. It is important to bear in mind that there is no logic of massive, clearly defined antagonistic blocs. Alliances prevail according to circumstances, which is not to say that they are not driven by an internal logic. As we shall see, Isayas has recently moved from the alliance uniting RSF, the United Arab Emirates and Ethiopia to the SAF-Egypt-Saudi Arabia bloc. He himself has not changed, and his relationship with Moscow, on the other hand, is stronger than ever.

Unlike Hemedti, who has few ideological ambitions and despite all compromises, Isayas remains an ideologue, a revolutionary with designs whose inconsistencies can certainly be pointed out, but who can take decisions contrary to his own interests just because they correspond to his program, or at least to the image he gives of it.

Another point that differentiates him from Hemedti: Eritrean gold was never for Wagner. Isayas did not deal with Prigozhin during his lifetime, and it is not possible to document the presence of Wagner's men in Eritrea. Isayas speaks directly with Vladimir Putin or Serguei Lavrov, no need to compromise with the 'Kremlin cook', as Dimitri Zuferey, co-author of the book *Wagner, Enquête au cœur du système Prigojine*, confirms, 'Wagner does regime maintenance for faltering dictators and Isayas Afwerki's does not need it'.[34] It is sufficiently solid by the grip of the autocrat and his party at all levels of Eritrean society.

While Isayas, Hemedti and Haftar, as we shall see, all remain within Putin's orbit, Isayas is a step above.

Libya and Yemen

Another key figure in the Wagner network's gold mining operations in Sudan is Alexander Sergeyevich Kuznetsov,[35] sanctioned by the European Union for his involvement in the paramilitary group's command.[36] He distinguished himself in Libya, where he was wounded in 2019 fighting alongside Marshal Haftar's Libyan National Army (LNA). Khalifa Belqasim Haftar Alferjani was one of Muammar Gaddafi's fellow fighters before breaking with him. Taken prisoner in Chad and then released, he remained in exile until 2011. He then returned to Libya to try his luck when it became clear that the star of the Guide of the Revolution would sooner or later crash, as it did on 20 October 2011. But in some respects, Haftar can be said to be Gaddafi's heir.

A look in the rear-view mirror. As a young officer in the Libyan army, Muammar Gaddafi became the de facto leader of Libya in 1969, following a coup d'état on 1 September. Until his death, Gaddafi was a fervent defender of pan-Arabism, but also of pan-Africanism understood as a struggle against 'Western and Zionist imperialism', in particular against French interests. In 2008, he proclaimed himself 'King of Kings', the traditional title of Ethiopian emperors (*Negusa Negest*). In 2009, the 'Guide' became head of the Organisation of the African Union as a rotating president, hoping to pass on his long-held dream of moving the headquarters of the African Union from Addis Ababa to Sirte, his hometown.

All these provocations especially pleased Isayas Afwerki, who personally fought against the Negus' troops when Eritrea still belonged to the Ethiopian Empire in the early 1970s. The friendship between the two heads of state was strong. Isayas made several trips to Tripoli, and in 2009, Libya, then a non-permanent member of the UN Security Council, was the only country not to vote in favour of sanctions against Eritrea. In 2011, when NATO had launched its military operation on March 19, and Gaddafi's fate had already been decided, it was considered for a time to exfiltrate him to Asmara.[37] The other possibility would have been Robert Mugabe's Zimbabwe, which in its time had already welcomed Mengistu Haile Mariam, the Derg tyrant responsible for the Red Terror, the brutal leader of Ethiopia driven out by the Tigrayans of the TPLF. 'The enemies of my enemies are the friends of my friends,'[38] Isayas Afwerki might say!

The second civil war in Libya from 2014 onwards pitted three rival governments against each other, then two, the Government of National Unity (GNU) in the West and the Libyan National Army (LNA) in the East. Khalifa Haftar and the LNA took control of eastern Libya, around Cyrenaica and the marshal's hometown Benghazi, a trafficking capital, the escape point for migrants from all over Africa, particularly Eritreans trying to flee the PFDJ regime. As mentioned above, it has been documented that senior members of the Eritrean army were directly involved in trafficking human beings to Libya, and more precisely to the Cyrenaica controlled by Marshal Haftar.

Although Haftar is master of Cyrenaica, his position has not been consolidated. This is how Wagner's men landed in Benghazi in May 2018, the first chapter in the Russian mercenaries' African anabasis.[39]

Khalifa Haftar and his sons are involved in all kinds of trafficking, from human beings to drugs, but gold takes pride of place.[40] These affairs are always directly linked to their political and strategic interests involving the RSF-Eritrea-UAE arc on the one hand or Russia[41] on the other. It should be noted, however, that the United Arab Emirates are steadfast in their desire to curb Iran's influence. They therefore ally themselves with North African leaders (Libya, Sudan, Eritrea) to capture mercenaries to send to Yemen to fight against the Houthis (a proxy for Iran), or to develop a military base in Africa (Ethiopia, Somaliland) right across from Yemen and Iran. Russia, on the other hand, supports anything that can create chaos and act as a barrier to the West. It proceeds in Libya as it does in Sudan, playing one group off against another and vice versa to obtain gold, oil and influence.[42] In this regard, Haftar has not always provided the expected resources; one of the plans drawn up by Prigozhin's men to make him more cooperative was even to unleash the Sudanese RSF against him.[43]

At the origin of this stormy relationship, we must look towards Canada. Indeed, on 3 December 2015, Khalifa Haftar signed a contract with the Canadian lobbying firm Dickens & Madson Canada Inc. which promised to act as an intermediary with the Kremlin to obtain funds and weapons. On 7 May 2019, a similar contract was signed between Dickens & Madson and Hemedti. For $6 million, Dickens & Madson's president commits himself to lobbying politicians and the press in order to change the image of Hemedti, to obtain agricultural commodities from the Russian Federation, as well as funds and fuel from Haftar in exchange for military assistance alongside the LNA.[44] Two months later, the Sudanese RSF landed in Libya in support of Haftar's LNA.[45] According to documents leaked by Al Jazeera, the United Arab Emirates organize the transport of fighters and 'various goods' from Darfur, the stronghold of Hemedti and the RSF, to Assab in Eritrea, then from Assab to Libya or Yemen.[46] The Eritrean port, which houses an Emirati military base, thus serves as a distribution platform for Hemedti's mercenaries.[47]

RSF and LNA are also supported (or instrumentalized, depending on the interpretation) by Wagner. Here it should be remembered that the Libyan gold circuit converges with that of the Central African Republic, a country almost entirely in the hands of the Wagnerians, joins Sudan and ends in the United Arab Emirates according to the diagram explained above.

Considering that the men of Haftar, Hemedti and Isayas find themselves together in Yemen in the coalition led by the United Arab Emirates to fight the Houthis, we can only note the overlap of the Prigozhin network and the Emirati alliance.[48] But the situation changes in 2023.

Isayas goes it alone (with Putin)

Two pivotal events: Yevgeny Prigozhin died on 23 August 2023, the prelude to the Kremlin taking control of his activities in Africa and the consequent abandonment of his former alliances, mainly also

UAE proxies; Hamas committed the pogrom of 7 October 2023, and the Houthis resumed their activity. Isayas then broke with his allies from the day before (Ethiopia, Emirates, RSF and LNA) and began to loudly proclaim his support for the Houthis (UAE's bête noire).

On 22 March 2024, the Russian ambassador to Eritrea, Igor N. Mozgo, received the heads of diplomatic missions of Egypt, Yemen, Qatar and Libya (the recognized government, rival of Haftar) in his embassy in Asmara to brief them on the 'special operation in Ukraine' and the situation in the Horn of Africa.[49]

Before this chosen audience who represents the exact opposite of the old coalition led by the Emirates, Ambassador Mozgo also expressed Eritrea's desire to see the West's presence in Africa reduced in favour of the permanent presence of the Russian fleet in the Red Sea. He specifies, 'Russian President Vladimir Putin's Maritime Doctrine could certainly be very promising, but everything depends on the negotiating position of the Eritrean side'.[50] This sentence is ambiguous; it can be terribly flattering if it implies that everything depends on the choice of Eritrea, that is to say Isayas, or it is a formal notice: choose the right side and the right friendships!

These statements were published by TASS, the main Russian news agency financed by the Kremlin. The sentence about Putin's naval doctrine does not appear in the Russian version,[51] so it is aimed internationally. On 11 June 2024, Ambassador Mozgo explains that relations between Russia and Eritrea have also strengthened because the latter 'have long waited for someone to dare slap the West "in its face' and put it in its place'.[52] This slap in the face is heard on diplomatic, military, media, but also economic and financial levels. And indeed, it is also the pocket that Russia wants to hit. This is verified the very day after the press release on 'the slap in the face of the West'. On 12 June 2024, the Moscow Stock Exchange announced that it would cease trading in the dollar and the euro. Russia and the BRICS begin the financial war of de-dollarization, the main weapon of which is gold.

The rise of the BRICS and the global peril in the Red Sea

The Russia-Africa Summit and the expansion of the BRICS

From 22 to 24 August 2023, the BRICS nations – Brazil, Russia, India, China and South Africa (hereafter 'the BRICS') – in other words the club of leading emerging countries in economic and demographic terms, met in Johannesburg.

The final declaration of this summit announced the extension of the club to six new members, Ethiopia, Saudi Arabia, the United Arab Emirates, Egypt, Iran and Argentina. Between the invitation and formal adhesion on 1 January 2024, Javier Milei was elected in Argentina, initiating a change of course for his country, which will not be joining the BRICS club after all. Saudi Arabia is dithering and still examining the terms of membership. The other four countries that did join at the beginning of 2024, namely Ethiopia the United Arab Emirates, Egypt and Iran, are all Red Sea Arena Middle Powers. The same is true of Saudi Arabia, if it makes up its mind. 'The term "Red Sea Arena" was coined in 2017 and picked up by diplomats seeking to pre-empt security threats across the adjoining regions. The shared plan was to convene a diplomatic forum that included all those with political, economic or security stakes in the Red Sea and Gulf of Aden, the Horn of Africa and the Arabian Peninsula.'[1]

All five new or potential members have been allies of Eritrea at one time or another in recent months. Indeed since 2018, Isayas Afwerki has been increasing his diplomatic visits to his Middle Eastern neighbours.

In Saudi Arabia first of all, on the sidelines of the war in Yemen, but also of the rapprochement with Ethiopia. Indeed, the peace agreement was even signed in Jeddah. Saudi Arabia's second-largest city gave it its name, the famous 'Jeddah Agreement' of 16 September 2018. King Salman then awarded the Order of Abdulaziz Al Saud medal, the kingdom's highest decoration, to the two heads of state for their 'commitment to peace'.[2]

But it's not just a matter of protocol. Ties on both sides of the Red Sea go back much further. At least since 2015, Eritrea has been cooperating with Saudi Arabia in its fight to contain Iran, engaging in particular against the Houthis in Yemen. The Eritrean Ministry of Communication announced on 6 August 2019,[3] that the country was strengthening its ties with the Saudi Kingdom in an Iron Alliance, following the normalization of its relations with Ethiopia. Ironically, Eritrea is presented as a factor for peace in the region. Eritrean government was toying with the idea of joining the Islamic Military Counter Terrorism Coalition (IMCTC) initiated in December 2015 by Mohammed bin Salman and still led by Saudi Arabia, but the latter has been cautious not to integrate too quickly a state whose government claims to be atheist Marxist-Leninist and which was sanctioned for funding terrorism. However, Eritrea's strategic position, with 1,000 kilometres of continental coastline on the Red Sea and the strategic archipelago of the Dahlak Islands just across from Yemen, merited an effort.

Relations with the United Arab Emirates are also intense and contradictory. The Red Sea Corporation, the financial extension of the PFDJ, the Eritrean single party, is based in Dubai, and since September 2015, too, the UAE has been developing a military base in the port of Assab,[4] again as part of the war in Yemen. The UAE is also Ethiopian prime minister's main supporter and backer. At the dawn of Abiy Ahmed's reign, Isayas Afwerki became his new best friend, or rather his accomplice, by engaging together in a conflict marred by multiple war crimes. A more or less formal alliance united the UAE, Eritrea, Ethiopia and the Amhara nationalists, cemented by interests that proved contradictory in the long term. Nevertheless, in June 2018, having just taken office and while working out his plans with Isayas and Amharas leaders, the Ethiopian prime minister visited Abu Dhabi. The Emirates granted a $1 billion loan to Ethiopia's National Bank and invested $2 billion in the country's economy.[5]

If Saudi Arabia and the UAE are on the same line regarding the Houthis, Iran and Qatar, it should be borne in mind that they may nevertheless be competing for regional influence. For example, in the Nile countries' battle over the Renaissance Dam, Saudi Arabia is closer to Egypt and Sudanese SAF,[6] while the UAE supports Ethiopia and the Sudanese RSF.

For many observers the young Ethiopian prime minister is under the thumb of the Eritrean president, an old hand in politics. So, given Isayas' long-standing friendships with China and Russia (the BRICS core group) but also with the Gulf states on the one hand, and his close reconciliation with Ethiopia on the other, he played the role of intermediary in this network of alliances by bringing together the BRICS and the Red Sea. It's then hardly surprising that Isayas Afwerki made the trip to Johannesburg for the BRICS summit. As president of one of the poorest countries in the world, his presence does not seem justified, unless one considers that he is the architect of the enlargement and one of the ideologues behind this rising club.

A long ideological march

Isayas' anti-Western ideology dates back to his youth in the 1960s, when he studied in China[7] and came into contact with the anti-colonial and revolutionary Marxist movements.[8] It was on this basis that was founded the EPLF, forerunner of the PFDJ.[9] There's nothing really original about his discourse, but it is formalized and internationalized thanks to Nevsun's lobbyists from 2014 onwards. At the same time, Vladimir Putin's Russia, in the midst of its anti-Western shift, is preparing to invade Crimea and extend its influence in Africa. An ideological backdrop was then needed to conquer the hearts of the South. Isayas Afwerki, the old pan-Africanist lion, was the ideal ally. His discourse was then carried throughout Africa by the Wagner channels of pro-Russian propaganda.

Neither Russia nor China ever voiced the slightest criticism about the Tigray war waged by Ethiopia and Eritrea. And in a further blowback after the invasion of Ukraine, Eritrea (along with the great democracies of North Korea, Belarus and Syria) refused to support the UN resolution condemning Russia, and at the Human Rights Council, Eritrea voted against an investigation on the violation committed in Ukraine, alone with . . . Russia.[10]

The Russia-Africa Summit, to be held on 27 and 28 July 2023 in St. Petersburg (less than a month before the Johannesburg BRICS meeting which saw the enlargement), takes things up a notch. Isayas Afwerki literally pledges allegiance to Vladimir Putin in the name of the World:

> Russia has a historic mission to play. On behalf of everybody in the world I can say who is the leader of this show – Mr Vladimir Putin is the leader of the show. Russia should take the lead because of the challenge that we are facing. I am not flattering anyone. I am not doing any favour to you. I say this is a global challenge and we have to overcome it by identifying the role of each and every one of us in the whole story.[11]

Eritrea is small and an economic dwarf, but the behind-the-scenes (nuisance) power of its president is all too often overlooked by analysts.

Isayas Afwerki thought he could control Abiy Ahmed and probably even Ethiopia itself. An Anschluss in favour of Asmara would have been highly unlikely, but symbolic control was probably the case from 2018 to 2022. Relations between the two heads of state began to strain when the Ethiopian federal government and the Tigray regional government entered ceasefire negotiations that would end the open fighting of the Tigray war with the signing of the Pretoria Agreement on 2 November 2022. Isayas would not have taken kindly to not having been invited. After all, he is the man behind the secret negotiations. He is Africa's Sherpa to Putin, the facilitator between Ethiopia and the BRICS.

The importance of Ethiopia's entry into the BRICS must be fully appreciated and understood as a key step in the long anti-Western march begun by Isayas Afwerki and opportunely used by Vladimir Putin. Ethiopia was part of Potepkine's plan[12] to expand Russian influence. Ethiopia is a prime target, not only for its demographic and economic weight, but also because Abyssinia occupies a special place among African nations, the only country on the continent not to have been colonized and embodied by a Black emperor. 'Ethiopianism' was one of the founding currents of pan-Africanism. *Aethiopia* was the kingdom of return for slaves and their descendants, the beacon of the continent, the voice of the Third World on the international stage. So, with Ethiopia, the whole of Africa joins the BRICS. Or at least, that's how they want the countries of the Global South to understand it. That was Isayas' plan, to offer Ethiopia to Putin. But the creature seems to have freed itself from Doctor Frankenstein.

The Tripartite Agreement and Somaliland

The question of access to ports on the Red Sea was at the heart of the negotiations which led to the reconciliation between Eritrea and Ethiopia in 2018[13] and had aroused the enthusiasm of mining companies who could already see borders disappearing and Ethiopian minerals transiting through Eritrean ports at lower cost. Indeed, since Eritrea's independence, landlocked Ethiopia has been dependent on Djibouti for its sea freight, and no longer has a navy. It therefore needed to regain access to Assab and Massawa.

The reconciliation between Eritrea and Ethiopia was immediately extended to Somalia, also hostile to Ethiopia since the 2006 intervention, in what came to be known as the Tripartite Agreement. On 5 September 2018, Abiy Ahmed, Isayas Afwerki and Farmaajo, visited the commercial port infrastructure at Massawa and the military infrastructure at Assab.[14] As they passed, they greeted a ship full of Bisha zinc.

The Tripartite Agreement also included a military component. After Asmara, the second meeting of Eritrean, Ethiopian and Somali leaders was held in Bahr Dar, thanks to the hospitality of the Amharas leaders, and it was undoubtedly on this occasion that the invasion of Tigray was envisaged in its most concrete aspects. It was decided, for example, that Somali recruits would go to Eritrea for training, in the knowledge that local trainers had already done a sadly effective job with the Amharas militiamen. They would then be deployed to Tigray, where they were likely to commit war crimes.[15]

On the Somali side, the architect of this arrangement was Fahad Yasin Haji Dahir, a former journalist for Al Jazeera, the Qatari media, who had become head of NISA, the Somali secret service. As a reminder, Abiy Ahmed is also a former intelligence officer, the Ethiopian INSA.[16] At the time, Fahad Yasin was extremely influential and Farmaajo was under his thumb. Yasin played into the hands of Qatar and Iran, giving the Al-Shabaab jihadists a free hand. He also used trickery to send recruits to Eritrea, promising them to train and work in Qatar to provide security for the 2022 soccer World Cup. They finally landed in Asmara rather than Doha.

Eritrea has been placed under UN sanctions for its alleged support of Al-Shabaab in destabilizing neighbouring Ethiopia, then ruled by a Tigrayan, and has an ambiguous relationship with Iran. Now it is back with an alliance in which cohabite Emirates-backed Ethiopia and Qatar-backed Somalia. This is madness. Isayas thought he could eat from all racks and stack alliances with Saudi Arabia, the UAE and the Tripartite Agreement. But this 'all at a time' soon proved untenable.

Access to the Red Sea has been a constant preoccupation for Ethiopian leaders, but on 13 October 2023, Abiy Ahmed suddenly became urgent, clear and aggressive: 'The lack of access to harbors "prevents Ethiopia from holding the place it ought to have, [. . .] If this is not going to happen, there will be no fairness and justice and if there is no fairness and justice, it's a matter of time, we will fight".[17] The prime minister goes on to cite the prestigious nineteenth-century general Ras Alula as a historical guarantor of the Red Sea as Ethiopia's 'natural boundary'.[18] Ras Alula was Tigrayan, and this reference was probably not chosen at random. At the time, Ras Alula was speaking out against the Italian conquest of Eritrea, considered an integral part of the Ethiopian Empire. To reuse the words of a Tigrayan hero (against whose descendants Abiy has just waged a war to the death) potentially against the Eritreans themselves (and not the Italian colonists at all) is more than audacious! Abiy is no stranger to twisting history to suit his political purposes.

He explains that Ethiopia as a landlocked country is like a prison for 150 million people. And then he links the question of the Red Sea to the issue of the Nile,[19] which is extremely tense with neighbouring Sudan and Egypt. So, in his belligerent mood against all his neighbours, is he threatening Eritrea to regain access to Assab? It seems the most logical eventuality, geographically speaking. In other words, will Ethiopia turn against its ally of the Tripartite Agreement? Yes, but not the one we were expecting.

On 1 January 2024, Ethiopia announced that it had signed a *Memorandum of Understanding* with Somaliland. Ethiopia would have access to a port in return for recognition of Somaliland. This surprise move was seen as hostile to Somalia. Indeed, after the massacre of the Isaaqs by other Somali clans between 1987 and 1989,[20] the latter claimed independence immediately after the collapse of Somalia's central government led by Siad Barre on 18 May 1991 from their territory in the north of Somalia, a wide coastal strip opening onto the Gulf of Aden. Since then, Somaliland has functioned as a de facto state, albeit a very successful one, but is not recognized by the international community. Somalia acts as if Somaliland were still part of its territory. So, recognition by Addis Ababa is a direct affront to Mogadishu, which is responding with force.

By choosing another port, Ethiopia has turned its back on Eritrea and confirmed the amputation of Somalia. The Tripartite Agreement is dead. Eritrea and Somalia close ranks against Ethiopia. But what happened?

7 October and the return of the Houthis

In September 2015, the United Arab Emirates gained a foothold in Assab by investing in the former Soviet naval base, which they renovated and modernized as part of the fight against Yemen's Houthis and indirectly against Iran, which supports them. From 2017, they are also developing the infrastructure to house their fleet of Chinese Wing-Loong II and CH-4 drones. In 2018, Abiy Ahmed was on the best terms with the rulers of Eritrea and the United Arab Emirates. And it was in this context of strategic amity that he visited Assab's infrastructure. In 2019, Emirati Wing-Loong IIs are used in Libya in support of Marshal Haftar.[21] They will also be used in Sudan in support of Hemedti's RSF, then also belonging to the glacis of Isayas' friendships. From 2020, the Ethiopian army will be using combat drones. Logically enough, given the strategic alliances mentioned here, rumour has it that these will be UAVs from the UAE's base in Assab. The OSINT website *Bellingcat* considers the hypothesis possible, but unverifiable.[22]

Under heavy international and domestic criticism for its involvement in the Yemen war, Abu Dhabi decided to close the Assab base in February 2021 and reshape its regional strategy.[23]

Then came 7 October 2023, and the massacre perpetrated by Hamas, another Tehran proxy, in southern Israel. The Houthis were reactivated. They block the southern Red Sea. Some of the world's freight had to be rerouted.

The Emirates regretted their departure from the southern shore of the Red Sea. So they need a new bridgehead, and that will be Berbera in Somaliland. DP World (Dubai Port World) is already established there, having been ejected from Djibouti. Ethiopia, also wanting to bypass Djibouti, is killing two birds with one stone. With their interests converging, Ethiopia will be the Emirates' new African ally, and too bad for Eritrea. Abiy Ahmed's enigmatic statements on his country's natural right to access the Red Sea date back to 14 October 2023. Negotiations with the Emirates began immediately after October 7.

Addis Ababa and Hargeisa remained vague as to the nature of the infrastructure, civilian or military, but Ethiopian deputy prime minister and foreign minister Demeke Mekonnen saw fit to specify that it would also be a military base on 12 January 2024.[24] On January 26, he resigned.

From early 2024, two blocks will take shape.[25] One is under Emirati patronage, with Ethiopia and Somaliland. Opposite, still in the Saudi fold, Somalia and Eritrea, two countries with a long tradition of enmity with Ethiopia, are looking to Egypt and Sudan, two other states that also have a dispute with the Abyssinian giant, over the construction of the Grand Renaissance Dam on the Nile (GERD).

On 11 November 2023, just between Abiy Ahmed's hostile announcements and the publication of the MoU with Somaliland in January, the office of Egyptian President Abdel Fattah El-Sisi announced that the head of state had spoken with his Eritrean counterpart at a meeting in Riyadh, the Saudi capital, to discuss 'the latest regional developments of mutual interest, particularly with regard to the Horn of Africa, Sudan, Somalia and Res [*sic*] Sea security issues'.[26] This press announcement was subsequently picked up by the semi-official Eritrean website TesfaNews,[27] which stated that the two presidents had in fact met with Hassan Sheikh Mohamud, the new president of Somalia, for discussions. Egypt replacing Ethiopia in a renewed tripartite alliance is symbolically very powerful. TesfaNews adds that Isayas Afwerki also met with General Abdel Fattah Al-Burhan, Chairman of Sudan's Transitional Sovereignty Council.

It was to overthrow Al-Burhan that Hemedti attempted a coup that degenerated into civil war on 15 April 2023, with the support of Isayas Afwerki and Abu Dhabi. Hemedti had made his fortune in gold mining in Sudan and was in business with Yevgeny Prigozhin, the creator and iconic leader of Wagner's Russian mercenaries. But after his defiance of the Kremlin, Prigozhin suffered a timely plane crash that left his friends in disgrace.[28] With the Emirates siding with Ethiopia over Eritrea, the regional planets were aligned for Moscow and Asmara to abandon Hemedti and turn their hearts to Al-Burhan.

It's not just a question of choosing one warlord against another. It's about two blocs growing stronger, and concessions being agreed and taken on a sea that's more strategic than ever. Thus, on 26 May 2024, Russia and Al-Burhan's Sudan signed an agreement allowing Moscow to establish a naval base in Port Sudan, while Iran leased infrastructure[29] there at the same time.

If Ethiopia left with the Emirates in its pocket, it also took France and the navy project with it. Indeed, on 12 and 13 March 2019, French president Emmanuel Macron visited Ethiopia. A military source ironically confided to me that President Macron had a real crush on the Ethiopian prime minister, in whom he recognized himself: young, forty-something (they're a year apart), dynamic, liberal, always well-dressed. Macron presents himself as his staunch ally and wants to build a navy for Ethiopia through the powerful Naval Group. The base was to have been in Eritrea,[30] but since the break-up, the project, far from being abandoned, has been transplanted to Somaliland. Naturally, diplomatic questions of sovereignty have arisen, and the French authorities are keeping a low profile also vis-à-vis Djibouti. Given Russia's anti-French campaign in Africa, the Port Soudan base project must also be seen in the context of this rivalry.

The latest twist: Russia owns the naval bases at Tartous and Latakia in Syria, but the fall of Bashar El Assad is likely to precipitate a redeployment to Russian naval forces. Port Sudan is becoming more strategic than ever at the gateway of Middle East.

In conclusion, it is clear that the United Arab Emirates, the fight against the Houthis and Iran, and the alliance with Ethiopia are definitely behind Isayas. On the other hand, the bond between the Eritrean and Sudanese presidents, as well as Moscow remains strong.

Eritrea, whose regime should have collapsed in 2010, but was saved by Bisha's gold, has become the centrepiece of a Great Game that fuels the deadliest conflicts of the twenty-first century (in Ethiopia, Yemen, Sudan). The civilian populations of these countries are the first to be affected, but it's the entire global economy that is impacted, with severe consequences all around the globe for the most economically vulnerable.

But who comes out on top in this clash of egos? Russia, of course, which is reaping great rewards in Africa by losing little, but also China. It's China that has won the day. It has managed to capture raw materials and develop strategic infrastructures without firing a shot and without overtly committing itself anywhere.

Armed conflicts are unfortunately well-known crises. On the other hand, there is a deeper, less visible, movement that will change the global economy and, more generally, the balance of the world: de-dollarization. And to wage this battle, China is thirsty for gold!

Conclusion

De-dollarization: Gold to overturn the world order

Crushing 'the elites of domination and monopoly'

Every year, on 24 May, Isayas Afwerki composes a speech to mark the anniversary of Eritrean independence. It should be noted that the countdown begins in 1991, the end of the war against the Derg waged alongside other opposition forces in Ethiopia, including the TPLF, and not from 1993, the year of the UN-supervised referendum that saw international recognition of the new state on the Red Sea. So, in 2024, on the thirty-third anniversary of independence and his reign, the Eritrean president has hardly a word for his fellow citizens, for his country, for the victims of armed conflict throughout the Horn of Africa, or for the thirsty, displaced and ruined by the great drought. No, true to his obsessions, he launches into a diatribe about the world order and the war waged by the 'elites of domination and monopoly'[1] to contain Russia and China. He adds, 'In the eyes of the elite of "domination and monopoly", Africa has always been, and continues to be, regarded as their exclusive enclave.' The meaning of this sentence is clear, despite the strange use of the word 'enclave'. Through slavery, colonization and resource exploitation, these elites keep Africa poor. This elite is the capitalist West. It's easy to argue, however, that Isayas is a splendid specimen of the global elite, who enslaves his people, invades the neighbouring countries and diverts all mineral wealth to his party without leaving a nugget for his people, who have never seen the golden colour of prosperity, the copper of Bisha in a smartphone relaying a free press or the fruit of his own fertile field fattened on potash from Colluli.

Isayas affirms his support for the Palestinian people, to whom other peoples of the Bab el-Mandeb Strait show their solidarity. Here he is talking about the Houthis. While it is they who are launching attacks on international ships, blocking traffic through the Suez Canal and forcing the biggest shipping companies to reroute their container ships and bulk carriers to the Cape of Good Hope, Isayas credits the 'Illicit interferences and naval stampedes' to the 'defunct forces of domination and monopoly'. Once again, the technique of accusatory inversion (AiM). NATO and the European Union are waging a secret war, supported by propaganda that conceals their decay. They are 'almost defunct', under 'intensive care', he says.

In fact, his 24 May speech is a copy-and-paste of his two discourses at the second Russia-Africa Summit held in St. Petersburg on 27 July and 28 July 2023[2] (the first one, held in Sochi in 2019, gave Nathalie Yamb a media breakthrough). During his two videotaped speeches, the Eritrean president repeats the same phrase about the defunct NATO conspiracy several times.[3] This statement is perfectly in line with Moscow's strategy of extending its prestige in Africa by using memorial diplomacy to present itself as the power not to have colonized the continent, but which, in the days of the USSR, even sided with oppressed peoples.[4] In a clever twist, the very words with which this is expressed are borrowed from French president Emmanuel Macron in his 7 November 2019 interview for with *The Economist* and then used against himself: 'What we are currently experiencing is the brain death of NATO.'[5] In so doing, Isayas Afwerki is not addressing his own population, who, deprived of all free press, cannot understand the allusion, but those in French-speaking Africa and the Sahel countries, where anti-French sentiment is growing. Isayas is a plaything in Moscow's African strategy, but an active one that has finally found a stage worthy of its disproportionate ambitions.

During this summit, he also hammers home to the world that there is no war between Russia and Ukraine, but a NATO attack on Russia for hegemony. Ukraine would be NATO's sacrificial victim in a containment war against Russia, the prelude to an offensive against China. NATO is spending billions, if not trillions, to this end, but this money is not pledged to any material or industrial value, it's just printed paper, he says. Putin smiles at this statement, and indeed, this sentence is crucial. Isayas goes on to say that the international monetary system dominated by the dollar and the euro has been NATO's hegemonic weapon, and that a new financial architecture is needed.

Isayas proposes a plan. Africa holds 60 per cent of the world's natural resources, while Russia has the technological and industrial edge to develop them. To change the world order, other 'free peoples' must be involved, like the Chinese. Vladimir Putin must be the leader of this new free world, he says solemnly.

The Russian president replies that he is in full agreement with such a plan, and that the perfect platform for its implementation is the BRICS alliance.

In an unsurprising twist of fate, the BRICS are due to hold their summit meeting one month later, from 22 August to 24 August 2023, in Johannesburg. During the summit, the club will issue formal invitations to six countries. The four who will officially accept are all from the Red Sea Arena (Ethiopia, Egypt, Iran and the United Arab Emirates). Isayas spoke at the meeting, using all his usual rhetorical palette and focusing on the issue of de-dollarization.

For if the gold of the Nubian Shield has been used to enrich crooked politicians, warlords and traffickers, if it has kept Isayas, Haftar, Hemedti or Al-Burhan in power, if it has financed wars, international terrorism and disinformation, today the BRICS are assigning it a historic destiny: the overthrow of the international monetary system. Gold will replace the dollar as collateral for their currencies.

It's the great return of the gold standard.

Gold against the dollar

The system of gold convertibility, which consisted of keeping the equivalent of the money supply in gold at the Central Bank and ensuring the convertibility of fiat money into metal, came to an end in July 1944 with the Bretton Woods agreements, which ushered in the post–Second World War hegemony of the dollar. At that time, the dollar remained the only currency convertible into gold, and became the standard for all other currencies. In 1971, the dollar in turn became a floating currency, no longer pegged to gold, but remaining the reference currency. This marked the end of the Bretton Woods system and the beginning of the floating fiat era.

And it is this very system that the BRICS leaders want to overthrow when they call for the subversion of the post–Second World War system, and not just to thwart geopolitical influence or curb Western values and style.

This could take several forms. One possibility would be for national banks to pledge their respective national currencies against gold. In fact, 2023 was a record year for gold purchases by central banks. This trend was driven by Russia, which was the biggest buyer of gold on the eve of the invasion of Ukraine,[6] and then by China, whose Central Bank (People's Bank of China, or PBoC) had announced in November 2022 that it was increasing its stock of gold every month.[7] As the petroyuan, an alternative to the petrodollar, is convertible into gold, this means that under this system, oil transactions can be carried out in gold without using the dollar.[8] Another possibility would be for the yuan to become a reference currency. This would be tantamount to a sort of Chinese-style Bretton Woods, but it doesn't exactly fit in with the multipolar policy advocated by the BRICS. This is why the idea of a common currency for the BRICS[9] was launched. The cryptocurrency model is also being watched with interest.[10] On 5 March 2024, Yuri Ushakov, former Russian ambassador to the United States and now Vladimir Putin's advisor, declared that 'BRICS will work to create an independent payment system based on digital currencies and blockchain'.[11]

While waiting for new technologies to change the world, on 12 June 2024, the Moscow Stock Exchange announced that it would cease all dollar and euro transactions.[12]

Similarly, on 28 July 2024, the office of Ethiopian prime minister Abiy Ahmed, who was present at the Johannesburg summit and whose country has just joined the BRICS, announced that the Ethiopian birr would become floating, abandoning the dollar. This announcement follows the National Bank of Ethiopia's reform aimed at replenishing its gold reserves. In Ethiopia, Ezana Mining Development PLC held a quasi-monopolistic position in the supply of gold to the National Bank of Ethiopia. Until then, the latter bought gold at 35 per cent above the market price, but from 6 May 2024, prices will be set according to the quantity of gold supplied, with tiers at 150 g (still 35 per cent above the market price), 1 kg (52 per cent) and 5 kg (60 per cent). The aim of this measure is to stimulate production and encourage the grouping of small producers to reach the critical 5 kg threshold and thus compete with Ezana. In this way, the Central Bank, in conjunction with the federal government, is seeking to break up trafficking and capture the gold that is disappearing into illegal networks bound for Eritrea and Sudan.

After two years of war, the Tigray gold will finally be used to bolster federal reserves and allow the birr to be de-dollarized, according to a plan drawn up by Isayas Afwerki, Vladimir Putin and Xi Jinping. A bitter conclusion.

Conclusion

Canadian and Australian mining companies have always been profit-seeking – that's the way capitalism works. But with the Nevsun trials, the company, to save itself, became the champion of the Eritrean regime. The discourse that was then produced subsequently entered the Russian soft and hard powers on a global scale. It's the paradox of liberalism that kills itself.

The mining companies' plan to promote or at least benefit from the rapprochement between Eritrea and Ethiopia within the framework of regional balances and imbalances was a huge fiasco, a huge mess. That part of the project completely failed. There is no cross-border exploitation of minerals in the Horn of Africa, and apparently not for a long time. No regional development. On the other hand, there have been a lot of casualties, and the gold from Shire or the potash from the Danakil wasn't worth it.

But something is on the way, perhaps a change of era.

I don't think that in 2014 Todd Romaine thought he was offering rhetorical ammunition to Vladimir Putin and the Wagnerians in their strategy of African expansion, or preparing for the de-dollarization of the world, but by an implausible domino effect beyond his control, he has contributed to it.

Epilogue

Political fiction

Is Europe next?

On April 2016, Nevsun acquired Reservoir Minerals Inc. for $365 million in cash and stock[1] and became the sole owner of Timok Upper Zone and 60.4 per cent owner of Timok Lower Zone, thanks to the cash flow generated by Bisha.[2] These mines exploit copper and gold deposits near Bor in eastern Serbia, not far from the Bulgarian and Romanian borders. This is Nevsun's only asset outside Eritrea.

In 2017, Todd Romaine participated in the seventh International Conference on Mining Resources in Serbia held on October 4, as welcomed by the Canadian Embassy in Serbia, North Macedonia and Montenegro. 'Mr. Todd Romaine from Nevsun Resources, presented responsible mining and best CSR [Corporate Social Responsibility] policies and practices.'[3]

Corporate social responsibility from a company on trial for forced labour and inhumane treatment must be fascinating.

Fascinating, too, is the way in which the mining companies of the Nevsun galaxy (which includes Danakali, since Todd Romaine worked there) choose the most Russian-friendly countries on their respective continents: Eritrea in Africa, Serbia in Europe. Serbia is the only European country not to have condemned the invasion of Ukraine, like Eritrea. These same companies then rise to a dominant or even monopolistic position before selling their shares, turnkey projects and good relations with the government in place to state-owned Chinese companies.

Indeed, when Nevsun accepted Zijin's offer in September 2018, the company sold Timok at the same time as Bisha, opening the doors of Serbia's gold and copper industry to China[4] to the delight of President Aleksandar Vučić, 'cantor of Serbian-Chinese friendship'.[5]

The repetition of the pattern is disturbing.

A Canadian story

If I were a conspiracy theorist, I'd say that Nevsun was knowingly used as a Trojan horse.

If I were a conspiracy theorist, I'd admire the inaction of the Canadian government, which prefers to favour its companies in contravention of everything its country is supposed to stand for, in terms of human rights and democracy, acting ultimately against its own side, NATO.

Inaction? But Todd Romaine is acting with the consent of the Canadian Foreign Affairs Department, isn't he? And when it came to recognizing the genocide of the Tigrayans, the Subcommittee on International Human Rights (SDIR) of the Standing Committee on Foreign Affairs and International Development was going to give a favourable opinion, but this recognition was actively blocked in high places, according to an inside source, who even mentioned the prime minister's office.

Each of the heads of state mentioned in this book, and each of the warlords, is responsible for the crimes he has committed; they are not Nevsun's creations. Nor is the gold circuit a Canadian creation, but in view of what has just been unfolded, through the actions of companies registered in this country and some of its nationals, Canada bears direct responsibility for the perpetuation of the Eritrean inferno and the genocide of the Tigrayans.

Notes

Introduction

1   Translated from the Greek version : Marcellin Berthelot and Marie-Émile Ruelle, Collection des anciens alchimistes grecs (Paris: G. Steinheil, 1888) t. 2, 243.

2   Charlotte Touati, 'Le Purgatoire dans les littératures d'Égypte et d'Afrique du Nord (Ier-IVe s. ap. J.-C.)' (PhD diss., Institute of History, Faculty of Humanities, University of Neuchâtel, 2012), https://libra .unine.ch/entities/publication/3fe63ca2-d70f-4f18-b561-e7fd48f43516/ details.

3   Charlotte Touati, 'A "Kerygma of Peter" behind the Apocalypse of Peter, the Pseudo-Clementine Romance and the Eclogae Propheticae of Clement of Alexandria', *Studia patristica* LXV (2013) ed. Markus Vinzent (Leuven, Paris, Walpole (Mass.): Peeters, 2013), 277–92.

4   I then explored the allegorization of holy war in patristic texts and the inner jihad or 'ijtihâd of Sufi poets, cf. Charlotte Touati, 'L'Allégorisation de la guerre sainte', *Revue de l'Histoire des Religions* 227/2 (2010): 231–47, https://doi.org/10.4000/rhr.7579.

5   Georges Goyon, *Le Papyrus de Turin dit 'des mines d'or' et le Wadi Hammamat* (Le Caire: Imprimerie de l'Institut Français d'Archéologie Orientale, 1949).

6   David N. Edwards, *The Kingdoms of Kush and Meroe: Cultural Encounters with Pharaonic Egypt, Nubia, and Axum* (Oxford: Oxford University Press, 2019); Timothy Kendall, 'Interactions between the Kingdom of Kush and the Red Sea Trade Network', *Journal of African Archaeology* 19/1 (2021): 45–68; Carolyn Fluehr-Lobban, 'Meroitic and Aksumite Interactions: Political and Cultural Exchange', *Northeast African Studies* 23/2 (2020): 120–39; Tekeste Negash, *The Rise of*

Aksum and the Decline of Meroe: Trade, War, and Diplomacy in Ancient Northeast Africa (New York: Routledge 2018); Emanuele Tacchini, 'New Perspectives on Meroitic-Axumite Relations: Archaeological Evidence and Historical Interpretations', *African Archaeological Review* 39/3 (2022): 275–95.

7   Peter R. Schmidt, Matthew Curtis and Zelalem Teka, *The Archaeology of Ancient Eritrea* (Champaign, IL: University of Illinois Press, 2008), 151–78.

8   Massimo Zaccaria, 'L'oro dell'eritrea, 1897-1914', *Africa* LX/1 (2005): 65–110.

9   Peter R. Johnson and Beraki Woldehaimanot, 'Development of the Arabian-Nubian Shield: Perspectives on Accretion and Deformation in the Northern East African Orogen and the Assembly of Gondwana', in *Proterozoic East Gondwana: Supercontinent Assembly and Breakup, Geological Society of London, Special Publications* 206, ed. Masaru Yoshida, Brian Frederick Windley and Somnath Dasgupta (Geological Society: London,2003), 289–325.

10   Charles Tucker Barrie, F. William Nielsen and Claude H. Aussant, 'The Bisha Volcanic-Associated Massive Sulfide Deposit, Western Nakfa Terrane, Eritrea', *Economic Geology* 102/4 (2007): 717–38; Vincent Bouchot and Jean-Pierre Milesi, 'La métallogénie de l'or : évolution des modèles et cibles prioritaires de la recherche au fil des années', *Géologues* 152 (2007): 40–8.

Chapter 1

1   Kjetil Tronvoll and Daniel Mekonnen, *The African Garrison State. Human Rights and Political Development in Eritrea* (Woodbridge: James Currey, 2014), 165–83; Alex de Waal, *The Real Politics of the Horn of Africa. Money, War and the Business of Power* (Cambridge: Polity Press, 2015), 143–50.

2   'Proclamation on National Service No. 82/1995 of 1995', *The Eritrean Gazette* 11 (23 October 1995), https://www.refworld.org/legal/ legislation/natlegbod/1995/en/32119.

3   Mirjam van Reisen, Makeda Saba and Klara Smits, '"Sons of Isaias": Slavery and Indefinite National Service in Eritrea', in *Mobile Africa: Human Trafficking and the Digital Divide*, ed. Mirjam van Reisen and Munyaradzi Mawere (Bamenda, Cameroon: Langaa Research & Publishing CIG, 2019), 115–75, https://www.researchgate.net/publication /336956190_Mobile_Africa_Human_Trafficking_and_the_Digital _Divide; Tronvoll and Mekonnen, *The African Garrison State*, 172–3.

4   Cf. Sara Palacios-Arapiles, 'Enslaved by their Own Government: Indefinite National Service in Eritrea', in *Enslaved Trapped and Trafficked in Digital Black Holes: Human Trafficking Trajectories to Libya*, ed. Mirjam van Reisen, Munyaradzi Mawere, Klara Smits and M. Wirtz (Bamenda, Cameroon: Langaa Research & Publishing CIG, 2023), 195–254,
     https://www.researchgate.net/publication/367254851_Enslaved_ Trapped_and_Trafficked_in_Digital_Black_Holes_Human_Trafficking _Trajectories_to_Libya; Nicole Hirt, 'Community Service or Forced Labour? The Eritrean National Service', in *Eritrea from Liberation to oppression*, ed. Katja Dorothea Buck and Mirjam van Reisen (Hamburg: EMV, mars 2017), 48–57 (52–54), https://raee.eu/wp-content/uploads /2022/01/EMW_English_version_2017.pdf.

5   Daniel Tesfa and Mirjam Van Reisen, 'Regional War by Design: The involvement of Eritrea in the Tigray War', in *Tigray. The Hysteresis of War*, Book 1, ed. Mirjam van Reisen and Munyaradzi Mawere (Bamenda, Cameroon: Langaa Research & Publishing CIG, 2024), 141–90, https://www.researchgate.net/publication/385202452_Tigray _The_Hysteresis_of_War_Book_1#pfb0.

6   Dan Connell, *Against All Odds – A Chronicle of the Eritrean Revolution with a New Update and Reappraisal* (Trenton, NJ: Red Sea Press, 1993, update 2021), https://danconnell.net/book/against-all-odds/I don't see the problem with 2021.

7   Dan Connell, *Conversations with Eritrean Political Prisoners* (Trenton, NJ: Red Sea Press, 2005).

8   Petros Tesfagorgis, Habte Hagos, Abraham Zere and Daniel Mekonnen, 'Mining and Repression in Eritrea: Corporate Complicity in Human Rights Abuses', *Eritrea Focus* (June 2018), 9–12, https://eritrea-focus.org/wp-content/uploads/2018/06/Mining-Repression-Eritrea-V1.pdf.

9   Léonard Vincent, *Les Erythréens* (Paris: Rivages, 2012). His online journal is also a valuable source of information and analysis: https://erythreens.wordpress.com.

10   Van Reisen, Saba and Smits, 'Sons of Isaias', 126.

11   What the experts call 'the deliberate impoverishment strategy', cf. Mirjam van Reisen, Meron Estefanos and Lena Reim, 'Human Trafficking in the Sinai: Mapping the Routes and Facilitators', in *Human Trafficking and Trauma in the Digital Era: The Ongoing Tragedy of the Trade in Refugees from Eritrea*, ed. Mirjam van Reisen and Munyaradzi Mawere (Bamenda, Cameroon: Langaa Research & Publishing CIG, 2017), 19–94 (21–30).

12   Matt Bryden, Jörg Roofthooft, Ghassan Schbley and Babatunde Taiwo, *Letter Dated 18 July 2011 from the Chairman of the Security Council Committee Pursuant to Resolutions 751 (1992) and 1907 (2009) Concerning Somalia and Eritrea Addressed to the President of the Security Council*, 18 July 2011, 109–10, https://digitallibrary.un.org/record/708002?ln=es&v=pdf; Mirjam van Reisen and Meron Estefanos, 'The Exodus from Eritrea and who is Benefiting', in *Human Trafficking and Trauma in the Digital Era: The Ongoing Tragedy of the Trade in Refugees from Eritrea*, ed. Mirjam van Reisen and Munyaradzi Mawere (Bamenda, Cameroon: Langaa Research & Publishing CIG, 2017), 95–192, https://www.researchgate.net/publication/316989834_Human_Trafficking_and_Trauma_in_the_Digital_Era_The_Ongoing_Tragedy_of_the_Trade_in_Refugees_from_Eritrea.

13   Van Reisen, Saba and Smits, 'Sons of Isaias', 130.

14   In a video posted on 13 February 2024, travel YouTuber Sabbatical showed how the port city of Massawa, an architectural gem, is left

abandoned and at the mercy of the elements. Nothing works there (running water, electricity, etc.), https://www.youtube.com/watch?v =dfVcnfaVKnI.

15 Hirt, 'Community Service or Forced Labour?', 49–51; Van Reisen, Saba and Smits, 'Sons of Isaias', 125–6; 136–7.

16 Human Rights Watch, '"They Are Making Us into Slaves, Not Educating Us" How Indefinite Conscription Restricts Young People's Rights, Access to Education in Eritrea', August 2019, https://www.hrw .org/sites/default/files/report_pdf/eritrea0819_web.pdf.

17 Human Rights Watch, 'They Are Making Us into Slaves', 30–2.

18 Human Rights Watch, 'They Are Making Us into Slaves', 17–9; van Reisen, Saba and Smits, 'Sons of Isaias', 120; 124.

19 Ibid., 120–5.

20 Resources relating to this case have been compiled by the Business & Human Rights Resource Centre: https://www.business-humanrights .org/en/latest-news/nevsun-lawsuit-re-bisha-mine-eritrea/.

21 Van Reisen, Saba and Smits, 'Sons of Isaias', 146–8; Human Rights Watch, 'They Are Making Us into Slaves', 20.

22 Tesfagorgis, Hagos, Zere and Mekonnen, 'Mining and Repression in Eritrea', 46–54.

23 Online resources, https://www.eepa.be/?page_id=29.

24 Online Ressources, https://raee.eu/publications/.

25 Equivalent to USD 160 official rate, USD 82 unofficial.

26 Van Reisen, Saba, Smits and 'Sons of Isaias', 139–40.

Chapter 2

1 Scott H. Delisi, 'Controlling the Market, Controlling the People: Hidri Trust Takes All', 27 June 2006, Wikileaks: 06ASMARA553_a.

2 Cf. Mirjam Van Reisen, Makeda Saba and Klara Smits, '"Sons of Isaias": Slavery and Indefinite National Service in Eritrea', in *Mobile Africa: Human Trafficking and the Digital Divide* (Bamenda, Cameroon: Langaa Research & Publishing CIG, 2019), 115–75 (129).

3　Van Reisen, Saba and Smits, 'Sons of Isaias', 126–31; Alex de Waal, *The Real Politics of the Horn of Africa. Money, War and the Business of Power* (Cambridge: Polity Press, 2015), 143–150.

4　On the inescapability of the national service in public and private economic participation, see Makeda Saba, 'Uncomfortable Aid: INGOs in Eritrea', in *Mobile Africa: Human Trafficking and the Digital Divide,* ed. Mijam van Reisen, Munyaradzi Mawere, Mia Stokmans and Kinfe Abraha Gebre-Egziabher (Bamenda, Cameroon: Langaa Research & Publishing CIG, 2019), 631–72, www.researchgate.net/publication /336956190_Mobile_Africa_Human_Trafficking_and_the_Digital _Divide.

5　This is one of the arguments he uses to convince investors to place their trust in his company, as illustrated by the presentation he gave at the UN Palais des Nations in Geneva: 'Demystifying Eritrea: The Ground Reality, Mining and Human Rights', 8 mars 2018, https://danakali.com .au/wp-content/uploads/2021/09/Company-Presentation-Demystifying -Eritrea-Thursday-08-March-2018.pdf.

6　Matt Bryden, Jörg Roofthooft, Ghassan Schbley and Babatunde Taiwo, *Letter Dated 18 July 2011 from the Chairman of the Security Council Committee Pursuant to Resolutions 751 (1992) and 1907 (2009) Concerning Somalia and Eritrea Addressed to the President of the Security Council*, 18 July 2011, 99, https://digitallibrary.un.org/record /708002?ln=es&v=pdf.

7　Ibid., 108. As for the Tigray smuggling operation, I've heard about it several times from eyewitnesses.

8　Klara Smits, '"You are the Ball – They are the Players": The Human Traffickers of Eritreans in Libya', in *Enslaved, Trapped and Trafficked in Digital Black Holes: Human Trafficking Trajectories to Libya*, ed. Mirjam van Reisen, Munyaradzi Mawere, Klara Smits and Morgane Wirtz (Bamenda, Cameroon: Langaa RCPIG, 2023), 451–520 (503–5), https:// www.researchgate.net/publication/367254851_Enslaved_Trapped_and _Trafficked_in_Digital_Black_Holes_Human_Trafficking_Trajectories _to_Libya; Mirjam van Reisen and Meron Estefanos, 'The Exodus from Eritrea and Who is Benefiting', in *Human Trafficking and Trauma in the Digital Era: The Ongoing Tragedy of the Trade in Refugees from Eritrea*, ed. Mirjam van Reisen, Munyaradzi Mawere (Bamenda, Cameroon: Langaa Research & Publishing CIG, 2017), 95–192; Amanda Poole, 'Ransoms, Remittances, and Refugees: The Gatekeeper State in Eritrea', in *Postliberation Eritrea* (Indiana University, 2018), https://iu .pressbooks.pub/postliberationeritrea/chapter/ransoms-remittances -and-refugees-the-gatekeeper-state-in-eritrea/; Bryden, Roofthooft, Schbley and Taiwo, *Letter Dated 18 July 2011 from the Chairman of the Security Council Committee Pursuant to Resolutions 751*, 109–10.

9 Saba, 'Uncomfortable Aid: INGOs in Eritrea'.

10 DeLisi, 'Controlling the Market, Controlling the People'.

11 Ibid., 68–90.

12 Cf. Harun Maruf and Dan Joseph, *Inside Al-Shabaab. The Secret History of Al-Qaeda's Most Powerful Ally* (Bloomington, IN: Indiana University Press, 2018), 36–7.

13 Bryden, Roofthooft, Schbley and Taiwo, *Letter Dated 18 July 2011 from the Chairman of the Security Council Committee Pursuant to Resolutions 751*, 77.

14 Scott H. DeLisi, 'Remittances and Hard Currency: Eritrea's Lifeline', 16 February 2007, Wikileaks: 07ASMARA158_a.

15 As early as October 2001, the Financial Action Task Force on Money Laundering (FATF) recommended a number of measures to combat money laundering through 'alternative remittance services or underground (or parallel) banking systems'. The result is the 40 AML/ CFT recommendations, cf. *The FATF Recommendations, International Standards on Combating Money Laudering and the Financing of Terrorism & Proliferation*, updated in October 2020: www.fatf-gafi .org/recommendations; Financial Action Task Force (FATF)/OECD, *The Role of Hawala and Other Similar Service Providers in Money Laundering and Terrorist Financing* (Paris, October 2013)https://www .fatf-gafi.org/content/dam/fatf-gafi/reports/Role-of-hawala-and-similar -in-ml-tf.pdf.coredownload.pdf; UNODC, *'We Don't Ask Questions': Hawala Payment System Vulnerable to Use by Organized Crime Groups, Including Opiate Traffickers and Migrant Smugglers* , Vienne,

11 September 2023, https://www.unodc.org/unodc/en/frontpage
/2023/September/we-dont-ask-questions_-hawala-payment-system
-vulnerable-to-use-by-organized-crime-groups--including-opiate
-traffickers-and-migrant-smugglers.html.

16 'The Hawala Alternative Remittance System and its Role
in Money Laundering', *Rapport au Congrès conformément à la Section
356(c) du USA Patriot Act, Financial Crimes Enforcement Network
rédigé en collaboration avec INTERPOL/FOPAC,* 31 December 2002,
5–8.

17 Egmont Group Financial Intelligence Unit, World Customs
Organization, *FIU Cooperation Handbook,* 2020, 14–17, https://
egmontgroup.org/wp-content/uploads/2021/09/2020_CUSTOMS_-
_FIU_Cooperation_Handbook.pdf.

18 DSP-Groep Amsterdam, Tilburg School of Humanities, Department of
Culture Studies, *The 2% Tax for Eritreans in the Diaspora. Facts, Figures
and Experiences in Seven European Countries*, June 2017,
https://www.tweedekamer.nl/kamerstukken/detail?id=2017D25761
&did=2017D25761.

19 DeLisi, 'Remittances and Hard Currency'.

20 Bryden, Roofthooft, Schbley and Taiwo, *Letter Dated 18 July 2011 from
the Chairman of the Security Council Committee Pursuant to Resolutions
751,* 110.

21 See this video soberly entitled 'No More' by Awel Said published on 13
August 2022, on Hidmona's YouTube channel, https://www.youtube
.com/watch?v=MoNwPZyUgzc.

22 Alex de Waal, *The Real Politics of the Horn of Africa,* 154.

23 'There is no government budget or public budgeting process in Eritrea,
and all public or private finances are collected and handled by PFDJ
individuals through private accounts,' cf. van Reisen, Saba and Smits,
'Sons of Isaias', 129.

24 Alex de Waal, *The Real Politics of the Horn of Africa,* 144.

25 Petros Tesfagorgis, Habte Hagos, Abraham Zere and Daniel Mekonnen,
'Mining and Repression in Eritrea: Corporate Complicity in Human
Rights Abuses', *Eritrea Focus* (June 2018), 28, https://eritrea-focus.org

/wp-content/uploads/2018/06/Mining-Repression-Eritrea-V1.pdf; DSP-Groep Amsterdam, Tilburg School of Humanities, Department of Culture Studies, *The 2% Tax for Eritreans in the diaspora.*

26 Tesfagorgis, Hagos, Zere and Mekonnen, 'Mining and Repression in Eritrea', 32.

27 Ronald K. McMullen, 'Eritrea – Major Australian Gold Strike', 7 May 2008, Wikileaks: 08ASMARA248_a; Ronald K. McMullen, 'Sanu Resources' Mining Prospects', 9 May 2008, Wikileaks: 08ASMARA252_a; Ronald K. McMullen, 'One Gold Mine Moving Forward', 10 November 2008, Wikileaks: 08ASMARA541_a; Ronald K. McMullen, 'Eritrea: German Banks Bailing on Bisha', 2 November 2009, Wikileaks:09ASMARA378_a.

28 'President of Eritrea is as Unique as His Country', *TesfaNews*, 13 May 2013, https://tesfanews.com/afwerqi-as-unique-as-his-country/.

29 Philmon Yohannes, 'Eritrea's Missing $1 Billion, *Martin Plaut*, 22 July 2013, https://martinplaut.com/2013/07/22/eritreas-missing-1-billion/.

30 UNHRC, *Report of the Detailed Findings of the Commission of Inquiry on Human Rights in Eritrea*, 5 June 2015, 58–9, https://www.refworld.org/docid/55758bab4.html.

31 Tesfagorgis, Hagos, Zere and Mekonnen, 'Mining and Repression in Eritrea', 32.

Chapter 3

1 Sun Peak Metals Corp., *2024 News Releases. Sun Peak Metals Provides Corporate Update – Exploration Work Expected to Resume on Shire Project*, 7 February 2014, https://sunpeakmetals.com/news/sun-peak-metals-provides-corporate-update-exploration-work-expected-to-resume-on-shire-project/?fbclid=IwAR1qBw7xydS0hnqPLNsnnBlomY9qg9_VZqLyGaYTG8D1I6Fwq2mUBaucWKs.

2 Ezana belongs to the EFFORT (Endowment Fund for the Rehabilitation of Tigray) consortium, whose operations are opaque and controversial, cf. Ashenafi Endale, 'Canadian Mining Co Prepares to Resume Tigray

Operations as Regional Officials Move to Revoke Concessions', *The Reporter*, 10 February 2024, https://www.thereporterethiopia.com /38647/.

3   Trish Saywell, 'Sun Peak Advances Shire Polymetallic Project in Ethiopia', *The Northern Miner*, 21 August 2020, https://northernminer .com/news/sun-peak-metals-advances-shire-project-in-ethiopia /1003821192/.

4   Daniel Tesfa, Mirjam van Reisen and Klara Smits, 'A Secret Deal to Conceal: The Eritrean Involvement in the Tigray War', in *Tigray. The Panarchy of War*, Book 1, ed. Mirjam van Reisen and Munyaradzi Mawere (Bamenda, Cameroon: Langaa Research & Publishing CIG, 2024), 53–100, https://www.researchgate.net/publication/385394550_A _Secret_Deal_to_Conceal_The_Eritrean_Involvement_in_the_Tigray _War.

5   His name also appears under the spelling 'Tomothy Butt', cf. United States Department of State, *U.S. Department of State Country Report on Human Rights Practices 2003 – Eritrea*, 25 February 2004, https://www .refworld.org/docid/403f57b010.html.

6   Melinda Tabler-Stone, 'The Mining Murder: An Insider Perspective', 14 October 2009, Wikileaks: 09ASMARA354_a.

7   Dan Connell, *Against All Odds – A Chronicle of the Eritrean Revolution with a New Update and Reappraisal* (Trenton, NJ: Red Sea Press, 1997, update 2021), 73–91.

8   Africa Mining Intelligence, 'Why Asmara Froze Mining Projects', *Africa Intelligence*, 15 September 2004; The Indian Ocean Newsletter, 'Eritrea Has Sights on Future Mining Profits', *Africa Intelligence*, 18 September 2004.

9   'The Eritrean National Mining Corporation Establishment Proclamation No 157/2006', *Gazette of Eritrean Laws Published by the Government of Eritrea*, Asmara, 18 December 2006.

10   'Mining in Eritrea', *Shaebia*, 10 mars 2006, https://web.archive.org/web /20060929110505/http://www.shaebia.org/artman/publish/article_4440 .html.

11 Melinda Tabler-Stone, 'Bisha Mining's Remaining Challenges', 7 October 2008, Wikileaks: 08ASMARA490_a.

12 Ronald K. McMullen, 'Chinese Move into Eritrea's Mining Sector', 6 August 2008, Wikileaks: 08ASMARA385_a; Ronald K. McMullen, 'Chinese Mining Woes in Eritrea', 25 June 2009, Wikileaks: 09ASMARA195_a.

13 Permanent Court of Arbitration, *Eritrea-Ethiopia Boundary Commission*, 30 November 2007, https://pca-cpa.org/en/cases/99/.

14 La Lettre de l'Océan Indien, 'Les prospecteurs de mines', *Africa Intelligence*, 3 November 1998.

15 McMullen, 'Chinese Move into Eritrea's Mining Sector'.

16 'Asmara Copper-Zinc-Gold-Silver Project', *Mining Technology*, 29 June 2015: https://www.mining-technology.com/projects/asmara -copper-zinc-gold-silver-project/; Africa Mining Intelligence, 'Eritrea ENAMCO Seeks a Repeat of Bisha Success Story', *Africa Intelligence*, 24 February 2015.

17 According to his LinkedIn page (consulted on 25 August 2024), David Daoud was senior exploration geologist at Nevsun from March 2003 to May 2005, a position he left to join Sunridge immediately.

18 Africa Mining Intelligence, 'A Key Year for Sunridge Gold', *Africa Intelligence*, 25 January 2012; Africa Mining Intelligence, 'Asmara's Gold: Sunridge Pulls Out All Stops', *Africa Intelligence*, 11 November 2013.

19 Senet, *Asmara Project Feasibility Study NI 43-101 Technical Report*, 16 May 2013, 27–8; 36, https://minedocs.com/12/Asmara_Feasibility _Sunridge_Corp.pdf.

20 Ronald K. McMullen, 'Sunridge Strikes Gold Near Asmara', 13 June 2008, Wikileaks: 08ASMARA317_a.

21 Sunridge Gold Corp, 'Sunridge Agrees to Sell Its 60% Interest in Asmara Mining Share Company', *Accesswire Company Update*, 6 November 2015, https://www.accesswire.com/433367/sunridge-agrees -to-sell-its-60-interest-in-asmara-mining-share-company; West Africa Newsletter, 'Qiu Xuejung Indulges in a Bit of Mining Diplomacy', *Africa Intelligence*, 5 May 2016.

22 'Eritrea Awards Three Mining Licences to Asmara Mining', *Mining Technology*, 19 October 2015, https://www.mining-technology.com/ marketdata/newseritrea-awards-three-mining-licences-asmara-mining -4697921/.

23 Africa Mining Intelligence, 'Former Sunridge Veterans Cross the Border to Strike Gold', *Africa Intelligence*, 16 April 2019.

24 Charles J. Greig and Jeffrey D. Rowe, *NI 43-101 Technical Report, A Geological Evaluation of the Meli Property, Tigray National Regional State, Northern Ethiopia*, 31 January 2020, 46, https://sunpeakmetals .com/site/assets/files/5593/2020-01-meli-tech-report.pdf.

25 Ibid., 46–51.

26 Saywell, 'Sun Peak Advances Shire Polymetallic Project in Ethiopia'.

27 An article in the meantime correlates with these statements, cf. Ashenafi Endale, 'Deadly Gold Rush: Military Commanders, Former Combatants, Foreign Players Scramble for Tigray's Bullion', *The Reporter*, 13 July 2024, https://www.thereporterethiopia.com/41076/.

28 Seamus Cornelius, 'Demystifying Eritrea Presentation', *Danakali Limited*, 8 mars 2018, https://danakali.com.au/wp-content/uploads /2021/09/Company-Presentation-Demystifying-Eritrea-Thursday-08 -March-2018.pdf.

29 François Christophe, 'Forget Objectivity: For the Atlantic Council, Eritrea's Prison State Isn't That Bad', *Medium*, December 2016, https:// frchristophe.medium.com/forget-objectivity-for-the-atlantic-council -eritreas-prison-state-isn-t-that-bad-be20f58ed315.

30 As an example, Human Rights Watch, *Hear No Evil, Forced Labor and Corporate Responsibility in Eritrea's Mining Sector*, 15 January 2013; P. Tesfagorgis, H. Hagos, A. Zere and D. Mekonnen, 'Mining and Repression in Eritrea: Corporate Complicity in Human Rights Abuses', *Eritrea Focus*, June 2018.

31 Cf. *infra* Chapter 5 'The first lobbying campaign to defend Nevsun and Isayas Afwerki'.

32 Georg Humbel, 'Sogar Gefolgsleute flüchten vor dem Regime: Der eritreische Botschafter hat in der Schweiz Asyl beantragt', *Neue Zürcher Zeitung*, 8 June 2024, https://www.nzz.ch/schweiz/sogar-gefolgsleute

-fluechten-vor-dem-regime-der-eritreische-botschafter-hat-in-der
-schweiz-asyl-beantragt-ld.1833594.

English translation also available: 'Even Supporters are Fleeing the Regime: The Eritrean Ambassador has Applied for Asylum in Switzerland', https://eritrea-focus.org/even-supporters-are-fleeing -the-regime-the-eritrean-ambassador-has-applied-for-asylum-in -switzerland/.

33 Cornelius, 'Demystifying Eritrea Presentation'.

34 Tesfa, van Reisen, and Smits, 'A Secret Deal to Conceal'.

35 Tom Gardner, *The Abiy Project. God, Power and War in the New Ethiopia* (London: C. Hurst & Co. Publishers Ltd., 2024), 9, 134.

36 'U.N. Chief Says Sanctions on Eritrea Likely to Become Obsolete', *Reuters*, 9 July 2018, https://www.reuters.com/article/world/u-n-chief-says -sanctions-on-eritrea-likely-to-become-obsolete-idUSKBN1JZ1UG/.

37 Nizar Manek, 'Eritrea Mulls Port as Ethiopia Rapprochement Spurs Investors', *Bloomberg*, 23 August 2018, https://www.bloomberg .com/news/articles/2018-08-23/eritrea-mulls-new-port-as-ethiopia -rapprochement-spurs-investors.

38 Seamus Cornelius, 'Proactive Investors One2One Investor Conference – London', Danakali Limited, 20 September 2018. The map is reproduced in 'Danakali's Potash Project Could be a Game Changer for Eritrea – UN', *Mining.com*, 30 January 2019, https://www.mining.com/ danakalis-potash-project-game-changer-eritrea-un/.

39 In the same document, Cornelius states: 'Danakali has a strong, effective working relationship with the Eritrean government'. The reasons for working with Colluli in Eritrea are then listed, including 'significant community support, safe and friendly [country], development focused, stable government, strong focus on health & education, no evidence of corruption', cf. Cornelius, 'Proactive Investors One2One Investor Conference – London', 27.

40 James Poole and Laura Millan, 'Nevsun Finds a White Knight in Zijin With $1.41 Billion Deal', *Bloomberg*, 5 September 2018, https://www .bloomberg.com/news/articles/2018-09-05/zijin-mining-to-buy-nevsun -resources-for-1-41-billion-in-cash.

41 *Joint Declaration on Comprehensive Cooperation Between Ethiopia, Somalia and Eritrea*, Asmara, 5 September 2018, https://www .peaceagreements.org/viewmasterdocument/2099.

42 Posted on 5 September 2018 Twitter (X) by Yemane G. Meskel, Eritrean Minister of Communication, with pictures, https://x.com/hawelti/ status/1037335660791820294.

43 Cristian Para and Prathivadi B. Anand, 'Analysis of the Potential Contributions of Colluli Potash Project to Sustainable Development Goals in Eritrea', *UNDP*, January 2019, https://www.undp.org/eritrea /publications/undp-eritrea-analysis-potential-contributions-colluli -potash-project-sustainable-development-goals-eritrea.

44 Cf. Alpha Exploration, *Kerkasha Exploration License – Eritrea*, https:// alpha-exploration.com/project/kerkasha-eritrea/.

45 West Africa Newsletter, 'Alasdair Smith Strikes for Gold Again', *Africa Intelligence*, 27 March 2018.

46 The Indian Ocean Newsletter, 'It's Open Season for Mining Permits', *Africa Intelligence*, 13 September 2008.

47 'Copper and Gold Finds Could End Up Breaking China's Monopoly', *Africa Intelligence*, 22 September 2020.

48 'Eritrean Mining Projects Return to Toronto Stock Exchange', *Africa Intelligence*, 5 October 2021.

49 'Alpha Exploration Explores "Last Frontier" in Eritrea', *Mining Journal*, 12 January 2022, 4, https://www.mining-journal.com/resourcestocks /resourcestocks/4072915/alpha-exploration-explores-last-frontier -eritrea.

50 Daniel Tesfa, Mirjam van Reisen and Klara Smits, 'A Secret Deal to Conceal: The Eritrean Involvement in the Tigray War', in *Tigray. The Panarchy of War*, Book 1, ed. Mirjam van Reisen and Munyaradzi Mawere (Bamenda, Cameroon: Langaa Research & Publishing CIG, 2024), 53–100 (64–7), https://www.researchgate.net/publication /385394550_A_Secret_Deal_to_Conceal_The_Eritrean_Involvement _in_the_Tigray_War.

51 Project presentation, https://cirdisumm.org/about-summ/.

52 'Addis Wants a Sector-by-Sector Approach to Minerals Management',
Africa Intelligence, 24 November 2020; Fitsum Areguy, 'Leaked Report
Accuses Canada of Covering for Mining Companies in War-Torn
Ethiopia', *The Breach*, 13 août 2021, https://breachmedia.ca/leaked
-report-accuses-canada-of-covering-for-mining-companies-in-war
-torn-ethiopia/.

Chapter 4

1 The NGO Business & Human Rights Resource Centre has set up a
timeline with resources relating to the Nevsun case, 'Nevsun Lawsuit
(re Bisha mine, Eritrea)', https://www.business-humanrights.org/en/
latest-news/nevsun-lawsuit-re-bisha-mine-eritrea/.

2 Mirjam van Reisen, Makeda Saba and Klara Smits, '"Sons of Isaias":
Slavery and Indefinite National Service in Eritrea', in *Mobile Africa:
Human Trafficking and the Digital Divide,* ed. Mirjam van Reisen,
Munyaradzi Mawere (Bamenda, Cameroon: Langaa Research &
Publishing CIG, 2019), 115–75 (127).

3 *Report of the Detailed Findings of the Commission of Inquiry on Human
Rights in Eritrea*, UNHRC, 5 June 2015, 413, https://www.refworld.org/
docid/55758bab4.html.

4 Human Rights Watch, *Hear No Evil, Forced Labor and Corporate
Responsibility in Eritrea's Mining Sector*, 15 January 2013, https://www
.hrw.org/report/2013/01/15/hear-no-evil/forced-labor-and-corporate
-responsibility-eritreas-mining-sector.

5 Ibid., 412–1.

6 Ibid., 306.

7 Ibid., 308; Van Reisen, Saba and Smits, 'Sons of Isaias', 139.

8 Business & Human Rights Resource Centre, 'Nevsun Lawsuit'.

9 Supreme Court of Canada, *Case in Brief: Nevsun Resources Ltd. v.
Araya*, 28 February 2020, https://decisions.scc-csc.ca/scc-csc/scc-csc/
en/item/18169/index.do; Beatrice A. Walton, 'Nevsun Resources Ltd.

v. Araya', *American Journal of International Law* 115/1 (2021): 107–14, https://doi.org/10.1017/ajil.2020.103.

10   Africa Mining Intelligence, 'All Complaints against Nevsun Lumped into the Same Case', *Africa Intelligence*, 24 March 2020.

11   Robert Wisner, 'Supreme Court of Canada Opens the Door to Novel International Human Rights Claims: The Uncertain Implications for Canadian Resource Companies', *McMillan Litigation Bulletin*, March 2020, https://mcmillan.ca/insights/supreme-court-of-canada-opens -the-door-to-novel-international-human-rights-claims-the-uncertain -implications-for-canadian-resource-companies/; Elisabeth Steyn, 'Slavery Charges against Canadian Mining Company Settled on the Sly', 26 October 2020, https://theconversation.com/slavery-charges-against -canadian-mining-company-settled-on-the-sly-148605.

12   Léonard Vincent, 'Canada: le procès d'une compagnie minière pour "esclavage" en Érythrée n'aura pas lieu', 13 October 2020, https://www .rfi.fr/fr/afrique/20201013-canada-le-proc%C3%A8s-d-une-compagnie -mini%C3%A8re-esclavage-en-%C3%A9rythr%C3%A9e-n-aura -pas-lieu?fbclid=IwAR2UMF3rY6MygiS6lkr6KQGscit2EbmrOLDB _5M7hMw5Gx7OYHscDr1_A6Q&ref=fb.

13   James Poole and Laura Millan, 'Nevsun Finds a White Knight in Zijin With $1.41 Billion Deal', *Bloomberg*, 5 September 2018, https://www .bloomberg.com/news/articles/2018-09-05/zijin-mining-to-buy-nevsun -resources-for-1-41-billion-in-cash.

14   https://www.rscollaboration.com/about-us.

15   To read an exemplary synthesis, just see the following article published on the PFDJ Youth website: Ruby Sandhu, 'Non-conformist Eritrea', *YoungPFDJ (YPFDJ)*, 18 April 2018, https://youngpfdj.wordpress.com /2018/04/13/non-conformist-eritrea/.

16   See *infra* chapiter 5, 'The first lobbying campaign to defend Nevsun and Isayas Afwerki'.

17   Supreme Court of Canada, *Bulletin of Proceedings*, 29 March 2018, 358–87, https://publications.gc.ca/collections/collection_2018/csc-scc/ JU8-1-2018-3-29.pdf.

18 West Africa Newsletter, 'Nevsun Escapes Asmara's Military Creditor', *Africa Intelligence*, 3 October 2017.

19 'Delizia Limited', *Cyprus Corporate Registry*, 22 February 2021, https:// cyprusregistry.com/companies/HE/101771.

20 US Department of Treasury, 'Russia-related Designations; Counter Narcotics Designation Update', 1 February 2023, https://ofac.treasury .gov/recent-actions/20230201; US Department of Treasury, 'Treasury Targets Global Sanctions Evasion Network Supporting Russia's Military-Industrial Complex', 1 February 2023, https://home.treasury .gov/news/press-releases/jy1241.

21 Graham Stack, 'Five Cyprus Golden Passport Holders Sanctioned for Russian Arms Trading', *Organized Crime and Corruption Reporting Project*, 7 February 2023, https://www.occrp.org/en/daily/17298-five -cyprus-golden-passports-holders-sanctioned-for-russian-arms-trading.

Chapter 5

1 For example, publications by Ann Garrison and Thomas C. Mountain on the *Black Agenda Report* website. Historically, the EPLF has long been popular with the revolutionary left, cf. Dan Connell, *Against All Odds – A Chronicle of the Eritrean Revolution with a New Update and Reappraisal* (Trenton, NJ: Red Sea Press, 1993, update 2021), 78.

2 Overseas Development Institute, *UK Approach to Eritrean Refugees: What is the Reality on the Ground?*, 2 November 2016, https://odi.org/en/events /uk-approach-to-eritrean-refugees-what-is-the-reality-on-the-ground/.

3 Ruby Sandhu, 'The Distorted Narrative, Media War and Eritrea's Culture of Silence', *Tesfanews*, 29 April 2016, https://tesfanews.com/ distorted-narrative-media-war-eritreas-silence-culture-i/.

4 *Detailed Findings of the Commission of Inquiry on Human Rights in Eritrea*, UNHRC, 8 June 2016, 50–8 (56–7): https://www.ohchr.org/sites /default/files/Documents/HRBodies/HRCouncil/CoIEritrea/A_HRC _32_CRP.1_read-only.pdf.

5   For the picture, see Léonard Vincent and Martin Plaut, 'Who are Eritrea's Foreign Friends?', *Martin Plaut*, 26 June 2017, https:// martinplaut.com/2017/06/26/who-are-eritreas-foreign-friends/.

6   Ministry of Information of Eritrea, 'Q&A with Mr. Todd Romaine, Vice President Corporate Social Responsibility, Nevsun Resources', *Shabait*, 21 September 2015, https://shabait.com/2015/09/21/qaa-with-mr -todd-romaine-vice-president-corporate-social-responsibility-nevsun -resources/.

7   François Christophe, 'Forget Objectivity: For The Atlantic Council, Eritrea's Prison State Isn't That Bad', *Medium*, December 2016, https:// frchristophe.medium.com/forget-objectivity-for-the-atlantic-council -eritreas-prison-state-isn-t-that-bad-be20f58ed315; François Christophe, 'Atlantic Council: The Eritrean Regime's US Spin Doctors?', in *Human Trafficking and Trauma in the Digital Era: The Ongoing Tragedy of the Trade in Refugees from Eritrea*, ed. Mirjam van Reisen and Munyaradzi Mawere (Bamenda, Cameroon: Langaa Research & Publishing CIG, 2017), 405–28, https://www.researchgate.net/publication/316989834 _Human_Trafficking_and_Trauma_in_the_Digital_Era_The_Ongoing _Tragedy_of_the_Trade_in_Refugees_from_Eritrea.

8   House of Commons Canada, *Subcommittee on International Human Rights of the Standing Committee on Foreign Affairs and International Development*, 5 June 2014, https://www.ourcommons.ca/ DocumentViewer/en/41-2/SDIR/meeting-32/evidence.

9   Sandhu, 'The Distorted Narrative, Media War and Eritrea's Culture of Silence'.

10   Bronwyn Bruton, 'Eritrea: A Neglected Regional Threat', Hearing Before the House Committee on Foreign Affairs, Subcommittee on Africa, Global Health, Global Human Rights, and International Organizations, Washington, DC, 14 September 2016, https://docs.house .gov/meetings/FA/FA16/20160914/105311/HHRG-114-FA16-Wstate -BrutonB-20160914.pdf; conclusions repeated in Bronwyn Bruton, 'Eritrea: Coming in from the Cold', *Atlantic Council*, 7 December 2016, https://www.atlanticcouncil.org/in-depth-research-reports/issue-brief/ eritrea-coming-in-from-the-cold/.

11   Bronwyn Bruton, 'It's Bad in Eritrea, But Not that Bad', *The New York Times*, 23 June 2016, https://www.nytimes.com/2016/06/24/opinion/its-bad-in-eritrea-but-not-that-bad.html.

12   Bruton, 'It's Bad in Eritrea, But Not that Bad'.

13   Hank Cohen, 'Time to Bring Eritrea in from the Cold', *African Arguments*, 16 December 2013, https://africanarguments.org/2013/12/time-to-bring-eritrea-in-from-the-cold-by-hank-cohen/.

14   'Eritrea: ጉዳይ ርክብ ምስ ሄርሞን ኮህን', *Asmarino Independant Media*, 4 July 2015, https://asmarino.com/news/4405-2015-07-04-02-39-34; for the English translation of the letter see 'Former Secretary of State for Africa Herman Cohen Paid to Lobby on Behalf of Eritrean President Isayas Afwerki', *Ethiopanorama*, 5 July 2015, https://ethiopanorama.com/?p=8370.

15   Michael Woldemariam, 'The Making of an African "Pariah": Eritrea in the International System', *Postliberation Eritrea*, Indiana University, 2018, https://iu.pressbooks.pub/postliberationeritrea/chapter/the-making-of-an-african-pariah-eritrea-in-the-international-system/.

16   'Update on the Eritrean Migration Situation with Felix Horne', *Event Recap*, Atlantic Council, 10 December 2015, https://www.atlanticcouncil.org/commentary/event-recap/update-on-the-eritrean-migration-situation-with-felix-horne/.

17   Tweet from 28 July 2016, https://twitter.com/pierremonegier/status/747773227359965184.

18   Since 1270, with the exception of Yohannes IV (1872–89).

19   Human Rights Watch, '"One Hundred Ways of Putting Pressure". Violations of Freedom of Expression and Association in Ethiopia', 24 March 2010, https://www.hrw.org/report/2010/03/24/one-hundred-ways-putting-pressure/violations-freedom-expression-and-association.

20   Daniel Tesfa and Mirjam van Reisen, 'Negative Stereotyping, Creation of a Threat, and Incitement to Genocide: Discourse Analysis of Hatespeech Disseminated in the Tigray War', in *Tigray. The Panarchy of War*, Book 1, ed. Mirjam van Reisen and Munyaradzi Mawere (Bamenda, Cameroon: Langaa Research & Publishing CIG, 2024), 145–85, https://www.researchgate.net/publication/385451336_Negative_Stereotyping

_Creation_of_a_Threat_and_Incitement_to_Genocide_Discourse
_Analysis_of_Hate-speech_Disseminated_in_the_Tigray_War.

Chapter 6

1 Daniel Berhane, 'Leaked Audio. Eritrea Funds ESAT and Ginbot 7', *The Horn Affairs*, 20 June 2013, https://hornaffairs.com/2013/06/20/leaked -audio-eritrea-funds-esat-berhanu-nega/.

2 Tom Gardner, *The Abiy Project. God, Power and War in the New Ethiopia* (London: C. Hurst and Company, 2024), 365, note 36.

3 Gardner, *The Abiy Project*, 133.

4 'Neamin Zeleke Tells ESAT "The Struggle for Freedom & Democracy Reached a Critical Stage"', *ESAT News*, 21 September 2015; The Indian Ocean Newsletter, 'Berhanu Nega Travels Secretly to the West', *Africa Intelligence*, 20 May 2016; The Indian Ocean Newsletter, 'Three Members of the Diaspora Killed in Asmara', *Africa Intelligence*, 20 October 2017; Martin Plaut and Sarah Vaughan, *Understanding Ethiopia's Tigray War* (London: C. Hurst and Company, 2023), 110.

5 Plaut and Vaughan, *Understanding Ethiopia's Tigray War*, 165. The relevant extract, a statement by Sisay Agena on July 1, 2020, is translated further on page 176.

6 Translation in Will Brown, 'Briton Released from Death Row Accused of Inciting Genocide in Ethiopia', *The Telegraph*, 28 November 2021, https://www.telegraph.co.uk/global-health/terror-and-security/briton -released-death-row-accused-inciting-genocide-ethiopia/.

7 Abiy Ahmed is a Pentecostal, a faith passed on by his mother, who brought him up to believe that he was God's chosen one and would become king. Cf. Gardner, 'Kingdom of God. Ethiopia's Pentecostal Turn', *The Abiy Project*, 41–9; Eliza Mackintosh, 'From Nobel Laureate to Global Pariah: How the World Got Abiy Ahmed and Ethiopia So Wrong', *CNN*, 5 November 2021, https://edition.cnn.com/2021/09/07/ africa/abiy-ahmed-ethiopia-tigray-conflict-cmd-intl/index.html.

8 For a study of the term's semantic shift, based on the graphitis left by invading troops inside the Martyrs' Commemoration Museum in Mekele, see: Daniel Tesfa and Mirjam van Reisen, '"Cannibals", "Daytime Hyenas", and "Not a Human Race" – "Woyane": The Semiotic Landscape of the Martyrs' Commemoration Museum', in *Tigray. The Panarchy of War*, Book 1, ed. Mirjam van Reisen and Munyaradzi Mawere (Bamenda, Cameroon: Langaa Research & Publishing CIG, 2024), 101–44, https://www.researchgate.net/publication/385406954_'Cannibals'_'Daytime_Hyenas'_and_'Not_a_Human_Race'_-_'Woyane'_The_Semiotic_Landscape_of_the_Martyrs'_Commemoration_Museum.

9 'Gov't Warns to Take Measures for Unconstitutional Power Grab', *Ethiopian News Agency*, 7 May 2020, https://www.ena.et/web/eng/w/en_14268; Simon Marks, 'Ethiopian Opposition, Prime Minister Accuse Each Other of Power Grab', *Voice of America*, 8 May 2020, https://www.voanews.com/a/africa_ethiopian-opposition-prime-minister-accuse-each-other-power-grab/6188969.html.

10 Interview on 9 February 2024.

11 Fugitive pilot interview on 30 October 2021.

12 Interview on 14 December 2021.

13 Interview on 25 September 2021.

14 Daniel Tesfa, Mirjam van Reisen and Klara Smits, 'A Secret Deal to Conceal: The Eritrean Involvement in the Tigray War', in *Tigray. The Panarchy of War*, Book 1, ed. Mirjam van Reisen and Munyaradzi Mawere (Bamenda, Cameroon: Langaa Research & Publishing CIG, 2024), 53–100 (64–7), https://www.researchgate.net/publication/385394550_A_Secret_Deal_to_Conceal_The_Eritrean_Involvement_in_the_Tigray_War.

Kristina Melicherová, Mirjam van Reisen, and Daniel Tesfa, '"Game Over": Key Markers of the Tigray War in Redefining the Region', in *Tigray. The Hysteresis of War*, Book 1, ed. Mirjam van Reisen and Munyaradzi Mawere (Bamenda, Cameroon: Langaa Research & Publishing CIG, 2024), 41–95, https://www.researchgate.net/publication/385300576_Game_Over_Key_Markers_of_the_Tigray_War_in_Redefining_the_Region.

15 Ministry of Information of Eritrea, 'President Isaias' Speech on Martyrs Day', *Shabait*, 20 June 2018, https://shabait.com/2018/06/20/president -isaias-speech-on-martyrs-day/.

16 Access to the Red Sea and Eritrean ports was the subject of verbal jousting between Abiy Ahmed and Isayas Afwerki in the autumn of 2023. The honeymoon between the two heads of state is now history. Ethiopia has finally signed a *Memorandum of Understanding* with Somaliland for access to the Red Sea, which has had the effect of shifting the debate to the question of the territorial sovereignty of Somalia, which does not recognize Somaliland's independence.

17 Cf. https://www.facebook.com/share/p/dVJkPPy1cNecHpDV/.

18 Gardner, *The Abiy Project*, 241–61; Plaut, Vaughan *Understanding Ethiopia's Tigray War*, 147–214.

19 Eliza Mackintosh, 'An Ethiopian Professor was Murdered by a Mob. A Lawsuit Alleges Facebook Fueled the Violence', *CNN*, 14 December 2022, https://edition.cnn.com/2022/12/14/tech/ethiopia-murdered -professor-lawsuit-meta-kenya-intl/index.html.

20 Jan Nyssen, Tesfaalem Ghebreyohannes, Emnet Negash, Hailemariam Meaza, Zbelo Tesfamariam, Amaury Frankl, Kiara Haegeman, Bert Van Schaeybroeck, Alem Redda, Fetien Abay, Sofie Annys and Biadgilgn Demissie, 'Impact of the Tigray War on Farming: Plight and Resilience', in Tigray. War in a Digital Black Hole, Book 1, ed. Mirjam van Reisen and Munyaradzi Mawere (Bamenda, Cameroon: Langaa Research & Publishing CIG, 2024), 145–72, https://www.researchgate .net/publication/385417372_Impact_of_the_Tigray_War_on_Farming _Plight_and_Resilience.

21 Alex de Waal, 'Steal, Burn, Rape, Kill', *London Review of Book* 43/12 (17 June 2021), https://www.lrb.co.uk/the-paper/v43/n12/alex-de-waal /steal-burn-rape-kill?fbclid=IwZXh0bgNhZW0CMTAAAR18nz6ai K3HK2HiNO2cHzEixxt4EQIPA9ZCCYuyMdJG4Rdgo0BvwRwb_4 _aem_wp6vm5s7CgOqQEGz04v2UQ.

22 Kristina Hook, Azeem Ibrahim OBE, Helena Kennedy KC, Nick Leddy, Melanie O'Brien and Ewelina U. Ochab, 'Genocide in Tigray: Serious Breaches of International Law in the Tigray Conflict, Ethiopia, and

Paths to Accountability', *New Lines Institute*, 3 June 2024, 65–71.105–6, https://newlinesinstitute.org/rules-based-international-order/genocide -in-tigray-serious-breaches-of-international-law-in-the-tigray-conflict -ethiopia-and-paths-to-accountability-2/.

23 https://eriyiakl.com/

24 Claire Wilmot, Ellen Tveteraas and Alexi Drew, 'Duelling Information Campaigns: The War over the Narrative on Tigray', *The Media Manipulation Casebook*, 20 août 2021, https://mediamanipulation.org/ case-studies/dueling-information-campaigns-war-over-narrative-tigray #footnote2_q179gxh.

25 Interviews and messages August 2023.

26 https://x.com/mission_russian/status/1471932037804212226?s=49&t= WcRdL1xBLluJI-WgN47ypg.

27 For a typical propaganda page, read: New Africa Institute, *Disinformation in Tigray: Manufacturing Consent for a Secessionist War*, 9 May 2021. Debunking of this report in: DFRLab, 'Eritrean Report Uses Fact-Checking Tropes to Dismiss Evidence as "Disinformation"', 23 juin 2021, https://medium.com/dfrlab/eritrean-report-uses -fact-checking-tropes-to-dismiss-evidence-as-disinformation -385718327481.

28 '"#No More" Campaign Should be Amplified: African Dev't Group President & CEO', *Ethiopian News Agency*, 27 November 2021, https://www.ena.et/web/eng/w/en_30941.

29 'Ethiopian, Russian News Agencies Sign Memorandum of Understanding', *Ethiopian News Agency*, 6 October 2022, https://www .ena.et/web/eng/w/en_38875.

30 Olivier Monnier, 'Or : les compagnies minières canadiennes à l'assaut de l'Afrique de l'Ouest', *Jeune Afrique*, 7 January 2019, https:// www.jeuneafrique.com/mag/692474/economie-entreprises/or-les -compagnies-minieres-a-lassaut-de-lafrique-de-louest/#:~:text=Young., -Nous%20nous%20attendons&text=TGC%20vise%20cette%20ann%C3 %A9e%20une,soci%C3%A9t%C3%A9%20atteindrait%20350%20000 %20onces.

31 'Jeff Pearce, Prof. Ann Fitzgerald Awarded for Defending Ethiopian Version of Truth Abroad', *Ethiopian News Agency*, 6 December 2021, https://www.ena.et/web/eng/w/en_31262.

32 This article is published one week after the #NoMore article and the interview with Kassoum Coulibali.

33 Bronwyn Bruton, 'To End Ethiopia's War, Biden Needs to Correct Course', *Foreign Policy*, 28 December, 2021, https://foreignpolicy.com /2021/12/28/ethiopia-tigray-abiy-tplf-war-biden-needs-to-correct -course/.

34 https://www.youtube.com/watch?v=rCoiSsR1qQE. And the same old line: "How can the US government engage "constructively"? 'Constructive' being a rhetorical element borrow to the Atlantic Council.

35 Tom Gardner, 'I was a War Reporter in Ethiopia. Then I Became the Enemy', *The Economist*, 24 June 2022, https://www.economist.com /1843/2022/06/24/i-was-a-war-reporter-in-ethiopia-then-i-became-the -enemy.

36 The MLI has stopped publishing its list of donors precisely in 2021. DeSmog's Climate Disinformation Database, precisely on the links between the MLI and the Canadian mining companies, https://www .desmog.com/macdonald-laurier-institute/.

37 Today's *Ethiopian Cable.*

38 'Mining: A Good Vein for Lobbyists?', *The Ethiopia Cable* 77 (28 April–4 May 2022), 1.

39 '"They Have Destroyed Tigray, Literally": Mulugeta Gebrehiwot Speaks from the Mountains of Tigray', *World Peace Foundation*, 29 janvier 2021, https://worldpeacefoundation.org/blog/they-have-destroyed -tigray-literally-mulugeta-gebrehiwot-speaks-from-the-mountains-of -tigray/.

40 This expression was even used in the international press. While the English-language press used the term 'Tigray rebels', the major French-language newspapers (Le Monde, RFI, Le Temps, TV5 Monde, etc.) made extensive use of 'TPLF rebels'.

41 Cf. Awet Tewelde Weldemichael, *Third World Colonialism and Strategies of Liberation. Eritrea and East Timor Compared* (Cambridge:

Cambridge University Press, 2012), 183–217; Dan Connell, *Against All Odds – A Chronicle of the Eritrean Revolution with a new Update and Reappraisal* (Trenton, NJ: Red Sea Press, 1997, update 2021), 78.

42 A request she repeated three weeks later to Philip Hammond, Willam Hague's successor, https://www.anagomes.eu/PublicDocs/13855c5d -81ea-44bc-94e2-9022654207b9.pdf.

43 https://www.europarl.europa.eu/doceo/document/E-7-2012-006967 _EN.html.

44 The Bisha mine should have earned the Eritrean government some $365 million in 2011.

45 Gardner, *The Abiy Project*, 134.

46 Fasil Yenealem, 'ዛሬ ሚስጢር ቢወጣ ችግር የለም', *Cherbole*, 9 July 2018, https://cherbole.wordpress.com/2018/07/09/%e1%8b%9b%e1%88%ac-%e1%88%9a%e1%88%b5%e1%8c%a2%e1%88%ad-%e1%89%a2%e1%8b%88%e1%8c%a3-%e1%89%bd%e1%8c%8d%e1%88%ad-%e1%8b%a8%e1%88%88%e1%88%9d-fasil-yenealem/.

47 'UN Secretary-General Antonio Guterres: Himself Part of the Problem?', *Globe News Net*, 29 October 2021, https://axumawian.com/ archives/12738.

48 Wilmot, Tveteraas, Drew, 'Duelling Information Campaigns'; S. E. Geb and Daniel Tesfa, 'Weaponising the Media: Exploring the Role of Ethiopian National Media in the Tigray War', in *Tigray. The Hysteresis of War*, Book 1, ed. Mirjam van Reisen and Munyaradzi Mawere (Bamenda, Cameroon: Langaa Research & Publishing CIG, 2024), 191–254, https://www.researchgate.net/publication/385202452_Tigray _The_Hysteresis_of_War_Book_1#pfb0.

Chapter 7

1 Kai Zhao, Huazhou Yao, Jiangxion Wang, Gebsha Fitwi Ghebretnsae and Wenshuai Xian, 'Genesis of the Koka Gold Deposit in Northwest Eritrea, NE Africa: Constraints from Fluid Inclusions and C–H–O–S

Isotopes', *Minerals* 9/201 (2019), https://www.mdpi.com/2075-163X/9/4/201.

2 Africa Energy Intelligence, 'Un permis dans l'Extrême-Nord', *Africa Intelligence*, 23 September 1998.

3 La Lettre de l'Océan Indien, 'Un consortium australien dans les mines', *Africa Intelligence*, 26 September 1998.

4 Africa Energy Intelligence, 'Un peu d'activité malgré la guerre', *Africa Intelligence*, 18 May 1999.

5 Africa Energy Intelligence, 'Genesis cède ses intérêts et Rift Resources fore', *Africa Intelligence*, 29 September 1999.

6 The Indian Ocean Newsletter, 'Mining Discoveries in Eritrea', *Africa Intelligence*, 15 March 2003.

7 'Koka, Zara. Eritrea, Main commodities: Au', *PorterGeo*, 2019, https://portergeo.com.au/database/mineinfo.asp?mineid=mn1648.

8 Africa Mining Intelligence, 'Why Asmara Froze Mining Projects', *Africa Intelligence*, 15 September 2004; The Indian Ocean Newsletter, 'Eritrea Has Sights on Future Mining Profits', *Africa Intelligence*, 18 September 2004.

9 Senet, *Asmara Project Feasibility Study NI 43-101 Technical Report*, 16 May 2013, 27–8; 36, https://minedocs.com/12/Asmara_Feasibility _Sunridge_Corp.pdf.

10 Sub-Sahara Resources NL, 'Sub-Sahara Delivers 1.04 Million oz Gold at the Koka Deposit in Eritrea with Scope for Expansion', *ASX Announcement*, 25 February 2008; Ronald K. McMullen, 'Eritrea – Major Australian Gold Strike', 7 May 2008, Wikileaks: 08ASMARA248_a.

11 McMullen, 'Eritrea – Major Australian Gold Strike'.

12 Ronald K. McMullen, 'One Gold Mine Moving Forward', 10 November 2008, Wikileaks: 08ASMARA541_a.

13 *Chalice Gold Annual Report*, 2009, 4, https://www.annualreports.com/HostedData/AnnualReportArchive/c/chalice-mining-limited_2009.pdf.

14 Cf. Jeremy Clarke, 'Three Mine Workers Shot Dead in Eritrea', *Reuters*, 7 October 2009, https://www.reuters.com/article/world/three-mine-workers-shot-dead-in-eritrea-idUSJOE5960GH/.

15 Melinda Tabler-Stone, 'Mine Workers Killed in Attack in Eritrea', 8 October 2009, Wikileaks: 09ASMARA350_a.

16 Melinda Tabler-Stone, 'The Mining Murder: An Insider Perspective', 14 October 2009, Wikileaks: 09ASMARA354_a.

17 Ronald K. McMullen, 'Sanu Resources' Mining Prospects', 9 May 2008, Wikileaks: 08ASMARA252_a.

18 Africa Mining Intelligence, 'ENAMCO Joins Chalice in Developing Koka', *Africa Intelligence*, 28 September 2011.

19 Chalice Gold Mines, *ASX Announcement*, https://announcements.asx .com.au/asxpdf/20120521/pdf/426cvk3pph36kn.pdf.

20 Africa Mining Intelligence, 'How ENAMCO Plans to Pay Chalice', *Africa Intelligence*, 11 January 2012.

21 South Boulder Mines LTD, *Potash for Produce*, November 2014, https:// www.bus-ex.com/article/south-boulder-mines.

22 The Indian Ocean Newsletter, 'It's Open Season for Mining Permits', *Africa Intelligence*, 13 September 2008; McMullen, 'One Gold Mine Moving Forward'.

23 West Africa Newsletter, 'South Boulder under Pressure in Eritrea', *Africa Intelligence*, 29 July 2014.

24 Africa Mining Intelligence, 'The Race to be First to Mine Danakil's Potash?', *Africa Intelligence*, 6 October 2015; 'Danakali Cuts Back on Costs to Launch Sulphate of Potash Project', *Africa Intelligence*, 15 December 2015.

25 Cristian Para and Prathivadi B. Anand, *Analysis of the Potential Contributions of Colluli Potash Project to Sustainable Development Goals in Eritrea*, UNDP, January 2019.

26 See above 'Summer 2018, Peace, Sun and Gold!'.

27 Back in 2013, when the company was still called South Boulder and managed by Liam Cornelius, Human Rights Watch questioned them about human rights violations in the mining sector in connection with the Nevsun affair: 'In a meeting with Human Rights Watch the head of South Boulder expressed no awareness of the human rights risks involved in his company's Eritrea operations and indicated that the company had not yet taken any measures to avoid the risks described

in this report. Human Rights Watch, *Hear No Evil, Forced Labor and Corporate Responsibility in Eritrea's Mining Sector*, 15 January 2013, https://www.hrw.org/report/2013/01/15/hear-no-evil/forced-labor-and -corporate-responsibility-eritreas-mining-sector.

28 Mirjam Van Reisen, Makeda Saba and Klara Smits, "'Sons of Isaias": Slavery and Indefinite National Service in Eritrea", in *Mobile Africa: Human Trafficking and the Digital Divide*, ed. Mirjam van Reisen and Munyaradzi Mawere (Bamenda, Cameroon: Langaa Research & Publishing CIG, 2019), 115–75 (128).

29 Ibid., 129.

30 '110 российских миллиардеров. Рейтинг', *Forbes*, 2023, https://www .forbes.ru/milliardery/487934-110-rossijskih-milliarderov-rejting -forbes-2023.

31 'Profile. Andrey Melnichenko & Family', *Forbes*, https://www.forbes .com/profile/andrey-melnichenko/.

32 Danakali, 'Rock Salt Production & New Generation Sodium Ion Batteries Opportunities', *ASX Release*, 20 December 2021, https:// danakali.com.au/wp-content/uploads/2021/12/02468821.pdf.

33 Li Yan, 'China's First High-capacity Sodium-ion Battery Storage Station is Launched', *China News Service*, 13 May 2024, https://www.ecns.cn/ business/2024-05-13/detail-iheamvqc7118696.shtml.

Chapter 8

1 'Rape Culture in Tigray Region of Ethiopia', *Radio Révolution Panafricaine*, 17 April 2021, https://www.radiorevolutionpanafricaine .com/single-post/rape-culture-in-tigray-region-of-ethiopia?fbclid=IwA R2G8XqJ4NHa89EOdo7nZYwKaDN3GSbFgsD92Nn3V10CdrjI8SO _9k1xGz4.

2 Depending on the source, 2RP's head office is advertised as being in Bamako (Mali), Douala (Cameroon), Malabo (Equatorial Guinea), and the telephone number advertised on the website features the country code for Mauritania.

3   Lucy Kassa, 'A Rape Survivor's Story Emerges from a Remote African War', *Los Angeles Times*, 11 February 2021, https://www.latimes.com /world-nation/story/2021-02-11/troops-accused-of-mass-rape-in -ethiopias-tigray-conflict.

4   Lucy Kassa, '"A Tigrayan Womb Should Never Give Birth": Rape in Tigray', *Al Jazeera*, 21 April 2021, https://aje.io/wl8t7.

5   This notion is typical of incitement to genocide and was theorized in particular after the Tutsi genocide in Rwanda, cf. Kenneth L. Marcus, 'Accusation in a Mirror', *Loyola University Chicago Law Journal* 43/2 (2012): 357–93.

6   Tessa Knight, 'Eritrean Report Uses Fact-Checking Tropes to Dismiss Evidence as "Disinformation"', *Digital Forensic Research Lab (DFRLab)*, 23 June 2021, https://medium.com/dfrlab/eritrean-report -uses-fact-checking-tropes-to-dismiss-evidence-as-disinformation -385718327481.

7   New Africa Institute, *Disinformation in Tigray: Manufacturing Consent for a Secessionist War* 19 May 2021, 18, https://newafricainstitute .medium.com/disinformation-in-tigray-manufacturing-consent-for-a -secessionist-war-summarized-report-cf4ea51c9910.

8   https://x.com/hawelti/status/1395356474465980416.

9   New Africa Institute, *Disinformation in Tigray*, 19.

10 Cf. https://x.com/HermelaTV/status/1457782940344094720.

11 Maxime Audinet, *Le lion, l'ours et les hyènes. Acteurs, pratiques et récits de l'influence informationnelle russe en Afrique subsaharienne francophone*, Institut de Recherche Stratégique de l'Ecole Militaire, Étude n°83 (2021), 49, https://www.irsem.fr/media/5-publications/ etude-irsem-83-audinet-le-lion-ok.pdf.

12 Cf. US Department of the Treasury, 'Treasury Escalates Sanctions Against the Russian Government's Attempts to Influence U.S. Elections', *Press Release*, 15 April 2021, https://home.treasury.gov/news/press -releases/jy0126.

13 Cf. Michael Weiss and Pierre Vaux, 'Russia is Using Undercover Racists to Exploit Africa's Anti-racist Political Revolt', *Daily Beast*, 8 September

2020, https://www.thedailybeast.com/prigozhin-is-using-afric-to
-exploit-africas-anti-colonial-political-revolt.

14 'Kémi Seba, condamné plusieurs fois pour incitation à la haine raciale,
déchu de la nationalité française', *Le Monde*, 9 July 2024, https://www
.lemonde.fr/societe/article/2024/07/09/le-militant-panafricaniste-kemi
-seba-dechu-de-la-nationalite-francaise_6248233_3224.html.

15 Benjamin Roger, '"Projet Kemi"' : quand Evgueni Prigojine finançait
Kemi Seba pour servir ses ambitions africaines', *Jeune Afrique*, 30
March 2023, https://www.jeuneafrique.com/1431514/politique/projet
-kemi-quand-evgueni-prigojine-financait-kemi-seba-pour-servir-ses
-ambitions-africaines/.

16 'Russie-Afrique: de Kemi Seba à Nathalie Yamb, les "influenceurs"
pro-Poutine du continent', *Jeune Afrique*, 31 March 2022, https://www
.jeuneafrique.com/1335015/politique/russie-afrique-de-kemi-seba-a
-nathalie-yamb-les-influenceurs-pro-poutine-du-continent/.

17 Kemi Seba is under investigation by the DGSI, the French domestic
intelligence service, and was taken into custody on 14 October 2024.
According to Le Monde, 'he was questioned as part of an investigation
opened for "intelligence with a foreign power [. . .] with a view to
stirring up hostilities or acts of aggression against France". Kemi Seba,
who was stripped of his French nationality in July, was also questioned
on suspicion of "intelligence with a foreign power [. . .] likely to harm
the fundamental interests of the nation"', 'Le «panafricaniste» Kemi
Seba soupçonné de liens avec le groupe paramilitaire russe Wagner', *Le
Monde*, 18 October 2024, https://www.lemonde.fr/afrique/article/2024
/10/18/le-panafricaniste-kemi-seba-soupconne-de-liens-avec-le-groupe
-paramilitaire-russe-wagner_6355265_3212.html.

18 US Department of State, 'Yevgeniy Prigozhin's Africa-Wide
Disinformation Campaign', 4 November 2022, https://www.state
.gov/disarming-disinformation/yevgeniy-prigozhins-africa-wide
-disinformation-campaign/.

19 Weiss and Vaux, 'Russia Is Using Undercover Racists', 24–30.

20 Nathalie Yamb, 'L'activiste qui se rêve comme le "cauchemar" de la
France', *TV5Monde*, 2 November 2022, https://information.tv5monde

.com/afrique/nathalie-yamb-lactiviste-qui-se-reve-comme-le
-cauchemar-de-la-france-1412317.

21 Radio Télévision Suisse, 'Nathalie Yamb, une Suissesse influenceuse de Poutine ?', *Temps Présent*, 23 March 2023, https://www.rts.ch/emissions /temps-present/2023/video/nathalie-yamb-une-suissesse-influenceuse -de-poutine-avion-contre-oiseau-attention-danger-26905125.html.

22 Nathalie Yamb, 'Sommet/Forum Russie-Afrique: le magistral discours de rupture de Nathalie Yamb (LIDER) à Sochi', *YouTube*, 26 October 2019, https://www.youtube.com/watch?v=4JO2uzrUec4.

23 It is interesting to place this program alongside the BRICS de-dollarization project.

24 Democracy 21, *How the Kremlin is Using Wagner to Launder Billions in African Gold*, The Blood Gold Report, December 2023, 10–2, https:// bloodgoldreport.com/wp-content/uploads/2023/12/The-Blood-Gold -Report-2023-December.pdf; Christophe Chatelot, 'Entre brutalité et prédation, comment Wagner pacifie la Centrafrique', *Le Monde*, 17 June 2024, https://www.lemonde.fr/afrique/article/2024/06/17/en -centrafrique-wagner-continue-de-prosperer_6240954_3212.html.

25 Kemi Seba officiel, 'Kemi Seba sur l'Ethiopie : genèse et perspective de la crise', *Afro Pertinent*, 7 August 2020, https://www.youtube.com/watch ?v=MEmv_yyHxK4.

26 '"#No More" Campaign Should be Amplified: African Dev't Group President & CEO', *Ethiopian News Agency*, 27 November 2021, https://www.ena.et/web/eng/w/en_30941.

27 Bartolomé Simon and Nicolas Quénel, 'Ce marchand d'influence russe qui formait de futurs journalistes français', *Le Point*, 22 February 2024, https://www.lepoint.fr/societe/ce-marchand-d-influence-russe-qui -formait-les-futurs-journalistes-francais-22-02-2024-2553171_23.php.

28 Mikhail Gamandiy-Egorov, 'Alliance des Etats du Sahel-Russie: la marche commune en avant', *Radio Révolution Panafricaine*, 7 June 2024, https://www.radiorevolutionpanafricaine.com/single-post/alliance-des -etats-du-sahel-russie-la-marche-commune-en-avant.

29 Translated from Russian 21 June 2014 by Robert Coalson, Central News, Radio Free Europe/Radio Liberty quoted in Valery Gerasimov,

'The Value of Science Is in the Foresight. New Challenges Demand Rethinking the Forms and Methods of Carrying out Combat Operations', *Military Review*, January-February 2016, https://www .armyupress.army.mil/portals/7/military-review/archives/english/ militaryreview_20160228_art008.pdf.

30 Mark Galeotti, 'The "Gerasimov Doctrine" and Russian Non-Linear War', *In Moscow's Shadow*, 6 July 2014, https://inmoscowsshadows .wordpress.com/2014/07/06/the-gerasimov-doctrine-and-russian-non -linear-war/

31 Mark Galeotti, 'The Mythical "Gerasimov Doctrine" and the Language of Threat', *Critical Studies on Security* 7/22 (2018): 157–61.

32 José Caballero, 'How Russia is Fighting for Allies among the Brics Countries Using "Memory Diplomacy"', *The Conversation*, 25 August 2023, https://theconversation.com/how-russia-is-fighting-for-allies -among-the-brics-countries-using-memory-diplomacy-212130?fbclid =IwZXh0bgNhZW0CMTAAAR0wELcvuqAtmjTpFVpjkIOkjTB_vXv dlG01yYESYtLNNCsS_5TAbpd6hJs_aem_pN69hcYme6u6SKvjgrzu0g.

Chapter 9

1 Democracy 21, *How the Kremlin is Using Wagner to Launder Billions in African Gold*, The Blood Gold Report, December 2023, 13–5, https:// bloodgoldreport.com/wp-content/uploads/2023/12/The-Blood-Gold -Report-2023-December.pdf.

2 Magdi El Gizouli interview with Radio Dabanga, 'Coup Critics Condemn Sudan Deputy's Visit to Russia', 1 March 2022, https://www .dabangasudan.org/en/all-news/article/coup-critics-condemn-sudan -deputy-s-visit-to-russia.

3 'Afwerki, Hemetti Discuss Eritrean Sudanese Relations', *Sudan Tribune*, 13 March 2023, https://sudantribune.com/article271830/. Abdelmonim Abu Idris, Chairman of the Sudan Journalists' Union, told Radio Dabanga at the time that this surprise visit served to seal a convergence of interests between the RSF, Eritrea and Russia, see 'Hemeti Visits

Eritrea to Discuss Bilateral Relations But Also to "Weave RSF Alliances"', *Radio Dabanga*, 14 March 2023, https://www.dabangasudan .org/en/all-news/article/hemeti-visits-eritrea-to-discuss-bilateral -relations-but-also-to-weave-rsf-alliances.

4 Matt Bryden, Jörg Roofthooft, Ghassan Schbley and Babatunde Taiwo, *Letter Dated 18 July 2011 from the Chairman of the Security Council Committee Pursuant to Resolutions 751 (1992) and 1907 (2009) Concerning Somalia and Eritrea Addressed to the President of the Security Council*, 18 July 2011, 109–10, https://digitallibrary.un.org/ record/708002?ln=es&v=pdf; Mirjam van Reisen and Meron Estefanos, 'The Exodus from Eritrea and Who is Benefiting', in *Human Trafficking and Trauma in the Digital Era. The Ongoing Tragedy of the Trade in Refugees from Eritrea*, ed. Mirjam van Reisen and Munyaradzi Mawere (Bamenda, Cameroon: Langaa RCPIG, 2017), 95–192, https://www .researchgate.net/publication/316989834_Human_Trafficking_and _Trauma_in_the_Digital_Era_The_Ongoing_Tragedy_of_the_Trade _in_Refugees_from_Eritrea.

5 Klara Smits, '"You are the Ball – They are the Players": The Human Traffickers of Eritreans in Libya', in *Enslaved, Trapped and Trafficked in Digital Black Holes: Human Trafficking Trajectories to Libya*, ed. Mirjam van Reisen, Munyaradzi Mawere, Klara Smits and Morgane Wirtz (Bamenda, Cameroon: Langaa RCPIG, 2023), 451–520 (503–5), https:// www.researchgate.net/publication/367254851_Enslaved_Trapped_and _Trafficked_in_Digital_Black_Holes_Human_Trafficking_Trajectories _to_Libya.

6 Salem Solomon, 'Observers See Several Motives for Eritrean Involvement in Yemen', *Voice of America*, 9 January 2016, https://www .voanews.com/a/observers-see-several-motives-eritrean-involvement -yemen/3138689.html; Richard Kent, Mohamed Aboelgheit and Nick Donovan, 'Exposing the RSF's Secret Financial Network', *Global Witness*, 9 December 2019, https://www.globalwitness.org/en/ campaigns/conflict-minerals/exposing-rsfs-secret-financial-network/; Richard Kent, Mohamed Aboelgheit and Nick Donovan, 'How the RSF Got their 4x4 Technicals: The Open Source Intelligence Techniques

Behind Our Sudan Exposé', *Global Witness*, 5 April 2020, https://www
.globalwitness.org/en/blog/how-the-rsf-got-their-4x4-technicals-the
-open-source-intelligence-techniques-behind-our-sudan-expos%C3
%A9/; 'Sudan Crisis: The Ruthless Mercenaries Who Run the Country
for Gold', *BBC News*, 20 July 2019, https://www.bbc.com/news/world
-africa-48987901.

7   Tom Gardner, *The Abiy Project. God, Power and War in the New
    Ethiopia* (London: C. Hurst and Company, 2024), 253.

8   *Joint Declaration on Comprehensive Cooperation Between Ethiopia,
    Somalia and Eritrea*, Asmara, 5 September 2018, https://www
    .peaceagreements.org/viewmasterdocument/2099.

9   https://www.facebook.com/share/p/dVJkPPy1cNecHpDV/.

10 Mehdi Labzaé, 'Wolqayt, la terre promise et ses limites. Mobilisations
    nationalistes amhara, foncier et bureaucratie dans la guerre civile
    éthiopienne (2016–2022)', *Critique Internationale* 99 (2023/2): 109–30
    (110).

11 Ahmed Soliman, 'Fighting Over "White Gold": Sesame in Ethiopia and
    Sudan', *Chatham House*, 4 April 2023, https://www.chathamhouse.org
    /2023/04/fighting-over-white-gold-sesame-ethiopia-and-sudan

12 Bryden, Roofthooft, Schbley and Taiwo, *Letter Dated 18 July 2011 from
    the Chairman of the Security Council Committee Pursuant to Resolutions
    751 (1992) and 1907 (2009) Concerning Somalia and Eritrea Addressed
    to the President of the Security Council*, 77 ; 'Neamin Zeleke Tells ESAT
    "The Struggle for Freedom & Democracy Reached a Critical Stage"',
    ESAT News, 21 September 2015.

13 When I was documenting cases of war rape among Tigrayan refugee
    women in Sudan, I collected several testimonies of this collaboration.
    Eritrean intelligence agents were visibly operating in Amhara units with
    Amhara uniforms. I then related this in the script for the virtual reality
    short film *Remember Tigray*.

14 Most recently, the assault by Amharas militiamen on SAF-held Al
    Fashaga just after the arrest of Ethiopian snipers embedded in the RSF
    demonstrates this alliance, cf. 'Ethiopian Militias Invade Sudanese
    Territory, Escalating Violence and Looting', *Sudan Tribune*, 24 June

2024, https://sudantribune.com/article287372/; Sudan Tribune, 'Sudanese Authorities Arrest Ethiopian Female Snipers', 20 June 2024, https://sudantribune.com/article287249/.

15 'The UAE Alchemist Who Turned Fields of Scrap into a Factory of Gold', *The National*, 7 April 2013, https://www.thenational.ae/business/the-uae-alchemist-who-turned-fields-of-scrap-into-a-factory-of-gold-1.305887.

16 https://cdn.occrp.org/projects/suisse-secrets-interactive/en/person/11/the-kaloti-family.

17 U.S. Department of the Treasury, 'Treasury Sanctions Military-Affiliated Companies Fueling Both Sides of the Conflict in Sudan', *Press Release*, 1 June 2023, https://home.treasury.gov/news/press-releases/jy1514.

18 Nima Elbagir, Barbara Arvanitidis, Tamara Qiblawi, Gianluca Mezzofiore, Mohammed Abo Al Gheit and Darya Tarasova, 'Russia is Plundering Gold in Sudan to Boost Putin's War Effort in Ukraine', *CNN*, 29 July 2022, https://edition.cnn.com/2022/07/29/africa/sudan-russia-gold-investigation-cmd-intl/index.html.

19 Kristina Enger, Floris J. A. de Klerk Wolters and Alex H. C. Wong, 'The Nuclei of the Global IFF Network: The Role of Global Commodity Trading Hubs in Defining the Global Patterns of Illicit Financial Flows', *Curbing Illicit Financial Flows from Resource-rich Developing Countries: Improving Natural Resource Governance to Finance the SDGs*, February 2020, 33, https://curbing-iffs.org/wp-content/uploads/2020/03/r4d-iff-wp03-2020.pdf.

20 Marc Ummel, 'Golden Detour. The Hidden Face of the Gold Trade between the United Arab Emirates and Switzerland', *Swissaid*, July 2020, https://swissaid.kinsta.cloud/wp-content/uploads/2020/07/SWISSAID-Goldstudie-EN_final-web.pdf; Marc Ummel, 'Beneath the Shine. A Tale of Two Gold Refiners', *Global Witness*, July 2020, https://www.globalwitness.org/en/campaigns/conflict-minerals/beneath-shine-tale-two-gold-refiners/.

21 Ronald K.McMullen, 'Eritrea: German Banks Bailing on Bisha', 2 November 2009, Wikileaks:09ASMARA378_a; Melinda Tabler-Stone,

‘Bisha Mining's Remaining Challenges’, 7 October 2008, Wikileaks: 08ASMARA490_a.

22　Schweizer Radio und Fernsehen, ‘Gold-Deal mit Eritrea’, *Rundschau*, 30 August 2017, https://www.srf.ch/play/tv/rundschau/video/gold-deal -mit-eritrea?urn=urn:srf:video:a7f475ef-f9e9-44ba-85ce-a4e330a5d0ac.

23　The US Departments of State, the Treasury, Labor, Commerce, and Homeland Security, the United States Agency for International Development, *Africa Gold Advisory*, 27 June 2023, https://ofac.treasury .gov/system/files/2023-06/africa_gold_advisory_06272023.pdf.

24　Mikhaïl Maglov, Timur Olevsky and Dmitry Treshchanin, ‘ЧАСТЬ 4. ТАЙНОЕ ЗАВОЕВАНИЕ АФРИКИ’, *Current Time TV*, 26 February 2019, https://www.currenttime.tv/a/yevgeny-prigozhin-investigation -chapter-4/29789953.html; Mohammed Amin, ‘Sudan's Darfur Draws Neighbours Back into a War that Never Ended’, *Middle East Eye*, 17 May 2023, https://www.middleeasteye.net/news/sudan-crisis -darfur-war-neighbours-never-ended; Samira Elsaidi, ‘Libya's Haftar “Rerouting” Supplies to Sudan's Rapid Support Forces’, *Middle East Eye*, 10 July 2023, https://www.middleeasteye.net/news/libya-sudan-haftar -rsf-supply-lines; ‘IntelBrief: Libyan Warlord Exploits Sudan Crisis’, *The Soufan Center*, 23 May 2023, https://thesoufancenter.org/intelbrief-2023 -may-23/; Democracy 21, *How the Kremlin is Using Wagner to Launder Billions in African Gold*, 15.

25　U.S. Department of the Treasury, ‘Treasury Targets Financier's Illicit Sanctions Evasion Activity’, *Press Release*, 15 July 2020, https://home .treasury.gov/news/press-releases/sm1058.

26　He is familiar with the ideologist Dugin, with whom he appears in photographs, and who is also close to Kemi Seba, cf. Fredrik Hellem, ‘How Russia Is Hijacking Pan-Africanism to Drive France out of Africa’, *Grea Dynamics*, 15 April 2021, https://greydynamics.com/how-russia -is-hijacking-pan-africanism-to-drive-france-out-of-africa/#h-russia -pan-africanism-and-kemi-seba; The Proekt Team, ‘Master and Chef. How Russia Interfered in Elections in Twenty Countries’, 11 April 2019, https://www.proekt.media/en/article-en/russia-african-elections/; Benjamin Roger, ‘“Projet Kemi”: quand Evgueni Prigojine finançait

Kemi Seba pour servir ses ambitions africaines', *Jeune Afrique*, 30 March 2023, https://www.jeuneafrique.com/1431514/politique/projet -kemi-quand-evgueni-prigojine-financait-kemi-seba-pour-servir-ses -ambitions-africaines/.

27 'Strategiâ razvitiâ "negroidnogo rasovogo šovinizma" ili prigožinskij otvet doktrine Gerasimova', *Dossier Center*, 21 May 2019, https:// dossier.center/e-prigozhin/article/prigozhinskij-otvet-doktrine -gerasimova/.

28 Maxime Audinet, *Le lion, l'ours et les hyènes. Acteurs, pratiques et récits de l'influence informationnelle russe en Afrique subsaharienne francophone*, Institut de Recherche Stratégique de l'Ecole Militaire, Étude n°83 (2021), 48–9, https://www.irsem.fr/media/5-publications/ etude-irsem-83-audinet-le-lion-ok.pdf.

29 Maglov, Olevsky and Treshchanin, 'ЧАСТЬ 4. ТАЙНОЕ ЗАВОЕВАНИЕ АФРИКИ'; Khadija Sharife, Lara Dihmis, 3Ayin and Erin Klazar, 'Documents Reveal Wagner's Golden Ties to Sudanese Military Companies', *Organized Crime and Corruption Reporting Project*, 2 November 2022, https://www.occrp.org/en/investigation/documents -reveal-wagners-golden-ties-to-sudanese-military-companies.

30 Elbagir, Arvanitidis, Qiblawi, Mezzofiore, Al Gheit and Tarasova, 'Russia is Plundering Gold in Sudan to Boost Putin's War Effort in Ukraine'.

31 Permanent Mission of the Russian Federation to the United Nations, 'Statement by Deputy Permanent Representative Anna Evstigneeva at UNSC Briefing on the Situation in Sudan', 25 April 2023, https:// russiaun.ru/en/news/250423_evst.

32 Samuel Ramani, 'As Fighting in Sudan Rages, Russia's Primary Goal is to Ensure Authoritarian Rule', *Middle East Institute*, 3 May 2023, https:// mei.edu/publications/fighting-sudan-rages-russias-primary-goal -ensure-authoritarian-rule.

33 'Afwerki, Hemetti Discuss Eritrean Sudanese Relations' ; Fathi Osman, 'Sudan: As the Generals Fight, Who's Playing Chess with the Old Islamists?', *African Arguments*, 15 May 2023, https://africanarguments .org/2023/05/sudan-as-the-generals-fight-whos-playing-chess-with-the -old-islamists/.

34　Interview on 5 December 2023.

35　Elbagir, Arvanitidis, Qiblawi, Mezzofiore, Al Gheit and Tarasova, 'Russia is Plundering Gold in Sudan to Boost Putin's War Effort in Ukraine'.

36　Josep Borrell i Fontelles, 'Council Implementing Decision (CFSP) 2021/2198 of 13 December 2021 Implementing Decision (CFSP) 2015/1333 Concerning Restrictive Measures in View of the Situation in Libya', *Official Journal of the European Union*, annex II.

37　'No African Red Carpet for King of Kings', *Reuters*, 8 March 2011, https://www.reuters.com/article/world/africa/no-african-red-carpet-for -king-of-kings-idUSLDE72717K/.

38　Robert Mugabe who, like Haftar and Hemedti, was also represented by Ari Ben Menashe, founder of Dickens and Madson, which I'll mention below, cf. 'Ari Ben-Menashe on Sudan, Mugabe & Haftar', *BBC*, 4 July 2019, https://www.bbc.co.uk/programmes/p07g0b3n.

39　Lou Osborn and Dimitri Zufferey, *Wagner. Enquête au cœur du système Prigojine* (Paris: Éditions du Faubourg, 2023), 193.

40　'Libye: Khalifa Haftar, son fils Saddam et le trafic d'or', *RFI*, 10 October 2020, https://www.rfi.fr/fr/afrique/20201010-libye-fils-haftar-trafic-or -turquie-emirats-arabes-unis.

41　Oscar Rickett, 'How the UAE Kept the Sudan War Raging', *African Arguments*, 21 février 2024, https://africanarguments.org/2024/02/how -the-uae-kept-the-sudan-war-raging/.

42　Anna Youranets, 'Не мы начали эту войну: как Хафтар разочаровал союзников', *Gazeta*, 10 June 2020, https://www.gazeta.ru/politics/2020 /06/09_a_13112863.shtml?updated.

43　Ilia Barabanov and Denis Korotkov, *La Mort est notre Business. La véritable histoire du groupe Wagner et de son fondateur Evgueni Prigojine* (Paris: Flammarion, 2024), 194.

44　Dickens and Madson (Canada), Inc., *Consultancy Agreement*, 7 May 2019, paragraph 1, https://efile.fara.gov/docs/6200-Exhibit-AB -20190617-8.pdf; Elsaidi, 'Libya's Haftar "Rerouting" Supplies to Sudan's Rapid Support Forces'.

45 '1,000 Sudanese Militiamen Arrive in Libya', *Radio Dabanga*, 25 July 2019, https://www.dabangasudan.org/en/all-news/article/1-000 -sudanese-militiamen-arrive-in-libya.

46 Al Jazeera, 'طائرات عسكرية إماراتية.. وثائق ومصادر خاصة للجزيرة نت تستخدم مطارات السودان وحميدتي يجند مرتزقة لأبو ظبي', 24 July 2019, https:// aja.me/z65ciy; Kaamil Ahmed, 'Haftar, Hemeti, and a Canadian Lobbyist's Libyan Connection', *Middle East Eye*, 2 août 2019, https:// www.middleeasteye.net/news/haftar-hemeti-and-lobbyists-libya -connection.

47 Confirmed by satellite imagery analysis: Jon Gambrell, 'UAE Dismantles Eritrea Base as it Pulls Back after Yemen War', *Associated Press*, 18 February 2021, https://apnews.com/article/eritrea-dubai-only -on-ap-united-arab-emirates-east-africa-088f41c7d54d6a397398b2a 825f5e45a.

48 Rickett, 'How the UAE Kept the Sudan War Raging'; Elis Gjevori, 'What the Wagner Group's Insurrection Means for the Middle East and Africa', *Middle East Eye*, 24 June 2023, https://www.middleeasteye.net/news/ wagner-group-russia-insurrection-middle-east-africa; Andreas Krieg, 'Gold, Arms and Mercenaries: On UAE's Shadowy Networks in Sudan', *Middle East Eye*, 1 May 2023, https://www.middleeasteye.net/opinion/ uae-sudan-shadowy-networks-cold-arms-mercenaries; Elsaidi, 'Libya's Haftar 'Rerouting' Supplies to Sudan's Rapid Support Forces'.

49 Ministry of Foreign Affairs of the Russian Federation, 'Russian Ambassador to Eritrea H.E. Mr. Igor N. Mozgo Held a Meeting with the Heads of Diplomatic Missions of Egypt, Yemen, Qatar and Libya', 29 March 2024, https://mid.ru/tv/?id=1806973&lang=en.

50 'Eritrea Supports Russia's Active Presence in Africa – Russian Ambassador', *TASS Russian News Agency*, 11 June 2024, https://tass .com/politics/1802057.

51 'Посол РФ заявил, что Эритрея выступает за активное присутствие России в Африке', *TASS Russian News Agency*, 11 June 2024, https://tass.ru/politika/21065909.

52 'Russian Ambassador Lauds Intensified Relations with Eritrea', *TASS Russian News Agency*, 11 June 2024, https://tass.com/politics/1802031.

Chapter 10

1   Alex de Waal, 'BRICS-Plus versus Pax Americana in the Red Sea Arena', *World Peace Foundation*, 3 February 2024, https://worldpeacef oundation.org/publication/brics-plus-versus-pax-americana-in-the-red -sea-arena/.

2   The official website of the Ministry of Communication is Shabait.com, but TesfaNews is also controlled by the PFDJ like all media in Eritrea. In this case, the latter quotes the former because the article is no longer available: Shabait (Eritrean Ministry of Information), 'Leaders of Eritrea and Ethiopia Receive Saudi Arabia's Highest Honour', *TesfaNews*, 16 September 2018, https://tesfanews.com/eritrea-ethiopia -leaders-received-saudi-arabia-highest-award/.

3   Shabait (Eritrean Ministry of Information), 'Saudi Coalition Forces Commander Met Eritrea President', *TesfaNews*, 6 August 2019, https:// tesfanews.com/saudi-anti-terrorism-coalition-forces-commander-meet -eritrea-president/; 'Eritrea, quell'alleanza di ferro con l'Arabia Saudita', *Rivista Africa*, 9 August 2019, https://www.africarivista.it/eritrea -quellalleanza-di-ferro-con-larabia-saudita/144503/.

4   Alex Almeida and Michael Knights, 'West of Suez for the United Arab Emirates, *War on the Rocks*, 2 September 2016, https://warontherocks .com/2016/09/west-of-suez-for-the-united-arab-emirates/; Stratfor Worldviews, 'The UAE Joins an Exclusive Club', 8 December 2016, https://worldview.stratfor.com/article/uae-joins-exclusive-club.

5   Aaron Maasho, 'UAE to Give Ethiopia $3 Billion in Aid and Investments', *Reuters*, 16 June 2018, https://www.reuters.com/ article/business/finance/uae-to-give-ethiopia-3-billion-in-aid-and -investments-idUSL8N1TH4GJ/.

6   All five states being members of the Council of Arab and African Coastal States of the Red Sea and the Gulf of Aden since 6 January 2020, under the patronage of Saudi Arabia, cf. 'Foreign Minister: The Council of Arab and African Coastal States of the Red Sea and the Gulf of Aden Is a Joint Action System for Coordination and Cooperation', *Saudi Press Agency*, 6 January 2020, https://www.spa.gov.sa/2019804.

7   Mohamed Kheir Omer, 'Isaias Afwerki: Beijing's Oldest Friend in the Horn', *African Arguments*, 25 July 2023, https://africanarguments.org /2023/07/isaias-afwerki-beijings-friend-in-the-horn/; Joshua Meservey, 'Eritrea's Growing Ties with China and Russia Highlight America's Inadequate Approach in East Africa', *Hudson Institute*, 17 July 2023, https://www.hudson.org/foreign-policy/eritreas-growing-ties-china -russia-highlight-americas-inadequate-approach-east-joshua-meservey.

8   Dan Connell, *Against All Odds – A Chronicle of the Eritrean Revolution with a New Update and Reappraisal* (Trenton, NJ: Red Sea Press, 1993, update 2021), 78–80.

9   Ibid., 73–91.

10 'Why Is Eritrea Backing Russian Aggression in Ukraine?', *The Economist*, 8 March 2022, https://www.economist.com/the-economist -explains/2022/03/08/why-is-eritrea-backing-russian-aggression-in -ukraine.

11 President of Russia, 'Meeting with President of Eritrea Isaias Afwerki', 28 July 2023, http://en.kremlin.ru/events/president/news/71830.

12 Maxime Audinet, *Le lion, l'ours et les hyènes. Acteurs, pratiques et récits de l'influence informationnelle russe en Afrique subsaharienne francophone*, Institut de Recherche Stratégique de l'Ecole Militaire, Étude n°83 (2021), 48–9, https://www.irsem.fr/media/5-publications/ etude-irsem-83-audinet-le-lion-ok.pdf.

13 Daniel Tesfa, Mirjam van Reisen and Klara Smits, 'A Secret Deal to Conceal: The Eritrean Involvement in the Tigray War', in *Tigray. The Panarchy of War*, Book 1, ed. Mirjam van Reisen and Munyaradzi Mawere (Bamenda, Cameroon: Langaa Research & Publishing CIG, 2024), 53–100, https://www.researchgate.net/publication/385394550_A _Secret_Deal_to_Conceal_The_Eritrean_Involvement_in_the_Tigray _War.

14 See Minister of Communication Yemane G. Meskel's Tweet, https://x. com/hawelti/status/1037335660791820294.

15 Lucy Kassa, 'Somali Troops Committed Atrocities in Tigray as New Alliance Emerged, Survivors Say', *The Globe and Mail*, 20 January

2022, https://www.theglobeandmail.com/world/article-somali-troops
-committed-atrocities-in-tigray-as-new-alliance-emerged/.

16 Tom Gardner, *The Abiy Project. God, Power and War in the New
Ethiopia* (London: C. Hurst and Company, 2024), 51–65.

17 Quotation translated in Antony Sguazzin, 'Why is Abiy Threatening
Ethiopia's Neighbors?: Next Africa', *Bloomsberg*, 20 October 2023,
https://www.bloomberg.com/news/newsletters/2023-10-20/why
-is-ethiopia-s-abiy-ahmed-demanding-access-to-the-sea. Original
speec recorded by the Ethiopian Broadcast Corporation, https://www
.facebook.com/EBCzena/videos/1057374018728263/.

18 Alex de Waal, 'Ethiopia PM Abiy Ahmed Eyes Red Sea Port, Inflaming
Tensions', *BBC*, 8 November 2023, https://www.bbc.com/news/world
-africa-67332811.

19 'Feature: "A Population of 150 Million Can't Live in a Geographic
Prison" – PM Abiy Ahmed', *Addis Standard*, 14 October 2023, https://
addisstandard.com/feature-a-population-of-150-million-cant-live-in-a
-geographic-prison-pm-abiy-ahmed/.

20 Robert Gersony, 'Why Somalis Flee. Synthesis of Accounts of Conflict
Experience in Northern Somalia by Somali Refugees, Displaced Persons
and Others', *Report Submitted to Robert L. Funseth, Acting Director
Bureau for Refugee Programs and Ambassador Herman J. Cohen, Assistant
Secretary of State Bureau for African Affairs*, August 1989; Ismail Einashe
and Matt Kennart, 'In the Valley of Death: Somaliland's Forgotten
Genocide', *The Nation*, 22 October 2018, https://www.thenation.com/
article/archive/in-the-valley-of-death-somalilands-forgotten-genocide/.

21 Arnaud Delalande, 'Remains of Chinese Made Missiles Found in
Tripoli Points to Wing Loongs Airstrikes', *AeroHisto – Aviation History*,
29 April 2019, https://aerohisto.blogspot.com/2019/04/remains-of
-chinese-made-missiles-found.html.

22 Wim Zwijnenburg, 'Are Emirati Armed Drones Supporting Ethiopia
from an Eritrean Air Base?', *Bellingcat*, 19 November 2020, https://www
.bellingcat.com/news/rest-of-world/2020/11/19/are-emirati-armed
-drones-supporting-ethiopia-from-an-eritrean-air-base/.

23   Jon Gambrell, 'UAE Dismantles Eritrea Base as it Pulls Back after
     Yemen War', *Associated Press*, 18 February 2021, https://apnews.com/
     article/eritrea-dubai-only-on-ap-united-arab-emirates-east-africa-088
     f41c7d54d6a397398b2a825f5e45a.

24   See the blog of the Ethiopian Ministry of Foreign Affairs, 'A week in the
     Horn', 12 January 2024, https://mfaethiopiablog.wordpress.com/2024
     /01/12/a-week-in-the-horn-34/.

25   Alex de Waal and Mulugeta Gebrehiwot Berhe, 'Ethiopia Back on
     the Brink. How Abiy's Reckless Ambition and Emirati Meddling are
     Fueling Chaos in the Horn', *Foreign Affairs*, 8 April 2024, https://www
     .foreignaffairs.com/ethiopia/ethiopia-back-brink.

26   The Arab Republic of Egypt Presidency, 'President El-Sisi Meets
     President of Eritrea Afwerki', 11 November 2023, https://www
     .presidency.eg/en/%D9%82%D8%B3%D9%85-%D8%A7%D9%84%D8
     %A3%D8%AE%D8%A8%D8%A7%D8%B1/%D8%A3%D8%AE%D8
     %A8%D8%A7%D8%B1-%D8%B1%D8%A6%D8%A7%D8%B3%D9
     %8A%D8%A9/news11112023-7/.

27   'President El-Sisi Meets President of Eritrea Afwerki', *TesfaNews*,
     12 November 2023, https://tesfanews.com/president-el-sisi-meets
     -president-afwerki-in-riyadh/.

28   Benoît Faucon, Joe Parkinson and Drew Hinshaw, 'Putin Moves to
     Seize Control of Wagner's Global Empire', *The Wall Street Journal*, 28
     June 2023, https://www.wsj.com/articles/putin-moves-to-seize-control
     -of-wagners-global-empire-26d49286.

29   'Sudan Confirms Agreements with Russia for Naval Base in Red Sea.
     Previous Deal Allowed Russia to Keep Up to Four Navy Ships Including
     Nuclear Powered Ones', *Radio Dabanga*, 29 May 2024, https://www
     .dabangasudan.org/en/all-news/article/sudan-general-confirms-red-sea
     -base-deal-with-russia-strengthens-ties-with-iran.

30   'Breaking News: Unconfirmed Reports Suggest An Ethiopian-Eritrean
     Federation Soon', *The Daily Horn News*, 29 March 2021, https://www
     .horndaily.com/2021/03/29/breaking-new-unconfirmed-reports
     -suggest-an-ethiopian-eritrean-federation-soon/.

Crushing 'the elites of domination and monopoly'

1 Eritrea Ministry of Information, 'Keynote Address by President Isaias Afwerki on the Occasion of the 33rd Independence Anniversary', *Asmara*, 24 May 2024: https://shabait.com/amp/2024/05/24/keynote -address-by-president-isaias-afwerki-on-the-occasion-of-the-33rd -independence-anniversary-asmara-24-may-2024/.

2 It was at the first Russia-Africa Summit in Sochi in October 2019 that Nathalie Yamb pulled off the coup that earned her the nickname 'Lady of Sochi'.

3 President of Russia, *Russia-Africa Summit*, 28 July 2023, http://en .kremlin.ru/events/president/news/71826.

4 Jose Caballero, 'How Russia is Fighting for Allies Among the Brics Countries Using "Memory Diplomacy"', *The Conversation*, 25 August 2023, https://theconversation.com/how-russia-is-fighting-for-allies -among-the-brics-countries-using-memory-diplomacy-212130?fbclid =IwZXh0bgNhZW0CMTAAAR0wELcvuqAtmjTpFVpjkIOkjTB _vXvdlG01yYESYtLNNCsS_5TAbpd6hJs_aem_pN69hcYme6u6SKv jgrzu0g; Jade McGlynn, 'Moscow Is Using Memory Diplomacy to Export Its Narrative to the World', *Foreign Policy*, 25 June 2021, https:// foreignpolicy.com/2021/06/25/russia-puting-ww2-soviet-ussr-memory -diplomacy-history-narrative/.

5 'Emmanuel Macron Warns Europe: NATO is Becoming Brain-Dead', *The Economist*, 7 November 2019, https://www.economist.com/europe /2019/11/07/emmanuel-macron-warns-europe-nato-is-becoming -brain-dead.

6 Zongyuan Zoe Liu and Mihaela Papa, *Can BRICS De-dollarize the Global Financial System?* (Cambridge: Cambridge University Press, 2022), 5.1, https://www.cambridge.org/core/elements/can-brics -dedollarize-the-global-financial-system/0AEF98D2F232072409E9556 620AE09B0?utm_campaign=shareaholic&utm_medium=copy_link &utm_source=bookmark.

7 Ronan Manly, 'Chinese Central Bank Accumulating Gold Again', *Bullionstar*, 11 January 2023, https://www.bullionstar.com/blogs/

ronan-manly/chinese-central-bank-kicks-off-new-round-of-gold
-accumulation/.

8 Cf. Liu and Papa, *Can BRICS De-dollarize the Global Financial System?*, 4.2.

9 Cf. Mohammed Saaida, 'BRICS Plus: De-dollarization and Global
Power Shifts in New Economic Landscape', *BRICS Journal of Economics*
5(1) (April 2024): 13–33 (19–24), https://doi.org/10.3897/brics-econ.5
.e117828;

    Melissa Pisitili, 'How Would a New BRICS Currency Affect the US
Dollar?', *Nasdaq*, 8 July 2024, https://www.nasdaq.com/articles/how
-would-new-brics-currency-affect-us-dollar-updated-2024; Célestin
Coquidé, José Lages and Dima L. Shepelyansky, 'Prospects of BRICS
Currency Dominance in International Trade', *Applied Network Science*
8:65 (2023), https://doi.org/10.1007/s41109-023-00590-3.

10 Cf. Matthieu Stricot, 'A New Currency to Dethrone the Dollar?', *CNRS
Le Journal*, 19 février 2024, https://news.cnrs.fr/articles/a-new-currency
-to-dethrone-the-dollar; Nathan Lewis, 'BRICS Making Good Progress
On Their Golden Path', *Forbes*, 24 January 2024, https://www.forbes
.com/sites/nathanlewis/2024/01/24/brics-making-good-progress-on
-their-golden-path/.

11 'Kremlin Announces Creation of Blockchain-Based Payment System
in BRICS', *TASS Russian News Agency*, 5 March 2024, https://tass.com/
politics/1755521.

12 https://x.com/BRICSinfo/status/1800915514891612570; Alexander
Marrow and Mark Trevelyan, 'Russia, Hit by New US Sanctions, Halts
Dollar and Euro Trade on Main Bourse', *Reuters*, 12 June 2024, https://
www.reuters.com/markets/europe/moscow-exchange-stop-trading
-dollars-after-latest-us-sanctions-2024-06-12/.

Epilogue: Political fiction

1 'Nevsun Resources to buy Reservoir Minerals for $365 million',
Reuters, 25 April 2016: https://www.reuters.com/article/business

/nevsun-resources-to-buy-reservoir-minerals-for-365-million
-idUSKCN0XM04Y/.

2   Peter Kukielski, 'Nevsun breaks ground on exploration decline and
    provides update on the Timok Project', *Nevsun Resources Ltd*, 5 juin
    2018: https://www.prnewswire.com/news-releases/nevsun-breaks
    -ground-on-exploration-decline-and-provides-update-on-the-timok
    -project-300659568.html.

3   https://www.facebook.com/100064573156593/posts
    /730835057114467/.

4   'Chinese company opens massive eco-friendly mine in Serbia', Xinhua,
    25 October 2021: http://www.china-ceec.org/eng/sbhz_1/202110/
    t20211029_10403551.htm

5   Jean-Baptiste Chastand, 'La Serbie, sas d'entrée vers l'Europe pour Pékin',
    Le Monde, 22 mars 2021: https://www.lemonde.fr/international/article
    /2021/03/19/la-serbie-sas-d-entree-vers-l-europe-pour-pekin_6073757
    _3210.html

Bibliography

Addis Standard, 'Feature: "A Population of 150 Million Can't Live in a Geographic Prison" – PM Abiy Ahmed', *Addis Standard*, 14 October 2023. https://addisstandard.com/feature-a-population-of-150-million-cant-live-in-a-geographic-prison-pm-abiy-ahmed/.

Africa Energy Intelligence, 'Genesis cède ses intérêts et Rift Resources fore', *Africa Intelligence*, 29 September 1999.

Africa Energy Intelligence, 'Un peu d'activité malgré la guerre', *Africa Intelligence*, 18 May 1999.

Africa Energy Intelligence, 'Un permis dans l'Extrême-Nord', *Africa Intelligence*, 23 September 1998.

Africa Energy Intelligence, 'Addis Wants a Sector-by-Sector Approach to Minerals Management', *Africa Intelligence*, 24 November 2020.

Africa Energy Intelligence, 'Copper and Gold Finds Could End Up Breaking China's Monopoly', *Africa Intelligence*, 22 September 2020.

Africa Energy Intelligence, 'Danakali Cuts Back on Costs to Launch Sulphate of Potash Project', *Africa Intelligence*, 15 December 2015.

Africa Energy Intelligence, 'Eritrean Mining Projects Return to Toronto Stock Exchange', *Africa Intelligence*, 5 October 2021.

Africa Mining Intelligence, 'All Complaints Against Nevsun Lumped into the Same Case', *Africa Intelligence*, 24 March 2020.

Africa Mining Intelligence, 'Asmara's Gold: Sunridge Pulls Out All Stops', *Africa Intelligence*, 11 November 2013.

Africa Mining Intelligence, 'ENAMCO Joins Chalice in Developing Koka', *Africa Intelligence*, 28 September 2011.

Africa Mining Intelligence, 'Eritrea ENAMCO Seeks a Repeat of Bisha Success Story', *Africa Intelligence*, 24 February 2015.

Africa Mining Intelligence, 'Former Sunridge Veterans Cross the Border to Strike Gold', *Africa Intelligence*, 16 April 2019.

Africa Mining Intelligence, 'How ENAMCO Plans to Pay Chalice', *Africa Intelligence*, 11 January 2012.

Africa Mining Intelligence, 'A Key Year for Sunridge Gold', *Africa Intelligence*, 25 January 2012.

Africa Mining Intelligence, 'The Race to be First to Mine Danakil's Potash?', *Africa Intelligence*, 6 October 2015

Africa Mining Intelligence, 'Why Asmara Froze Mining Projects', *Africa Intelligence*, 15 September 2004.

Ahmed, Kaamil, 'Haftar, Hemeti, and a Canadian Lobbyist's Libyan Connection', *Middle East Eye*, 2 août 2019. https://www.middleeasteye .net/news/haftar-hemeti-and-lobbyists-libya-connection.

Al Jazeera, 'وثائق ومصادر خاصة للجزيرة نت.. طائرات عسكرية إماراتية تستخدم مطارات', السودان وحميدتي يجند مرتزقة لأبو ظبي 24 July 2019. https://aja.me/z65ciy.

Almeida, Alex and Michael Knights, 'West of Suez for the United Arab Emirates, *War on the Rocks*, 2 September 2016. https://warontherocks .com/2016/09/west-of-suez-for-the-united-arab-emirates/.

Alpha Exploration, *Kerkasha Exploration License – Eritrea*. https://alpha -exploration.com/project/kerkasha-eritrea/.

Amin, Mohammed, 'Sudan's Darfur Draws Neighbours Back into a War that Never Ended', *Middle East Eye*, 17 May 2023. https://www.middleeasteye .net/news/sudan-crisis-darfur-war-neighbours-never-ended.

The Arab Republic of Egypt Presidency, 'President El-Sisi Meets President of Eritrea Afwerki', 11 November 2023. https://www.presidency.eg/en/ %D9%82%D8%B3%D9%85-%D8%A7%D9%84%D8%A3%D8%AE %D8%A8%D8%A7%D8%B1/%D8%A3%D8%AE%D8%A8%D8%A7 %D8%B1-%D8%B1%D8%A6%D8%A7%D8%B3%D9%8A%D8%A9/ news11112023-7/.

Areguy, Fitsum, 'Leaked Report Accuses Canada of Covering for Mining Companies in War-Torn Ethiopia', *The Breach*, 13 août 2021. https:// breachmedia.ca/leaked-report-accuses-canada-of-covering-for-mining -companies-in-war-torn-ethiopia/.

Asmarino Independant Media, 'Eritrea: ጉዳይ ርእሰ ምስ ፌርምን ኩባን', *Asmarino Independant Media*, 4 July 2015. https://asmarino.com/news/4405-2015 -07-04-02-39-34.

Atlantic Council, 'Update on the Eritrean Migration Situation with Felix Horne', *Event Recap*, Atlantic Council, 10 December 2015. https://www.atlanticcouncil.org/commentary/event-recap/update-on-the-eritrean-migration-situation-with-felix-horne/.

Audinet, Maxime, *Le lion, l'ours et les hyènes. Acteurs, pratiques et récits de l'influence informationnelle russe en Afrique subsaharienne francophone*, Institut de Recherche Stratégique de l'Ecole Militaire, Étude n°83 (2021). https://www.irsem.fr/media/5-publications/etude-irsem-83-audinet-le-lion-ok.pdf.

Barabanov, Ilia and Denis Korotkov, *La Mort est notre Business. La véritable histoire du groupe Wagner et de son fondateur Evgueni Prigojine* (Paris: Flammarion, 2024).

Barrie, Charles Tucker, F. William Nielsen and Claude H Aussant, 'The Bisha Volcanic-Associated Massive Sulfide Deposit, Western Nakfa Terrane, Eritrea', *Economic Geology* 102/4 (2007): 717–38.

BBC News, 'Sudan Crisis: The Ruthless Mercenaries Who Run the Country for Gold', *BBC News*, 20 July 2019. https://www.bbc.com/news/world-africa-48987901.

BBC News, 'Ari Ben-Menashe on Sudan, Mugabe & Haftar', *BBC News*, 4 July 2019. https://www.bbc.co.uk/programmes/p07g0b3n.

Berhane, Daniel, 'Leaked Audio. Eritrea Funds ESAT and Ginbot 7', *The Horn Affairs*, 20 June 2013. https://hornaffairs.com/2013/06/20/leaked-audio-eritrea-funds-esat-berhanu-nega/.

Borrell i Fontelles, Josep, 'Council Implementing Decision (CFSP) 2021/2198 of 13 December 2021 Implementing Decision (CFSP) 2015/1333 Concerning Restrictive Measures in View of the Situation in Libya', *Official Journal of the European Union*.

Berthelot, Marcellin, and Marie-Émile Ruelle, *Collection des anciens alchimistes grecs* (Paris: G. Steinheil, 1888).

Bouchot, Vincent and Jean-Pierre Milesi, 'La métallogénie de l'or : évolution des modèles et cibles prioritaires de la recherche au fil des années', *Géologues* 152 (2007): 40–8.

Brown, Will, 'Briton Released From Death Row Accused of Inciting Genocide in Ethiopia', *The Telegraph*, 28 November 2021. https://www

.telegraph.co.uk/global-health/terror-and-security/briton-released-death
-row-accused-inciting-genocide-ethiopia/.

Bruton, Bronwyn, 'Eritrea: Coming in From the Cold', *Atlantic Council*,
7 December 2016. https://www.atlanticcouncil.org/in-depth-research
-reports/issue-brief/eritrea-coming-in-from-the-cold/.

Bruton, Bronwyn, 'Eritrea: A Neglected Regional Threat', Hearing Before
the House Committee on Foreign Affairs, Subcommittee on Africa,
Global Health, Global Human Rights, and International Organizations,
Washington, DC, September 14, 2016. https://docs.house.gov/meetings
/FA/FA16/20160914/105311/HHRG-114-FA16-Wstate-BrutonB
-20160914.pdf.

Bruton, Bronwyn, 'It's bad in Eritrea, but not that bad', *The New York Times*,
23 June 2016. https://www.nytimes.com/2016/06/24/opinion/its-bad-in
-eritrea-but-not-that-bad.html.

Bruton, Bronwyn, 'To End Ethiopia's War, Biden Needs to Correct Course',
Foreign Policy, 28 December, 2021. https://foreignpolicy.com/2021/12/28
/ethiopia-tigray-abiy-tplf-war-biden-needs-to-correct-course/.

Bryden, Matt, Jörg Roofthooft, Ghassan Schbley and Babatunde Taiwo,
*Letter dated 18 July 2011 from the Chairman of the Security Council
Committee pursuant to resolutions 751 (1992) and 1907 (2009) concerning
Somalia and Eritrea addressed to the President of the Security Council*, 18
July 2011, 109–10. https://digitallibrary.un.org/record/708002?ln=es&v
=pdf.

Caballero, José, 'How Russia is Fighting for Allies Among the Brics
Countries Using "Memory Diplomacy"', *The Conversation*, 25 August
2023. https://theconversation.com/how-russia-is-fighting-for-allies
-among-the-brics-countries-using-memory-diplomacy-212130?fbclid
=IwZXh0bgNhZW0CMTAAAR0wELcvuqAtmjTpFVpjkIOkjTB_vXv
dlG01yYESYtLNNCsS_5TAbpd6hJs_aem_pN69hcYme6u6SKvjgrzu0g.

Chastand, Jean-Baptiste, 'La Serbie, sas d'entrée vers l'Europe pour Pékin', *Le
Monde*, 22 mars 2021. https://www.lemonde.fr/international/article/2021
/03/19/la-serbie-sas-d-entree-vers-l-europe-pour-pekin_6073757_3210
.html.

Chatelot, Christophe, 'Entre brutalité et prédation, comment Wagner
pacifie la Centrafrique', *Le Monde*, 17 June 2024. https://www.lemonde

.fr/afrique/article/2024/06/17/en-centrafrique-wagner-continue-de
-prosperer_6240954_3212.html.

Christophe, François, 'Atlantic Council: The Eritrean Regime's US Spin
Doctors?', in *Human Trafficking and Trauma in the Digital Era: The
Ongoing Tragedy of the Trade in Refugees from Eritrea*, ed. Mirjam
van Reisen and Munyaradzi Mawere (Bamenda, Cameroon: Langaa
Research & Publishing CIG, 2017), 405–28. https://www.researchgate
.net/publication/316989834_Human_Trafficking_and_Trauma_in_the
_Digital_Era_The_Ongoing_Tragedy_of_the_Trade_in_Refugees_from
_Eritrea.

Christophe, François, 'Forget Objectivity: For The Atlantic Council,
Eritrea's Prison State Isn't That Bad', *Medium*, December 2016. https://
frchristophe.medium.com/forget-objectivity-for-the-atlantic-council
-eritreas-prison-state-isn-t-that-bad-be20f58ed315.

Clarke, Jeremy, 'Three Mine Workers Shot Dead in Eritrea', *Reuters*, 7
October 2009. https://www.reuters.com/article/world/three-mine
-workers-shot-dead-in-eritrea-idUSJOE5960GH/.

Cohen, Hank, 'Time to Bring Eritrea in from the Cold', *African Arguments*,
16 December 2013. https://africanarguments.org/2013/12/time-to-bring
-eritrea-in-from-the-cold-by-hank-cohen/.

Connell, Dan, *Against All Odds – A Chronicle of the Eritrean Revolution with
a new Update and Reappraisal* (Trenton, NJ: Red Sea Press, 1997, update
2021).

Connell, Dan, *Conversations with Eritrean Political Prisoners* (Trenton, NJ:
Red Sea Press, 2005).

Coquidé, Célestin, José Lages and Dima L. Shepelyansky, 'Prospects of
BRICS Currency Dominance in International Trade', *Applied Network
Science* 8:65 (2023). https://doi.org/10.1007/s41109-023-00590-3.

Cornelius, Seamus, 'Demystifying Eritrea: The Ground Reality, Mining
and Human Rights', 8 mars 2018. https://danakali.com.au/wp-content
/uploads/2021/09/Company-Presentation-Demystifying-Eritrea
-Thursday-08-March-2018.pdf.

Cornelius, Seamus, 'Proactive Investors One2One Investor Conference –
London', Danakali Limited, 20 September 2018. The Map is Reproduced
in 'Danakali's Potash Project Could be a Game Changer for Eritrea –

UN', *Mining.com*, 30 January 2019. https://www.mining.com/danakalis
   -potash-project-game-changer-eritrea-un/.

The Daily Horn News, 'Breaking News: Unconfirmed Reports Suggest
   An Ethiopian-Eritrean Federation Soon', *The Daily Horn News*, 29
   mars 2021. https://www.horndaily.com/2021/03/29/breaking-new
   -unconfirmed-reports-suggest-an-ethiopian-eritrean-federation-soon/.

Delalande, Arnaud, 'Remains of Chinese Made Missiles Found in Tripoli
   Points to Wing Loongs Airstrikes', *AeroHisto – Aviation History*, 29 April
   2019. https://aerohisto.blogspot.com/2019/04/remains-of-chinese-made
   -missiles-found.html.

Delisi, Scott H., 'Controlling the Market, controlling the people: Hidri Trust
   takes all', 27 June 2006, Wikileaks: 06ASMARA553_a.

Delisi, Scott H., 'Remittances and Hard Currency: Eritrea's Lifeline', 16
   February 2007, Wikileaks: 07ASMARA158_a.

'Delizia Limited', *Cyprus Corporate Registry*, 22 February 2021. https://
   cyprusregistry.com/companies/HE/101771.

Democracy 21, *How the Kremlin is using Wagner to launder billions in
   African gold*, The Blood Gold Report, December 2023, 10–2. https://
   bloodgoldreport.com/wp-content/uploads/2023/12/The-Blood-Gold
   -Report-2023-December.pdf.

De Waal, Alex, 'BRICS-Plus versus Pax Americana in the Red Sea Arena',
   World Peace Foundation, February 2024, 3. https://worldpeacefoundation
   .org/publication/brics-plus-versus-pax-americana-in-the-red-sea-arena/.

De Waal, Alex, 'Ethiopia PM Abiy Ahmed Eyes Red Sea Port, Inflaming
   Tensions', *BBC*, 8 novembre 2023. https://www.bbc.com/news/world
   -africa-67332811.

De Waal, Alex, *The Real Politics of the Horn of Africa. Money, War and the
   business of Power* (Cambridge: Polity Press, 2015)

De Waal, Alex, 'Steal, Burn, Rape, Kill', *London Review of Book* 43/12 (17
   June 2021). https://www.lrb.co.uk/the-paper/v43/n12/alex-de-waal/steal
   -burn-rape-kill?fbclid=IwZXh0bgNhZW0CMTAAAR18nz6aiK3HK
   2HiNO2cHzEixxt4EQIPA9ZCCYuyMdJG4Rdgo0BvwRwb_4_aem_wp6
   vm5s7CgOqQEGz04v2UQ.

De Waal, Alex and Mulugeta Gebrehiwot Berhe, 'Ethiopia Back on the
   Brink. How Abiy's Reckless Ambition -and Emirati Meddling- are

Fueling Chaos in the Horn', *Foreign Affairs*, 8 April 2024. https://www
.foreignaffairs.com/ethiopia/ethiopia-back-brink.

Dossier Center, 'Strategiâ razvitiâ "negroidnogo rasovogo šovinizma" ili
prigožinskij otvet doktrine Gerasimova', *Dossier Center*, 21 May 2019.
https://dossier.center/e-prigozhin/article/prigozhinskij-otvet-doktrine
-gerasimova/.

DSP-groep Amsterdam, Tilburg School of Humanities, Department
of Culture Studies, *The 2% Tax for Eritreans in the diaspora. Facts,
figures and experiences in seven European Countries*, June 2017. https://
www.tweedekamer.nl/kamerstukken/detail?id=2017D25761&did
=2017D25761.

The Economist, 'Emmanuel Macron Warns Europe: NATO is Becoming
Brain-Dead', *The Economist*, 7 November 2019. https://www.economist
.com/europe/2019/11/07/emmanuel-macron-warns-europe-nato-is
-becoming-brain-dead.

The Economist, 'Why is Eritrea Backing Russian Aggression in Ukraine?',
The Economist, 8 March 2022. https://www.economist.com/the
-economist-explains/2022/03/08/why-is-eritrea-backing-russian
-aggression-in-ukraine.

Edwards, David N., *The Kingdoms of Kush and Meroe: Cultural Encounters
with Pharaonic Egypt, Nubia, and Axum* (Oxford: Oxford University
Press, 2019).

Egmont Group Financial Intelligence Unit, World Customs Organization,
FIU Cooperation Handbook, 2020, 14–7. https://egmontgroup.org/
wp-content/uploads/2021/09/2020_CUSTOMS_-_FIU_Cooperation
_Handbook.pdf.

Einashe, Ismail and Matt Kennart, 'In the Valley of Death: Somaliland's
Forgotten Genocide', *The Nation*, 22 October 2018. https://www
.thenation.com/article/archive/in-the-valley-of-death-somalilands
-forgotten-genocide/.

Elbagir, Nima, Barbara Arvanitidis, Tamara Qiblawi, Gianluca Mezzofiore,
Mohammed Abo Al Gheit and Darya Tarasova, 'Russia is Plundering
Gold in Sudan to Boost Putin's War Effort in Ukraine', *CNN*, 29 July
2022. https://edition.cnn.com/2022/07/29/africa/sudan-russia-gold
-investigation-cmd-intl/index.html.

Elsaidi, Samira, 'Libya's Haftar "Rerouting" Supplies to Sudan's Rapid Support Forces', *Middle East Eye*, 10 July 2023. https://www.middleeasteye.net/news/libya-sudan-haftar-rsf-supply-lines.

Enger, Kristina, Floris J. A. de Klerk Wolters and Alex H. C. Wong, 'The Nuclei of the Global IFF Network: The Role of Global Commodity Trading Hubs in Defining the Global Patterns of Illicit Financial Flows', *Curbing Illicit Financial Flows from Resource-rich Developing Countries: Improving Natural Resource Governance to Finance the SDGs*, February 2020. https://curbing-iffs.org/wp-content/uploads/2020/03/r4d-iff-wp03-2020.pdf.

Endale, Ashenafi, 'Canadian Mining Co Prepares to Resume Tigray Operations as Regional Officials Move to Revoke Concessions', *The Reporter*, 10 February 2024. https://www.thereporterethiopia.com/38647/.

The Eritrean Gazette, 'Proclamation on National Service No. 82/1995 of 1995', *The Eritrean Gazette* 11 (23 October 1995). https://www.refworld.org/legal/legislation/natlegbod/1995/en/32119.

ESAT News, 'Neamin Zeleke Tells ESAT "The Struggle for Freedom & Democracy Reached a Critical Stage"', *ESAT News*, 21 September 2015.

Ethiopanorama, 'Former Secretary of State for Africa Herman Cohen Paid to Lobby on Behalf of Eritrean President Isayas Afwerki', *Ethiopanorama*, 5 July 2015. https://ethiopanorama.com/?p=8370.

Ethiopian Ministry of Foreign Affairs, 'A Week in the Horn', 12 January 2024. https://mfaethiopiablog.wordpress.com/2024/01/12/a-week-in-the-horn-34/.

Ethiopian News Agency, 'Ethiopian, Russian News Agencies Sign Memorandum of Understanding', *Ethiopian News Agency*, 6 October 2022. https://www.ena.et/web/eng/w/en_38875.

Ethiopian News Agency, 'Gov't Warns to Take Measures for Unconstitutional Power Grab', *Ethiopian News Agency*, 7 May 2020. https://www.ena.et/web/eng/w/en_14268.

Ethiopian News Agency, '"#No More" Campaign Should be Amplified: African Dev't Group President & CEO', *Ethiopian News Agency*, 27 November 2021. https://www.ena.et/web/eng/w/en_30941.

Ethiopian News Agency, Pearce, Prof. Ann Fitzgerald Awarded for Defending Ethiopian Version of Truth Abroad', *Ethiopian News Agency*, 6 December 2021. https://www.ena.et/web/eng/w/en_31262.

The FATF Recommendations, International Standards on Combating Money Laudering and the Financing of Terrorism & Proliferation, updated in October 2020: www.fatf-gafi.org/recommendations.

Faucon, Benoît, Joe Parkinson and Drew Hinshaw, 'Putin Moves to Seize Control of Wagner's Global Empire', *The Wall Street Journal*, 28 June 2023. https://www.wsj.com/articles/putin-moves-to-seize-control-of-wagners-global-empire-26d49286.

Financial Action Task Force (FATF)/OECD, *The Role of Hawala and Other Similar Service Providers in Money Laundering and Terrorist Financing*, Paris, October 2013. https://www.fatf-gafi.org/content/dam/fatf-gafi/reports/Role-of-hawala-and-similar-in-ml-tf.pdf.coredownload.pdf.

Fluehr-Lobban, Carolyn, 'Meroitic and Aksumite Interactions: Political and Cultural Exchange', *Northeast African Studies* 23/2 (2020): 120–39.

Galeotti, Mark, 'The "Gerasimov Doctrine" and Russian Non-Linear War', *In Moscow's Shadow*, 6 July 2014. https://inmoscowsshadows.wordpress.com/2014/07/06/the-gerasimov-doctrine-and-russian-non-linear-war/.

Galeotti, Mark, 'The Mythical "Gerasimov Doctrine" and the Language of Threat', *Critical Studies on Security* 7/22 (2018): 157–61.

Gamandiy-Egorov, Mikhail, 'Alliance des Etats du Sahel-Russie: la marche commune en avant', *Radio Révolution Panafricaine*, 7 June 2024. https://www.radiorevolutionpanafricaine.com/single-post/alliance-des-etats-du-sahel-russie-la-marche-commune-en-avant.

Gambrell, Jon, 'UAE Dismantles Eritrea Base as It Pulls Back after Yemen War', *Associated Press*, 18 February 2021. https://apnews.com/article/eritrea-dubai-only-on-ap-united-arab-emirates-east-africa-088f41c7d54d6a397398b2a825f5e45a.

Gardner, Tom, *The Abiy Project. God, Power and War in the New Ethiopia* (London: C. Hurst and Company, 2024).

Gardner, Tom, 'I Was a War Reporter in Ethiopia. Then I Became the Enemy', *The Economist*, 24 June 2022. https://www.economist.com/1843/2022/06/24/i-was-a-war-reporter-in-ethiopia-then-i-became-the-enemy.

Gazette of Eritrean Laws, 'The Eritrean National Mining Corporation
     Establishment Proclamation No 157/2006', *Gazette of Eritrean Laws
     Published by the Government of Eritrea*, Asmara, 18 December 2006.
Geb, S. E. and Daniel Tesfa, 'Weaponising the Media: Exploring the Role of
     Ethiopian National Media in the Tigray War', in *Tigray. The Hysteresis
     of War*, Book 1, ed. Mirjam van Reisen and Munyaradzi Mawere
     (Bamenda, Cameroon: Langaa Research & Publishing CIG, 2024),
     191–254. https://www.researchgate.net/publication/385202452_Tigray
     _The_Hysteresis_of_War_Book_1#pfb0.
Gerasimov, Valery, 'The Value of Science Is in the Foresight. New
     Challenges Demand Rethinking the Forms and Methods of Carrying out
     Combat Operations', *Military Review*, January–February 2016. https://
     www.armyupress.army.mil/portals/7/military-review/archives/english/
     militaryreview_20160228_art008.pdf.
Gersony, Robert, 'Why Somalis Flee. Synthesis of Accounts of Conflict
     Experience in Northern Somalia by Somali Refugees, Displaced Persons
     and Others', Report Submitted to Robert L. Funseth, Acting Director
     Bureau for Refugee Programs and Ambassador Herman J. Cohen,
     Assistant Secretary of State Bureau for African Affairs, August 1989.
Gjevori, Elis, 'What the Wagner Group's Insurrection Means for the
     Middle East and Africa', *Middle East Eye*, 24 June 2023. https://www
     .middleeasteye.net/news/wagner-group-russia-insurrection-middle-east
     -africa.
Globe News Net, 'UN Secretary-General Antonio Guterres: Himself Part of
     the Problem?', *Globe News Net*, 29 October 2021. https://axumawian.com
     /archives/12738.
Goyon, Georges, *Le Papyrus de Turin dit 'des mines d'or' et le Wadi
     Hammamat* (Le Caire: Imprimerie de l'Institut Français d'Archéologie
     Orientale, 1949).
Greig, Charles J. and Jeffrey D. Rowe, *NI 43-101 Technical Report, A
     Geological Evaluation of the Meli Property, Tigray National Regional State,
     Northern Ethiopia*, 31 January 2020, 46. https://sunpeakmetals.com/site/
     assets/files/5593/2020-01-meli-tech-report.pdf.
'The Hawala Alternative Remittance System and its Role
     in Money Laundering', *Rapport au Congrès conformément à la Section*

356(c) du USA Patriot Act, Financial Crimes Enforcement Network rédigé en collaboration avec INTERPOL/FOPAC, 31 December 2002.

Hellem, Fredrik, 'How Russia Is Hijacking Pan-Africanism to Drive France out of Africa', *Grea Dynamics*, 15 April 2021. https://greydynamics.com/how-russia-is-hijacking-pan-africanism-to-drive-france-out-of-africa/#h-russia-pan-africanism-and-kemi-seba.

Hirt, Nicole, 'Community Service or Forced Labour? The Eritrean National Service', in *Eritrea from Liberation to oppression*, ed. Katja Dorothea Buck and Mirjam van Reisen (Hamburg: EMV, mars 2017), 48–57 (52–4). https://raee.eu/wp-content/uploads/2022/01/EMW_English_version_2017.pdf.

Hook, Kristina, Azeem Ibrahim O. B. E., Helena Kennedy K. C., Nick Leddy, Melanie O'Brien and Ewelina U. Ochab, 'Genocide in Tigray: Serious Breaches of International Law in the Tigray Conflict, Ethiopia, and Paths to Accountability', *New Lines Institute*, 3 June 2024. https://newlinesinstitute.org/rules-based-international-order/genocide-in-tigray-serious-breaches-of-international-law-in-the-tigray-conflict-ethiopia-and-paths-to-accountability-2/.

House of Commons Canada, *Subcommittee on International Human Rights of the Standing Committee on Foreign Affairs and International Development*, 5 June 2014. https://www.ourcommons.ca/DocumentViewer/en/41-2/SDIR/meeting-32/evidence.

Human Rights Watch, *Hear No Evil, Forced Labor and Corporate Responsibility in Eritrea's Mining Sector*, 15 January 2013. https://www.hrw.org/report/2013/01/15/hear-no-evil/forced-labor-and-corporate-responsibility-eritreas-mining-sector.

Human Rights Watch, '"One Hundred Ways of Putting Pressure". Violations of Freedom of Expression and Association in Ethiopia', 24 March 2010. https://www.hrw.org/report/2010/03/24/one-hundred-ways-putting-pressure/violations-freedom-expression-and-association.

Human Rights Watch, '"They Are Making Us into Slaves, Not Educating Us" How Indefinite Conscription Restricts Young People's Rights, Access to Education in Eritrea', August 2019. https://www.hrw.org/sites/default/files/report_pdf/eritrea0819_web.pdf.

Humbel, Georg, 'Sogar Gefolgsleute flüchten vor dem Regime: Der eritreische Botschafter hat in der Schweiz Asyl beantragt', *Neue Zürcher Zeitung*, 8 June 2024. https://www.nzz.ch/schweiz/sogar-gefolgsleute-fluechten-vor-dem-regime-der-eritreische-botschafter-hat-in-der-schweiz-asyl-beantragt-ld.1833594.

Humbel, Georg, 'Even Supporters Are Fleeing the Regime: The Eritrean Ambassador Has Applied for Asylum in Switzerland'. https://eritrea-focus.org/even-supporters-are-fleeing-the-regime-the-eritrean-ambassador-has-applied-for-asylum-in-switzerland/.

The Indian Ocean Newsletter, 'Berhanu Nega Travels Secretly to the West', *Africa Intelligence*, 20 May 2016.

The Indian Ocean Newsletter, 'Eritrea Has Sights on Future Mining Profits', *Africa Intelligence*, 18 September 2004.

The Indian Ocean Newsletter, 'It's Open Season for Mining Permits', *Africa Intelligence*, 13 September 2008.

The Indian Ocean Newsletter, 'Mining Discoveries in Eritrea', *Africa Intelligence*, 15 mars 2003.

The Indian Ocean Newsletter, 'Three Members of the Diaspora Killed in Asmara', *Africa Intelligence*, 20 October 2017.

Jeune Afrique, 'Russie-Afrique: de Kemi Seba à Nathalie Yamb, les "influenceurs" pro-Poutine du continent', *Jeune Afrique*, 31 March 2022. https://www.jeuneafrique.com/1335015/politique/russie-afrique-de-kemi-seba-a-nathalie-yamb-les-influenceurs-pro-poutine-du-continent/.

Johnson, Peter R. and Beraki Woldehaimanot, 'Development of the Arabian-Nubian Shield: Perspectives on Accretion and Deformation in the Northern East African Orogen and the Assembly of Gondwana', in *Proterozoic East Gondwana: Supercontinent Assembly and Breakup, Geological Society of London, Special Publications* 206, ed. Masaru Yoshida, Brian Frederick Windley and Somnath Dasgupta (Geological Society: London, 2003), 289–325.

Joint Declaration on Comprehensive Cooperation Between Ethiopia, Somalia and Eritrea, Asmara, 5 September 2018. https://www.peaceagreements.org/viewmasterdocument/2099.

Kassa, Lucy, 'A Rape Survivor's Story Emerges from a Remote African War', *Los Angeles Times*, 11 February 2021. https://www.latimes.com/world

-nation/story/2021-02-11/troops-accused-of-mass-rape-in-ethiopias
-tigray-conflict.

Kassa, Lucy, 'Somali Troops Committed Atrocities in Tigray as New Alliance Emerged, Survivors Say', *The Globe and Mail*, 20 January 2022. https://www.theglobeandmail.com/world/article-somali-troops -committed-atrocities-in-tigray-as-new-alliance-emerged/.

Kassa, Lucy, '"A Tigrayan Womb Should Never Give Birth": Rape in Tigray', *Al Jazeera*, 21 April 2021. https://aje.io/wl8t7.

Kendall, Timothy, 'Interactions between the Kingdom of Kush and the Red Sea Trade Network', *Journal of African Archaeology* 19/1 (2021): 45–68.

Kent, Richard, Mohamed Aboelgheit and Nick Donovan, 'Exposing the RSF's Secret Financial Network', *Global Witness*, 9 December 2019. https://www.globalwitness.org/en/campaigns/conflict-minerals/exposing -rsfs-secret-financial-network/.

Kent, Richard, Mohamed Aboelgheit and Nick Donovan, 'How the RSF Got Their 4x4 Technicals: The Open Source Intelligence Techniques Behind Our Sudan Exposé', *Global Witness*, 5 April 2020. https://www .globalwitness.org/en/blog/how-the-rsf-got-their-4x4-technicals-the -open-source-intelligence-techniques-behind-our-sudan-expos%C3 %A9/.

Kheir Omer, Mohamed, 'Isaias Afwerki: Beijing's Oldest Friend in the Horn', *African Arguments*, 25 July 2023. https://africanarguments.org/2023/07/ isaias-afwerki-beijings-friend-in-the-horn/.

Knight, Tessa, 'Eritrean Report Uses Fact-Checking Tropes to Dismiss Evidence as "Disinformation"', *Digital Forensic Research Lab (DFRLab)*, 23 June 2021. https://medium.com/dfrlab/eritrean-report-uses-fact -checking-tropes-to-dismiss-evidence-as-disinformation-385718327481.

Krieg, Andreas, 'Gold, Arms and Mercenaries: On UAE's Shadowy Networks in Sudan', *Middle East Eye*, 1 May 2023. https://www .middleeasteye.net/opinion/uae-sudan-shadowy-networks-cold-arms -mercenaries.

Kukielski, Peter, 'Nevsun Breaks Ground on Exploration Decline and Provides Update on the Timok Project', *Nevsun Resources Ltd*, 5 juin 2018. https://www.prnewswire.com/news-releases/nevsun-breaks

-ground-on-exploration-decline-and-provides-update-on-the-timok
   -project-300659568.html.
Labzaé, Mehdi, 'Wolqayt, la terre promise et ses limites. Mobilisations
   nationalistes amhara, foncier et bureaucratie dans la guerre civile
   éthiopienne (2016-2022)', *Critique Internationale* 99 (2023/2): 109–30.
La Lettre de l'Océan Indien, 'Les prospecteurs de mines', *Africa Intelligence*,
   3 November 1998.
La Lettre de l'Océan Indien, 'Un consortium australien dans les mines',
   Africa Intelligence, 26 September 1998.
Le Monde, 'Kémi Seba, condamné plusieurs fois pour incitation à la haine
   raciale, déchu de la nationalité française', *Le Monde*, 9 July 2024. https://
   www.lemonde.fr/societe/article/2024/07/09/le-militant-panafricaniste
   -kemi-seba-dechu-de-la-nationalite-francaise_6248233_3224.html.
Le Monde, 'Le «panafricaniste» Kemi Seba soupçonné de liens avec le
   groupe paramilitaire russe Wagner', *Le Monde*, 18 October 2024. https://
   www.lemonde.fr/afrique/article/2024/10/18/le-panafricaniste-kemi
   -seba-soupconne-de-liens-avec-le-groupe-paramilitaire-russe-wagner
   _6355265_3212.html.
Lewis, Nathan, 'BRICS Making Good Progress On Their Golden Path',
   Forbes, 24 January 2024. https://www.forbes.com/sites/nathanlewis/2024
   /01/24/brics-making-good-progress-on-their-golden-path/.
Liu, Zongyuan Zoe and Mihaela Papa, *Can BRICS De-dollarize the Global
   Financial System?* (Cambridge: Cambridge University Press, 2022),
   5.1. https://www.cambridge.org/core/elements/can-brics-dedollarize
   -the-global-financial-system/0AEF98D2F232072409E9556620AE09B0
   ?utm_campaign=shareaholic&utm_medium=copy_link&utm_source
   =bookmark.
Maasho, Aaron, 'UAE to Give Ethiopia $3 Billion in Aid and Investments',
   Reuters, 16 June 2018. https://www.reuters.com/article/business
   /finance/uae-to-give-ethiopia-3-billion-in-aid-and-investments
   -idUSL8N1TH4GJ/.
Mackintosh, Eliza, 'An Ethiopian Professor Was Murdered by a Mob. A
   Lawsuit Alleges Facebook Fueled the Violence', *CNN*, 14 December 2022.
   https://edition.cnn.com/2022/12/14/tech/ethiopia-murdered-professor
   -lawsuit-meta-kenya-intl/index.html.

Mackintosh, Eliza, 'From Nobel Laureate to Global Pariah: How the World Got Abiy Ahmed and Ethiopia So Wrong', *CNN*, 5 November 2021. https://edition.cnn.com/2021/09/07/africa/abiy-ahmed-ethiopia-tigray -conflict-cmd-intl/index.html.

Maglov, Mikhaïl, Timur Olevsky and Dmitry Treshchanin, 'ЧАСТЬ 4. ТАЙНОЕ ЗАВОЕВАНИЕ АФРИКИ', *Current Time TV*, 26 February 2019. https://www.currenttime.tv/a/yevgeny-prigozhin-investigation -chapter-4/29789953.html

Manek, Nizar, 'Eritrea Mulls Port as Ethiopia Rapprochement Spurs Investors', *Bloomberg*, 23 August 2018. https://www.bloomberg .com/news/articles/2018-08-23/eritrea-mulls-new-port-as-ethiopia -rapprochement-spurs-investors.

Manly, Ronan, 'Chinese Central Bank Accumulating Gold Again', *Bullionstar*, 11 January 2023. https://www.bullionstar.com/blogs/ ronan-manly/chinese-central-bank-kicks-off-new-round-of-gold -accumulation/.

Marcus, Kenneth L., 'Accusation in a Mirror', *Loyola University Chicago Law Journal* 43/2 (2012).

Marks, Simon, 'Ethiopian Opposition, Prime Minister Accuse Each Other of Power Grab', *Voice of America*, 8 May 2020. https://www.voanews .com/a/africa_ethiopian-opposition-prime-minister-accuse-each-other -power-grab/6188969.html.

Marrow, Alexander and Mark Trevelyan, 'Russia, Hit by New US Sanctions, Halts Dollar and Euro Trade on Main Bourse', *Reuters*, 12 June 2024. https://www.reuters.com/markets/europe/moscow-exchange-stop -trading-dollars-after-latest-us-sanctions-2024-06-12/.

Maruf, Harun and Dan Joseph, *Inside Al-Shabaab. The Secret History of Al-Qaeda's Most Powerful Ally* (Bloomington, IN: Indiana University Press, 2018).

McGlynn, Jade, 'Moscow Is Using Memory Diplomacy to Export Its Narrative to the World', *Foreign Policy*, 25 June 2021. https:// foreignpolicy.com/2021/06/25/russia-puting-ww2-soviet-ussr-memory -diplomacy-history-narrative/.

McMullen, Ronald K., 'Chinese Mining Woes in Eritrea', 25 June 2009, Wikileaks: 09ASMARA195_a.

McMullen, Ronald K., 'Chinese Move into Eritrea's Mining Sector', 6 August 2008, Wikileaks: 08ASMARA385_a.

McMullen, Ronald K., 'Eritrea: German banks Bailing on Bisha', 2 November 2009, Wikileaks:09ASMARA378_a.

McMullen, Ronald K., 'Eritrea – Major Australian gold strike', 7 May 2008, Wikileaks: 08ASMARA248_a.

McMullen, Ronald K., 'One Gold Mine Moving Forward', 10 November 2008, Wikileaks: 08ASMARA541_a.

McMullen, Ronald K., 'Sanu Resources' Mining Prospects', 9 May 2008, Wikileaks: 08ASMARA252_a.

McMullen, Ronald K., 'Sunridge Strikes Gold Near Asmara', 13 June 2008, Wikileaks: 08ASMARA317_a.

Melicherová, Kristina, Mirjam van Reisen and Daniel Tesfa, '"Game Over": Key Markers of the Tigray War in Redefining the Region', in *Tigray. The Hysteresis of War*, Book 1, ed. Mirjam van Reisen and Munyaradzi Mawere (Bamenda, Cameroon: Langaa Research & Publishing CIG, 2024), 41–95 (55–56). https://www.researchgate.net/publication/385300576_Game_Over_Key_Markers_of_the_Tigray_War_in__Redefining_the_Region.

Meservey, Joshua, 'Eritrea's Growing Ties with China and Russia Highlight America's Inadequate Approach in East Africa', *Hudson Institute*, 17 July 2023. https://www.hudson.org/foreign-policy/eritreas-growing-ties-china-russia-highlight-americas-inadequate-approach-east-joshua-meservey.

Mining Journal, 'Alpha Exploration Explores "Last Frontier" in Eritrea', *Mining Journal*, 12 January 2022, 4. https://www.mining-journal.com/resourcestocks/resourcestocks/4072915/alpha-exploration-explores-last-frontier-eritrea.

Mining Journal, 'Asmara Copper-Zinc-Gold-Silver Project', *Mining Technology*, 29 June 2015. https://www.mining-technology.com/projects/asmara-copper-zinc-gold-silver-project/.

Mining Journal, 'Eritrea Awards Three Mining Licences to Asmara Mining', *Mining Technology*, 19 October 2015. https://www.mining-technology.com/marketdata/newseritrea-awards-three-mining-licences-asmara-mining-4697921/.

Ministry of Foreign Affairs of the Russian Federation, 'Russian Ambassador to Eritrea H.E. Mr. Igor N. Mozgo held a meeting with the heads of diplomatic missions of Egypt, Yemen, Qatar and Libya', 29 March 2024. https://mid.ru/tv/?id=1806973&lang=en.

Ministry of Information of Eritrea, *Keynote Address by President Isaias Afwerki on the Occasion of the 33rd Independence Anniversary*, Asmara, 24 May 2024. https://shabait.com/amp/2024/05/24/keynote-address-by-president-isaias-afwerki-on-the-occasion-of-the-33rd-independence-anniversary-asmara-24-may-2024/.

Ministry of Information of Eritrea, 'Leaders of Eritrea and Ethiopia receive Saudi Arabia's highest Honour', *TesfaNews*, 16 September 2018. https://tesfanews.com/eritrea-ethiopia-leaders-received-saudi-arabia-highest-award/.

Ministry of Information of Eritrea, 'President Isaias' Speech on Martyrs Day', *Shabait*, 20 June 2018. https://shabait.com/2018/06/20/president-isaias-speech-on-martyrs-day/

Ministry of Information of Eritrea, 'Q&A with Mr. Todd Romaine, Vice President Corporate Social Responsibility, Nevsun Resources', *Shabait*, 21 September 2015. https://shabait.com/2015/09/21/qaa-with-mr-todd-romaine-vice-president-corporate-social-responsibility-nevsun-resources/.

Ministry of Information of Eritrea, 'Saudi Coalition Forces Commander Met Eritrea President', *TesfaNews*, 6 August 2019. https://tesfanews.com/saudi-anti-terrorism-coalition-forces-commander-meet-eritrea-president/.

Monnier, Olivier, 'Or : les compagnies minières canadiennes à l'assaut de l'Afrique de l'Ouest', *Jeune Afrique*, 7 January 2019. https://www.jeuneafrique.com/mag/692474/economie-entreprises/or-les-compagnies-minieres-a-lassaut-de-lafrique-de-louest/#:~:text=Young.,-Nous%20nous%20attendons&text=TGC%20vise%20cette%20ann%C3%A9e%20une,soci%C3%A9t%C3%A9%20atteindrait%20350%20000%20onces.

The National, 'The UAE Alchemist Who Turned Fields of Scrap into a Factory of Gold', *The National*, 7 April 2013. https://www.thenationalnews.com/business/the-uae-alchemist-%20who-turned-fields-of-scrap-into-a-factory-of-gold-%201.305887

Negash, Tekeste, *The Rise of Aksum and the Decline of Meroe: Trade, War, and Diplomacy in Ancient Northeast Africa* (New York: Routledge, 2018).

New Africa Institute, *Disinformation in Tigray: Manufacturing Consent for a Secessionist War*, 9 May 2021. Debunking of this report in: DFRLab, 'Eritrean Report Uses Fact-Checking Tropes to Dismiss Evidence as "Disinformation"', 23 juin 2021. https://medium.com/dfrlab/eritrean-report-uses-fact-checking-tropes-to-dismiss-evidence-as-disinformation-385718327481.

Nyssen, Jan, Tesfaalem Ghebreyohannes, Emnet Negash, Hailemariam Meaza, Zbelo Tesfamariam, Amaury Frankl, Kiara Haegeman, Bert Van Schaeybroeck, Alem Redda, Fetien Abay, Sofie Annys and Biadgilgn Demissie, 'Impact of the Tigray War on Farming: Plight and Resilience', in *Tigray. War in a Digital Black Hole*, Book 1, ed. Mirjam van Reisen and Munyaradzi Mawere (Bamenda, Cameroon: Langaa Research & Publishing CIG, 2024), 145–72. https://www.researchgate.net/publication/385417372_Impact_of_the_Tigray_War_on_Farming_Plight_and_Resilience.

Osborn, Lou and Dimitri Zufferey, *Wagner. Enquête au cœur du système Prigojine* (Paris: Éditions du Faubourg, 2023).

Osman, Fathi, 'Sudan: As the Generals Fight, Who's Playing Chess with the Old Islamists?', *African Arguments*, 15 mai 2023. https://africanarguments.org/2023/05/sudan-as-the-generals-fight-whos-playing-chess-with-the-old-islamists/.

Overseas Development Institute, *UK Approach to Eritrean Refugees: What is the Reality on the Ground?*, 2 November 2016. https://odi.org/en/events/uk-approach-to-eritrean-refugees-what-is-the-reality-on-the-ground/.

Palacios-Arapiles, Sara, 'Enslaved by their Own Government: Indefinite National Service in Eritrea', *Enslaved Trapped and Trafficked in Digital Black Holes: Human Trafficking Trajectories to Libya*, ed. Mirjam van Reisen, Munyaradzi Mawere, Klara Smits, Wirtz, M. (Bamenda, Cameroon: Langaa Research & Publishing CIG, 2023), 195-254. https://www.researchgate.net/publication/367254851_Enslaved_Trapped_and_Trafficked_in_Digital_Black_Holes_Human_Trafficking_Trajectories_to_Libya.

Para, Cristian and Prathivadi B. Anand, 'Analysis of the Potential Contributions of Colluli Potash Project to Sustainable Development Goals in Eritrea', *UNDP*, January 2019. https://www.undp.org/eritrea/publications/undp-eritrea-analysis-potential-contributions-colluli-potash-project-sustainable-development-goals-eritrea.

Permanent Court of Arbitration, *Eritrea-Ethiopia Boundary Commission*, 30 November 2007. https://pca-cpa.org/en/cases/99/.

Permanent Mission of the Russian Federation to the United Nations, 'Statement by Deputy Permanent Representative Anna Evstigneeva at UNSC Briefing on the Situation in Sudan', 25 April 2023. https://russiaun.ru/en/news/250423_evst.

Pisitili, Melissa, 'How Would a New BRICS Currency Affect the US Dollar?', *Nasdaq*, 8 July 2024. https://www.nasdaq.com/articles/how-would-new-brics-currency-affect-us-dollar-updated-2024.

Plaut, Martin and Sarah Vaughan, *Understanding Ethiopia's Tigray War* (London: Hurst and Company, 2023).

Poole, Amanda, 'Ransoms, Remittances, and Refugees: The Gatekeeper State in Eritrea', *Postliberation Eritrea*, Indiana University, 2018. https://iu.pressbooks.pub/postliberationeritrea/chapter/ransoms-remittances-and-refugees-the-gatekeeper-state-in-eritrea/.

Poole, James and Laura Millan, 'Nevsun Finds a White Knight in Zijin With $1.41 Billion Deal', *Bloomberg*, 5 September 2018. https://www.bloomberg.com/news/articles/2018-09-05/zijin-mining-to-buy-nevsun-resources-for-1-41-billion-in-cash.

President of Russia, 'Meeting with President of Eritrea Isaias Afwerki', 28 July 2023. http://en.kremlin.ru/events/president/news/71830.

President of Russia, *Russia-Africa Summit*, 28 July 2023. http://en.kremlin.ru/events/president/news/71826.

The Proekt Team, 'Master and Chef. How Russia Interfered in Elections in Twenty Countries', 11 April 2019. https://www.proekt.media/en/article-en/russia-african-elections/.

Radio Dabanga, 'Coup Critics Condemn Sudan Deputy's Visit to Russia', *Radio Dabanga*, 1 March 2022. https://www.dabangasudan.org/en/all-news/article/coup-critics-condemn-sudan-deputy-s-visit-to-russia.

Radio Dabanga, 'Hemeti Visits Eritrea to Discuss Bilateral Relations But Also to "Weave RSF Alliances"', *Radio Dabanga*, 14 March 2023. https://www.dabangasudan.org/en/all-news/article/hemeti-visits-eritrea-to-discuss-bilateral-relations-but-also-to-weave-rsf-alliances

Radio Dabanga, 'Sudan Confirms Agreements with Russia for Naval Base in Red Sea. Previous Deal Allowed Russia to Keep Up to Four Navy Ships Including Nuclear Powered Ones', *Radio Dabanga*, 29 May 2024. https://www.dabangasudan.org/en/all-news/article/sudan-general-confirms-red-sea-base-deal-with-russia-strengthens-ties-with-iran.

Radio Dabanga, '1,000 Sudanese Militiamen Arrive in Libya', *Radio Dabanga*, 25 July 2019. https://www.dabangasudan.org/en/all-news/article/1-000-sudanese-militiamen-arrive-in-libya.

Radio Télévision Suisse, 'Nathalie Yamb, une Suissesse influenceuse de Poutine ?', *Temps Présent*, 23 March 2023. https://www.rts.ch/emissions/temps-present/2023/video/nathalie-yamb-une-suissesse-influenceuse-de-poutine-avion-contre-oiseau-attention-danger-26905125.html.

Ramani, Samuel, 'As Fighting in Sudan Rages, Russia's Primary Goal is to Ensure Authoritarian Rule', *Middle East Institute*, 3 May 2023. https://mei.edu/publications/fighting-sudan-rages-russias-primary-goal-ensure-authoritarian-rule.

'Rape Culture in Tigray Region of Ethiopia', *Radio Révolution Panafricaine*, 17 April 2021. https://www.radiorevolutionpanafricaine.com/single-post/rape-culture-in-tigray-region-of-ethiopia?fbclid=IwAR2G8XqJ4NHa8 9EOdo7nZYwKaDN3GSbFgsD92Nn3V10CdrjI8SO_9k1xGz4.

Reisen, Mirjam van and Meron Estefanos, 'The Exodus from Eritrea and Who is Benefiting', in *Human Trafficking and Trauma in the Digital Era: The Ongoing Tragedy of the Trade in Refugees from Eritrea*, ed. Mirjam van Reisen and Munyaradzi Mawere (Bamenda, Cameroon: Langaa Research & Publishing CIG, 2017), 95–192. https://www.researchgate.net/publication/316989834_Human_Trafficking_and_Trauma_in_the_Digital_Era_The_Ongoing_Tragedy_of_the_Trade_in_Refugees_from_Eritrea.

Reisen, Mirjam van, Meron Estefanos and Lena Reim, 'Human Trafficking in the Sinai: Mapping the Routes and Facilitators', in *Human Trafficking and Trauma in the Digital Era: The Ongoing Tragedy of the Trade in*

Refugees from Eritrea, ed. Mirjam van Reisen and Munyaradzi Mawere (Bamenda, Cameroon: Langaa Research & Publishing CIG, 2017), 19–94.

Reisen, Mirjam van, Makeda Saba and Klara Smits, '"Sons of Isaias": Slavery and Indefinite National Service in Eritrea', in *Mobile Africa: Human Trafficking and the Digital Divide*, ed. Mirjam van Reisen and Munyaradzi Mawere (Bamenda, Cameroon: Langaa Research & Publishing CIG, 2019), 115–75. https://www.researchgate.net/ publication/336956190_Mobile_Africa_Human_Trafficking_and_the _Digital_Divide.

Reuters, 'Nevsun Resources to Buy Reservoir Minerals for $365 Million', *Reuters*, 25 April 2016. https://www.reuters.com/article/business /nevsun-resources-to-buy-reservoir-minerals-for-365-million -idUSKCN0XM04Y/.

Reuters, 'No African Red Carpet for King of Kings', *Reuters*, 8 March 2011. https://www.reuters.com/article/world/africa/no-african-red-carpet-for -king-of-kings-idUSLDE72717K/.

Reuters, 'U.N. Chief Says Sanctions on Eritrea Likely to Become Obsolete', *Reuters*, 9 July 2018. https://www.reuters.com/article/ world/u-n-chief-says-sanctions-on-eritrea-likely-to-become-obsolete -idUSKBN1JZ1UG/.

RFI, 'Libye: Khalifa Haftar, son fils Saddam et le trafic d'or', *RFI*, 10 October 2020. https://www.rfi.fr/fr/afrique/20201010-libye-fils-haftar-trafic-or -turquie-emirats-arabes-unis.

Rickett, Oscar, 'How the UAE Kept the Sudan War Raging', African Arguments, 21 février 2024. https://africanarguments.org/2024/02/how -the-uae-kept-the-sudan-war-raging/.

Rivista Africa, 'Eritrea, quell'alleanza di ferro con l'Arabia Saudita', *Rivista Africa*, 9 August 2019. https://www.africarivista.it/eritrea-quellalleanza -di-ferro-con-larabia-saudita/144503/.

Roger, Benjamin, '"Projet Kemi" : quand Evgueni Prigojine finançait Kemi Seba pour servir ses ambitions africaines', *Jeune Afrique*, 30 March 2023. https://www.jeuneafrique.com/1431514/politique/projet-kemi-quand -evgueni-prigojine-financait-kemi-seba-pour-servir-ses-ambitions -africaines/.

Saaida, Mohammed, 'BRICS Plus: De-dollarization and Global Power
	Shifts in New Economic Landscape', *BRICS Journal of Economics* 5:1
	(April 2024): 13–33 (19–24). https://doi.org/10.3897/brics-econ.5
	.e117828.

Saba, Makeda, 'Uncomfortable aid: INGOs in Eritrea', in *Mobile Africa:
	Human Trafficking and the Digital Divide*, ed. Mijam van Reisen,
	Munyaradzi Mawere, Mia Stokmans and Kinfe Abraha Gebre-Egziabher
	(Bamenda, Cameroon: Langaa Research & Publishing CIG, 2019),
	631–72: www.researchgate.net/publication/336956190_Mobile_Africa
	_Human_Trafficking_and_the_Digital_Divide.

Sandhu, Ruby, 'The Distorted Narrative, Media War and Eritrea's Culture
	of Silence', *Tesfanews*, 29 April 2016. https://tesfanews.com/distorted
	-narrative-media-war-eritreas-silence-culture-i/.

Sandhu, Ruby, 'Non-conformist Eritrea', *YoungPFDJ (YPFDJ)*, 18 April
	2018. https://youngpfdj.wordpress.com/2018/04/13/non-conformist
	-eritrea/.

Saudi Press Agency, 'Foreign Minister: The Council of Arab and African
	Coastal States of the Red Sea and the Gulf of Aden is a Joint Action
	System for Coordination and Cooperation', *Saudi Press Agency*, 6 January
	2020. https://www.spa.gov.sa/2019804.

Saywell, Trish, 'Sun Peak Advances Shire Polymetallic Project in Ethiopia',
	The Northern Miner, 21 August 2020. https://northernminer.com/news/
	sun-peak-metals-advances-shire-project-in-ethiopia/1003821192/.

Schmidt, Peter R., Matthew Curtis and Zelalem Teka, *The Archaeology
	of Ancient Eritrea* (Champaign, IL: University of Illinois Press, 2008),
	151–78.

Schweizer Radio und Fernsehen, 'Gold-Deal Mit Eritrea', *Rundschau*, 30
	August 2017. https://www.srf.ch/play/tv/rundschau/video/gold-deal-mit
	-eritrea?urn=urn:srf:video:a7f475ef-f9e9-44ba-85ce-a4e330a5d0ac.

Senet, *Asmara Project Feasibility Study NI 43-101 Technical Report*, 16 May
	2013. https://minedocs.com/12/Asmara_Feasibility_Sunridge_Corp.pdf.

Sguazzin, Antony, 'Why is Abiy Threatening Ethiopia's Neighbors?: Next
	Africa', *Bloomsberg*, 20 October 2023. https://www.bloomberg.com/
	news/newsletters/2023-10-20/why-is-ethiopia-s-abiy-ahmed-demanding
	-access-to-the-sea.

Shaebia, 'Mining in Eritrea', *Shaebia*, 10 mars 2006. https://web.archive.org /web/20060929110505/http://www.shaebia.org/artman/publish/article _4440.html.

Sharife, Khadija, Lara Dihmis, 3Ayin and Erin Klazar, 'Documents Reveal Wagner's Golden Ties to Sudanese Military Companies', *Organized Crime and Corruption Reporting Project*, 2 November 2022. https://www .occrp.org/en/investigation/documents-reveal-wagners-golden-ties-to -sudanese-military-companies.

Simon, Bartolomé and Nicolas Quénel, 'Ce marchand d'influence russe qui formait de futurs journalistes français', *Le Point*, 22 February 2024. https://www.lepoint.fr/societe/ce-marchand-d-influence-russe-qui -formait-les-futurs-journalistes-francais-22-02-2024-2553171_23.php.

Smits, Klara, '"You Are the Ball – They Are the Players": The Human Traffickers of Eritreans in Libya', in *Enslaved, Trapped and Trafficked in Digital Black Holes: Human Trafficking Trajectories to Libya*, ed. Mirjam van Reisen, Munyaradzi Mawere, Klara Smits and Morgane Wirtz (Bamenda, Cameroon: Langaa RCPIG, 2023), 451–520 (503–5). https:// www.researchgate.net/publication/367254851_Enslaved_Trapped_and _Trafficked_in_Digital_Black_Holes_Human_Trafficking_Trajectories _to_Libya.

Soliman, Ahmed, 'Fighting Over "White Gold": Sesame in Ethiopia and Sudan', *Chatham House*, 4 April 2023. https://www.chathamhouse.org /2023/04/fighting-over-white-gold-sesame-ethiopia-and-sudan.

Solomon, Salem, 'Observers See Several Motives for Eritrean Involvement in Yemen', *Voice of America*, 9 January 2016. https://www.voanews.com /a/observers-see-several-motives-eritrean-involvement-yemen/3138689 .html.

The Soufan Center, 'IntelBrief: Libyan Warlord Exploits Sudan Crisis', *The Soufan Center*, 23 May 2023. https://thesoufancenter.org/intelbrief-2023 -may-23/.

South Boulder Mines LTD, *Potash for Produce*, November 2014. https:// www.bus-ex.com/article/south-boulder-mines.

Stack, Graham, 'Five Cyprus Golden Passport Holders Sanctioned for Russian Arms Trading', *Organized Crime and Corruption Reporting Project*, 7 February 2023. https://www.occrp.org/en/daily/17298

-five-cyprus-golden-passports-holders-sanctioned-for-russian-arms
-trading.

Steyn, Elisabeth, 'Slavery Charges against Canadian Mining Company
Settled on the Sly', 26 October 2020. https://theconversation.com/slavery
-charges-against-canadian-mining-company-settled-on-the-sly-148605.

Stratfor Worldviews, 'The UAE Joins an Exclusive Club', 8 December 2016.
https://worldview.stratfor.com/article/uae-joins-exclusive-club.

Stricot, Matthieu, 'A New Currency to Dethrone the Dollar?', *CNRS Le
Journal*, 19 February 2024. https://news.cnrs.fr/articles/a-new-currency
-to-dethrone-the-dollar.

Sudan Tribune, 'Afwerki, Hemetti Discuss Eritrean Sudanese Relations',
Sudan Tribune, 13 March 2023. https://sudantribune.com/article271830/

Sudan Tribune, 'Ethiopian Militias Invade Sudanese Territory, Escalating
Violence and Looting', *Sudan Tribune*, 24 June 2024. https://
sudantribune.com/article287372/.

Sudan Tribune, 'Sudanese Authorities Arrest Ethiopian Female Snipers',
Sudan Tribune, 20 June 2024. https://sudantribune.com/article287249/.

Sun Peak Metals Corp., *2024 News Releases. Sun Peak Metals Provides
Corporate Update – Exploration Work Expected to Resume on Shire
Project*, 7 February 2014. https://sunpeakmetals.com/news/sun-peak
-metals-provides-corporate-update-exploration-work-expected-to
-resume-on-shire-project/?fbclid=IwAR1qBw7xydS0hnqPLNsnn
BlomY9qg9_VZqLyGaYTG8D1I6Fwq2mUBaucWKs.

Sunridge Gold Corp, 'Sunridge Agrees To Sell Its 60% Interest in Asmara
Mining Share Company', *Accesswire Company Update*, 6 November
2015. https://www.accesswire.com/433367/sunridge-agrees-to-sell-its-60
-interest-in-asmara-mining-share-company.

Supreme Court of Canada, *Bulletin of Proceedings*, 29 March 2018, 358–87.
https://publications.gc.ca/collections/collection_2018/csc-scc/JU8-1
-2018-3-29.pdf.

Supreme Court of Canada, *Case in Brief: Nevsun Resources Ltd. v. Araya*,
28 February 2020. https://decisions.scc-csc.ca/scc-csc/scc-csc/en/item
/18169/index.do.

Tabler-Stone, Melinda, 'Bisha Mining's Remaining Challenges', 7 October
2008, Wikileaks: 08ASMARA490_a.

Tabler-Stone, Melinda, 'Mine Workers Killed in Attack in Eritrea', 8 October 2009, Wikileaks: 09ASMARA350_a.

Tabler-Stone, Melinda, 'The Mining Murder: An Insider Perspective', 14 October 2009, Wikileaks: 09ASMARA354_a.

Tacchini, Emanuele, 'New Perspectives on Meroitic-Axumite Relations: Archaeological Evidence and Historical Interpretations', *African Archaeological Review* 39/3 (2022): 275–95.

TASS Russian News Agency, 'Eritrea Supports Russia's Active Presence in Africa — Russian Ambassador', 11 June 2024. https://tass.com/politics/1802057.

TASS Russian News Agency, 'Kremlin Announces Creation of Blockchain-Based Payment System in BRICS', *TASS Russian News Agency*, 5 March 2024. https://tass.com/politics/1755521.

TASS Russian News Agency, 'Посол РФ заявил, что Эритрея выступает за активное присутствие России в Африке', *TASS Russian News Agency*, 11 June 2024. https://tass.ru/politika/21065909.

TASS Russian News Agency, 'Russian Ambassador Lauds Intensified Relations with Eritrea', *TASS Russian News Agency*, 11 June 2024. https://tass.com/politics/1802031.

Tesfa, Daniel and Mirjam Van Reisen, '"Cannibals", "Daytime Hyenas", and "Not a Human Race" – "Woyane": The Semiotic Landscape of the Martyrs' Commemoration Museum', in *Tigray. The Panarchy of War*, Book 1, ed. Mirjam van Reisen and Munyaradzi Mawere (Bamenda, Cameroon: Langaa Research & Publishing CIG, 2024), 101–44. https://www.researchgate.net/publication/385406954_'Cannibals'_'Daytime_Hyenas'_and_'Not_a_Human_Race'_-_'Woyane'_The_Semiotic_Landscape_of_the_Martyrs'_Commemoration_Museum.

Tesfa, Daniel and Mirjam Van Reisen, 'Negative Stereotyping, Creation of a Threat, and Incitement to Genocide: Discourse Analysis of Hatespeech Disseminated in the Tigray War', in *Tigray. The Panarchy of War*, Book 1, ed. Mirjam van Reisen and Munyaradzi Mawere (Bamenda, Cameroon: Langaa Research & Publishing CIG, 2024), 145–85. https://www.researchgate.net/publication/385451336_Negative_Stereotyping_Creation_of_a_Threat_and_Incitement_to_Genocide_Discourse_Analysis_of_Hate-speech_Disseminated_in_the_Tigray_War.

     Bibliography

Tesfa, Daniel and Mirjam Van Reisen, 'Regional War by Design: The involvement of Eritrea in the Tigray War', in *Tigray. The Hysteresis of War*, Book 1, ed. Mirjam van Reisen and Munyaradzi Mawere (Bamenda, Cameroon: Langaa Research & Publishing CIG, 2024), 141–90. https://www.researchgate.net/publication/385202452_Tigray _The_Hysteresis_of_War_Book_1#pfb0.

Tesfa, Daniel, Mirjam van Reisen and Klara Smits, 'A Secret Deal to Conceal: The Eritrean Involvement in the Tigray War', in *Tigray. The Panarchy of War*, Book 1, ed. Mirjam van Reisen and Munyaradzi Mawere (Bamenda, Cameroon: Langaa Research & Publishing CIG, 2024), 53–100. https://www.researchgate.net/publication/385394550_A _Secret_Deal_to_Conceal_The_Eritrean_Involvement_in_the_Tigray _War.

Tesfagorgis, Petros, Habte Hagos, Abraham Zere and Daniel Mekonnen, 'Mining and Repression in Eritrea: Corporate Complicity in Human Rights Abuses', *Eritrea Focus* (June 2018): 9–12. https://eritrea-focus.org/ wp-content/uploads/2018/06/Mining-Repression-Eritrea-V1.pdf.

TesfaNews, 'President El-Sisi Meets President of Eritrea Afwerki', *TesfaNews*, 12 November 2023. https://tesfanews.com/president-el-sisi-meets -president-afwerki-in-riyadh/.

TesfaNews, 'President of Eritrea is as Unique as His Country', *TesfaNews*, 13 May 2013. https://tesfanews.com/afwerqi-as-unique-as-his -country/.

Touati, Charlotte, 'A "Kerygma of Peter" behind the Apocalypse of Peter, the Pseudo- Clementine Romance and the Eclogae Propheticae of Clement of Alexandria', *Studia patristica* LXV (2013) ed. Markus Vinzent (Leuven, Paris, Walpole (Mass.): Peeters, 2013), 277–92. https://libra.unine.ch/ entities/publication/3fe63ca2-d70f-4f18-b561-e7fd48f43516/details.

Touati, Charlotte, 'Le Purgatoire dans les littératures d'Égypte et d'Afrique du Nord (Ier-IVe s. ap. J.-C.)' (PhD diss., Institute of History, Faculty of Humanities, University of Neuchâtel, 2012).

Touati, Charlotte, 'L'Allégorisation de la guerre sainte', *Revue de l'Histoire des Religions* 227/2 (2010): 231–47. https://doi.org/10.4000/rhr.7579.

Touati, Charlotte, 'Mining: A Good Vein for Lobbyists ?', *The Ethiopia Cable* 77(28 April-4 May 2022), 1.

Tronvoll, Kjetil and Daniel Mekonnen, *The African Garrison State. Human Rights and political development in Eritrea* (Woodbridge: James Currey, 2014), 165–83.

TV5Monde, 'Nathalie Yamb, L'activiste qui se rêve comme le "cauchemar" de la France', *TV5Monde*, 2 November 2022. https://information .tv5monde.com/afrique/nathalie-yamb-lactiviste-qui-se-reve-comme-le -cauchemar-de-la-france-1412317.

Ummel, Marc, 'Beneath the Shine. A Tale of Two Gold Refiners', *Global Witness*, July 2020. https://www.globalwitness.org/en/campaigns/conflict -minerals/beneath-shine-tale-two-gold-refiners/.

Ummel, Marc, 'Golden Detour. The Hidden Face of the Gold Trade between the United Arab Emirates and Switzerland', *Swissaid*, July 2020. https://swissaid.kinsta.cloud/wp-content/uploads/2020/07/SWISSAID -Goldstudie-EN_final-web.pdf.

UNHRC, *Detailed Findings of the Commission of Inquiry on Human Rights in Eritrea*, 8 June 2016, 50–8 (56–7). https://www.ohchr.org/sites/default /files/Documents/HRBodies/HRCouncil/CoIEritrea/A_HRC_32_CRP .1_read-only.pdf.

UNHRC, *Report of the Detailed Findings of the Commission of Inquiry on Human Rights in Eritrea*, 5 June 2015. https://www.refworld.org/docid /55758bab4.html.

United States Department of State, *U.S. Department of State Country Report on Human Rights Practices 2003 – Eritrea*, 25 February 2004. https:// www.refworld.org/docid/403f57b010.html.

UNODC, *'We Don't Ask Questions': Hawala Payment System Vulnerable to Use by Organized Crime Groups, Including Opiate Traffickers and Migrant Smugglers* , Vienne, 11 September 2023. https://www.unodc.org/unodc/ en/frontpage/2023/September/we-dont-ask-questions_-hawala-payment -system-vulnerable-to-use-by-organized-crime-groups--including-opiate -traffickers-and-migrant-smugglers.html.

US Department of State, 'Yevgeniy Prigozhin's Africa-Wide Disinformation Campaign', 4 November 2022. https://www.state.gov/disarming -disinformation/yevgeniy-prigozhins-africa-wide-disinformation -campaign/.

US Department of State, the Treasury, Labor, Commerce, and Homeland Security, the United States Agency for International Development, *Africa Gold Advisory*, 27 June 2023. https://ofac.treasury.gov/system/files/2023-06/africa_gold_advisory_06272023.pdf.

US Department of the Treasury, 'Russia-related Designations; Counter Narcotics Designation Update', 1 February 2023. https://ofac.treasury.gov/recent-actions/20230201.

US Department of the Treasury, 'Treasury Escalates Sanctions Against the Russian Government's Attempts to Influence U.S. Elections', *Press release*, 15 April 2021. https://home.treasury.gov/news/press-releases/jy0126.

US Department of the Treasury, 'Treasury Sanctions Military-Affiliated Companies Fueling Both Sides of the Conflict in Sudan', *Press Release*, 1 June 2023. https://home.treasury.gov/news/press-releases/jy1514.

US Department of the Treasury, 'Treasury Targets Financier's Illicit Sanctions Evasion Activity', *Press Release*, 15 July 2020. https://home.treasury.gov/news/press-releases/sm1058.

US Department of the Treasury, 'Treasury Targets Global Sanctions Evasion Network Supporting Russia's Military-Industrial Complex', 1 February 2023. https://home.treasury.gov/news/press-releases/jy1241.

Vincent, Léonard, 'Canada: le procès d'une compagnie minière pour "esclavage" en Érythrée n'aura pas lieu', 13 October 2020. https://www.rfi.fr/fr/afrique/20201013-canada-le-proc%C3%A8s-d-une-compagnie-mini%C3%A8re-esclavage-en-%C3%A9rythr%C3%A9e-n-aura-pas-lieu?fbclid=IwAR2UMF3rY6MygiS6lkr6KQGscit2EbmrOLDB_5M7hMw5Gx7OYHscDr1_A6Q&ref=fb.

Vincent, Léonard, *Les Erythréens* (Paris: Rivages, 2012).

Vincent, Léonard and Martin Plaut, 'Who Are Eritrea's Foreign Friends?', *Martin Plaut*, 26 June 2017. https://martinplaut.com/2017/06/26/who-are-eritreas-foreign-friends/.

Walton, Beatrice A., 'Nevsun Resources Ltd. v. Araya', *American Journal of International Law* 115/1 (2021): 107–14. https://doi.org/10.1017/ajil.2020.103

Weiss, Michael and Pierre Vaux, 'Russia is Using Undercover Racists to Exploit Africa's Anti-racist Political Revolt', *Daily Beast*, 8 September

2020. https://www.thedailybeast.com/prigozhin-is-using-afric-to-exploit
-africas-anti-colonial-political-revolt.

Weldemichael, Awet Tewelde, *Third World Colonialism and Strategies of Liberation. Eritrea and East Timor Compared* (Cambridge: Cambridge University Press, 2012).

West Africa Newsletter, 'Alasdair Smith Strikes for Gold Again', *Africa Intelligence*, 27 March 2018.

West Africa Newsletter, 'Nevsun Escapes Asmara's Military Creditor', *Africa Intelligence*, 3 October 2017.

West Africa Newsletter, 'Qiu Xuejung Indulges in a Bit of Mining Diplomacy', *Africa Intelligence*, 5 May 2016.

West Africa Newsletter, 'South Boulder under Pressure in Eritrea', *Africa Intelligence*, 29 July 2014.

Wilmot, Claire, Ellen Tveteraas and Alexi Drew, 'Duelling Information Campaigns: The War over the Narrative on Tigray', *The Media Manipulation Casebook*, 20 août 2021. https://mediamanipulation.org/
case-studies/dueling-information-campaigns-war-over-narrative-tigray
#footnote2_q179gxh.

Wisner, Robert, 'Supreme Court of Canada Opens the Door to Novel International Human Rights Claims: The Uncertain Implications for Canadian Resource Companies', *McMillan Litigation Bulletin*, March 2020. https://mcmillan.ca/insights/supreme-court-of-canada-opens
-the-door-to-novel-international-human-rights-claims-the-uncertain
-implications-for-canadian-resource-companies/.

Woldemariam, Michael, 'The Making of an African "Pariah": Eritrea in the International System', *Postliberation Eritrea*, Indiana University, 2018. https://iu.pressbooks.pub/postliberationeritrea/chapter/the-making-of
-an-african-pariah-eritrea-in-the-international-system/.

World Peace Foundation, '"They Have Destroyed Tigray, Literally": Mulugeta Gebrehiwot Speaks from the Mountains of Tigray', *World Peace Foundation*, 29 janvier 2021. https://worldpeacefoundation.org/
blog/they-have-destroyed-tigray-literally-mulugeta-gebrehiwot-speaks
-from-the-mountains-of-tigray/.

Xinhua, 'Chinese Company Opens Massive Eco-Friendly Mine in Serbia', *Xinhua*, 25 October 2021. http://www.china-ceec.org/eng/sbhz_1 /202110/t20211029_10403551.htm.

Yan, Li, 'China's First High-Capacity Sodium-Ion Battery Storage Station is Launched', *China News Service*, 13 May 2024. https://www.ecns.cn/ business/2024-05-13/detail-iheamvqc7118696.shtml.

Yenealem, Fasil, 'ዛሬ ሚኒስጢር ቢወጣ ችግር የለም', *Cherbole*, 9 July 2018. https:// cherbole.wordpress.com/2018/07/09/%e1%8b%9b%e1%88%ac-%e1%88 %9a%e1%88%b5%e1%8c%a2%e1%88%ad-%e1%89%a2%e1%8b%88%e1 %8c%a3-%e1%89%bd%e1%8c%8d%e1%88%ad-%e1%8b%a8%e1%88 %88%e1%88%9d-fasil-yenealem/.

Yohannes, Philmon, 'Eritrea's Missing $1 Billion, *Martin Plaut*, 22 July 2013. https://martinplaut.com/2013/07/22/eritreas-missing-1-billion/.

Youranets, Anna, 'Не мы начали эту войну: как Хафтар разочаровал союзников', *Gazeta*, 10 June 2020. https://www.gazeta.ru/politics/2020 /06/09_a_13112863.shtml?updated.

Zaccaria, Massimo, 'L'oro dell'eritrea, 1897-1914', *Africa* LX/1 (2005): 65–110.

Zhao, Kai, Huazhou Yao, Jiangxion Wang, Gebsha Fitwi Ghebretnsae and Wenshuai Xian, 'Genesis of the Koka Gold Deposit in Northwest Eritrea, NE Africa: Constraints from Fluid Inclusions and C–H–O–S Isotopes', *Minerals* 9/201 (2019). https://www.mdpi.com/2075-163X/9/4/201.

Zwijnenburg, Wim, 'Are Emirati Armed Drones Supporting Ethiopia from an Eritrean Air Base?', *Bellingcat*, 19 November 2020. https://www .bellingcat.com/news/rest-of-world/2020/11/19/are-emirati-armed -drones-supporting-ethiopia-from-an-eritrean-air-base/.

Index